Building Skills for Competency-Based Teaching

Building Skills for Competency-Based Teaching

LEO D. LEONARD
ROBERT T. UTZ

The University of Toledo

HARPER & ROW, PUBLISHERS
New York, Evanston, San Francisco, London

Sponsoring Editor: Lane Akers
Project Editor: Alice M. Solomon
Designer: Jared Pratt
Production Supervisor: Valerie Klima

BUILDING SKILLS FOR COMPETENCY-BASED TEACHING

Library of Congress Cataloging in Publication Data

Leonard, Leo D.
    Building skills for competency-based teaching.

    1. Curriculum planning.   2. Motivation in
education.   3.   Educational tests and measurements.
I.   Utz, Robert T., joint author.   II.   Title.
LB1570.L46   375'.001   73-13197
ISBN 0-06-043979-3

To Marilynn, Sharon, Richard,
Kristine, and Thomas

Contents

Preface

This book is a model for developing a competency-based curriculum. The competency-based curriculum developed in this book is structured to allow maximum growth for *each individual* student. To achieve this, behavioral objectives, pretests, individualized learning activities, and posttest problems are presented. A number of other related problems are considered, such as nongrading, flexible scheduling, and continuous progress. Behavior modification techniques are suggested because they provide a systematic means of modifying behavior in the classroom. The competency-based model is based on the philosophy that curriculum can be written in discreet units of instruction (behavioral objectives) so that the student's performance can be easily measured during the course of instruction. Because the teacher is readily able to determine the strengths and weaknesses of each student, he is better able to plan appropriate learning activities for the child.

In contrast to more traditional approaches, competency-based instruction provides a *systematic way to plan curriculum.* The competency-based model provides a skeletal structure for curriculum planning. It does not dictate a priori methodologies, learning activities, teacher staffing, or physical classroom arrangements. *Teachers themselves* must make the decisions about the best way to implement the objectives. The competency-based curriculum uses more individualized instruction than traditional approaches do in order to provide each student with the necessary experiences to develop his skills in a given subject area. This is done by carefully developing behavioral objectives that provide the requisite skills for both his intellectual and emotional growth.

In the competency-based model developed in this book, the authors have provided a set of behavioral objectives for each chapter. These objectives indicate the basic skills to be achieved by the reader. The objectives are discussed, and numerous examples are provided. The final part of the chapter gives the reader a chance to evaluate himself on the skills listed in the chapter's objectives.

Each chapter discusses one segment of what actually takes place in the classroom. For example, there is a chapter on developing student self-discipline. Other chapters relate to assessing learning needs, developing behavioral objectives, curriculum planning, and evaluation. Although these topics are discussed separately, it is continually stressed that these areas are related. Problems in one area affect other areas. Therefore, a teacher needs at least minimal skills in each area if the classroom experience is to be successful.

The book can be used by *both* prospective and experienced teachers who want to obtain skills in developing competency-based instruction. Although the book is aimed toward the individual teacher, several sections discuss how a school system or academic department can evaluate its curriculum and plan a large-scale, systematic approach that allows for the experiences, opportunities, and learning goals desired. Briefly outlined in the final chapter are examples of how a district can begin to plan for change using this model. These examples have been drawn from two school systems: the Catholic Diocese of Toledo and the Clark County School System in Las Vegas, Nevada. These school systems have used the competency-based model in their curriculum development, and their assistance is sincerely appreciated.

The authors would also like to express their appreciation to the College of Education at The University of Toledo, which provided an opportunity for testing and developing ideas. In particular, the authors wish to thank Dean George Dickson, Stuart Cohen, Castelle Gentry, Edward Nussel, William Wiersma, John Turpin, and their other colleagues. Special thanks are given to Lane Akers of Harper & Row, Publishers, for his encouragement and assistance and to James Cooper of The University of Houston for his critique and recommendations for the manuscript.

Leo D. Leonard
Robert T. Utz

Foreword

It is virtually impossible for a teacher to graduate from a teacher education program without hearing the phrase "individualized instruction" scores of times. Teachers are admonished to individualize instruction to meet the needs of their students. It is very difficult to argue against this admonition, knowing as we do that humans learn at different rates of speed and through different instructional processes and modes. Although teachers agree that individualized instruction is a desirable goal and are committed to the notion at a verbal level, most find the concept difficult to operationalize in their classrooms. Why? Although some teachers claim that time and/or administrative constraints prevent them, the more likely reason is that many teachers don't know how to individualize instruction.

This book attempts to provide the reader with some of the basic strategies and competencies needed to individualize instruction. Leo Leonard and Robert Utz have identified five skill areas that they believe are essential to the individualization process: *developing student self-discipline, applying learning concepts, taxonomies of learning and educational objectives, building a curriculum, and evaluation.* Within each of these areas the authors have identified specific behavioral objectives that the reader is expected to achieve in order to demonstrate that he has acquired the basic competencies to individualize instruction.

This book is unique in that it models the very processes it urges teachers to practice in their own classrooms. Each chapter is organized as a learning module—a self-contained learning package—consisting of (1) behavioral objectives that the learner is expected to demonstrate, (2) appropriate learning activities to help the learner achieve the objectives, (3) a pretest to assess the entering level of competency with respect to the objectives, and (4) a posttest, similar to the pretest, that evaluates the competency level after the learner has engaged in the learning activities. A sequence of pretesting, stating learner objectives, designing appropriate learning activities, and evaluating the learner's level of achievement with respect to the objectives is referred to by the authors as a *competency-based curriculum,* and it is an effective means for individualizing instruction. Thus the reader is not only taught some of the skills necessary to individualize instruction, but he also simultaneously experiences the process as he progresses through the book. As teachers have long urged teacher educators, Leo Leonard and Robert Utz are practicing what they preach!

Recognizing that the sum of the parts frequently does not equal the whole (despite what both the old and new math may tell us), the authors have included a final synthesizing chapter that requires the reader to pull together what he has learned in the previous chapters and to produce a cluster of learning modules in a subject area of his own choice. An example module drawn from an elementary school curriculum is included as a guide to the reader in developing his own modules.

When people are asked to change their own behavior and operating styles, as this book asks the reader to do, they ask for reassurance that the new behaviors they are to practice really work. If the reader is concerned that a couple of education professors are using him to test some new theories they have about individualized instruction, he can put his mind at ease. Leo D. Leonard and Robert T. Utz are presenting their ideas to the reader only after they have shaped and refined them while working with teachers to implement competency–based curriculums in both public and parochial school districts. Their ideas have been tested with good results in a classroom context.

Individualized instruction, long a major goal of schools and teachers, is no longer an educator's dream but an obtainable reality. Equipped with the proper skills and understanding, teachers can make dramatic improvements in their instruction. *Building Skills for Competency-Based Teaching* can help teachers develop both a conceptual understanding of the individualization process and the practical skills necessary to implement it in their classrooms.

James M. Cooper
UNIVERSITY OF HOUSTON

Building Skills for Competency-Based Teaching

The Competency-Based Model

INTRODUCTION

Some time back, when the authors were in the midst of pointing out the merits of a behavioral-objectives approach, a question came from the floor. "What are the behavioral objectives of this course?" a student asked. After responding but not really answering the question, the authors did a little reflecting and came up with an unavoidable conclusion: to teach behavioral objectives meaningfully, teacher educators must utilize them in their own teaching. For in teaching, the *process* is the thing; the teacher or prospective teacher cannot be persuaded that a particular approach to teaching is of merit unless the teacher extolling the merits of that approach can exemplify the process which that approach entails. The impact of teaching method on the future behavior of teachers is hard to overemphasize.[1] We are reminded of a teacher who attempted to teach the inquiry method by three hours of lecture every week. To teach an educational process without using it is analogous to the two-packs-a-day man exhorting his teenage son not to take up that filthy habit of smoking.

Before we go any further, let's clarify the meaning of two terms which are central to our entire approach. The first of these is *behavioral objectives*. When we use this term, we mean a specification of educational goals which includes (1) the person to perform the behavior; (2) the type of behavior the person is to perform; (3) the given conditions under which he will perform it; (4) some criteria for evaluating the success of that performance. An example of a behavioral objective would be this:

Given a 30-minute time limit, the student will write correct solutions to at least seven out of ten arithmetic word problems, each of which requires both addition and subtraction.

Our second critical term is *competency-based curriculum*. This refers to a curriculum or learning program that identifies its behavioral objectives, suggests appropriate methodologies, and then assesses the student to determine its effectiveness in reaching those objectives. A competency-based curriculum is individualized, and therefore it may vary with regard to each student's point of entry, particular learning method, and rate of completion. Each of the components is continually reassessed to determine what revision might be needed. A competency-based curriculum is *not a method of teaching;* it is a means by which to assess the effectiveness of *any* educational method in reaching its desired results. Our discussion in the next several pages will clarify the full meaning of the competency-based curriculum and its various components.

Why behavioral objectives? Beyond the fact that their use promotes a more effective means of learning,[2] the authors believe that a behavioral-objectives approach has other merits. Most importantly, they communicate what is going on in a learning situation. Whether we are students or teachers, we know more about where we are, where we are going, and how we are going to get there. From the student's standpoint, a curriculum based on behavioral objectives enables him to focus more clearly on his educational goals and the means by which he may attain them. Anxiety about what test questions the instructor is going to ask is greatly reduced; test items and equivalent practice activities are taken directly from the behavioral objectives. Seen from the teacher's perspective, a behavioral-objectives approach furnishes greater insight into what went on in Miss Green's fifth grade class last year and what will go on in seventh grade classes next year. Moreover, the total process of utilizing behavioral objectives (that is, competency-based instruction) forces the teacher or teaching team continually to reexamine their goals, methods, and results for their degree of merit in the learning process.

Perhaps we can best demonstrate the functionality of our approach by an analogy. Let's assume we have the job of a truck driver whose task is to figure a way to get to a new destination. If we were to approach the solution to our problem in a haphazard way, we might start out "sometime in the morning," taking a road which was "generally in the right direction," toward our imaginary destination of Springdale. After several hours on the road, we might find that our lack of planning had resulted in any number of problems. We might find ourselves on the wrong road, out of gas, or too late to reach Springdale by the required arrival time. This "somehow we'll get there" approach seems to characterize many of our endeavors in education, and the results almost always come up short for students and teachers.

How might we approach our truck driver's problem if we were to tackle it in a way analogous to a competency-based approach? We would start by looking at the three critical questions. Where are we going? How are we going to get there? How do we know when we've arrived? In the instance of the first question, we need specifically to identify the location of Springdale, how many miles it is from our starting point and what time we are expected to arrive. To cope with the question of how we are going to get there, we must study our map to determine the best route and must be sure that our truck is in good working order. From all this data, we determine our starting time, our route, and our stopping points. To meet the specifications of the last question, we must identify a means of determining whether we have arrived at our designated destination and whether we have arrived at our expected arrival time.

Many teachers, unfortunately, more closely follow the first approach in their own teaching. When we fail to define our goals clearly, we don't know where we're going, we don't know how to get there, and we don't know when we've arrived. We start each school year with some vague notions about what did and did not "work" last year, and make some equally imprecise changes which we hope will enable us to do better. Rather than lingering in such a sea of ambiguity, we are arguing that the truck driver's second approach, analogous to a competency-based curriculum, is a better way to get the job done.

A MODEL OF OPERATION

Any educational program involving behavioral objectives must concern itself with the total learning program; all the facets are necessarily interrelated. To illustrate this critical point, we need to examine a model of our approach, Figure 1, to see how the competency-based curriculum is designed to function.[3]

Selection of Behavioral Objectives

The first step in the model is the selection of the appropriate behavioral objectives. How do we determine what these are to be? This determination is made by answering another question that relates to

FIGURE 1

A Competency-Based Curriculum: An Operational Model

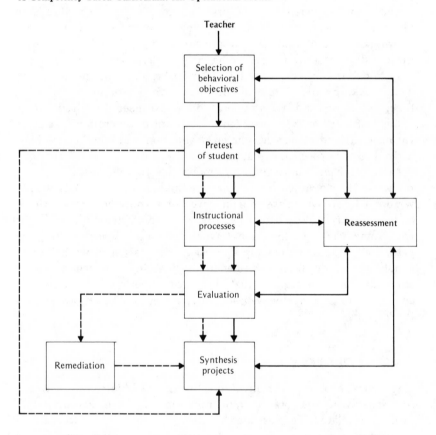

the *learning* behavior of the student. What skills, concept mastery, and so on, do we wish the student to have when he completes the educational program under consideration? What kind of skills do we see as necessary? In our case, several sources were utilized in the selection of skills. First, we see the need for the demonstration of skills which directly relate to functioning in a real classroom. A second conscious and unconscious source of influence in our selection of behavioral objectives was the authors' experience in public school classrooms; what we deem important had its influence in our selection. A third source was the concern of teachers and teachers in training about what *they* saw as important classroom skills.

The inclusion of certain objectives and the exclusion of others is not meant to deny the possible importance of those excluded; the relatively narrow scope of this book precludes the possibility of a comprehensive set of objectives for teacher education. All behavioral objectives, of course, must eventually fall under the critical examination of the ultimate test: whether or not their attainment leads to success in the classroom. We will explore this point further a little later.

How do teachers approach the problem of selecting appropriate behavioral objectives? The criteria for selecting objectives in math, science, social studies or any other curricular area are essentially the same. The skills which teachers wish the students to demonstrate at the conclusion of the unit must be specifically identified in the behavioral objectives. Some of the many input sources for determining those objectives might be texts, curriculum guides, students, parents, school district requirements, and the general input of the teacher, his teaching team and/or colleagues in his subject areas.

The Skill Areas in This Book

In our case, the skills we deem important to effective classroom functioning fall into five areas, each of which we have developed in a separate chapter. Certainly one can argue that educational skills do not readily compartmentalize themselves and that many educational problems must be confronted with skills that bridge across these chapters. With these points the authors agree; nonetheless, we would also argue that the development of the skills necessary to cope with these broad problems is initially best handled through the concept approach utilized in the chapters. Therefore we have identified five areas: *Developing student self-discipline, applying learning concepts, taxonomies of learning and educational objectives, building a curriculum, and evaluation.* The last three chapters focus on skills utilized in developing a competency-based curriculum, whereas the first two develop skills that are applicable to classrooms using any kind of curriculum organization.

The inclusion of chapters relating to classroom discipline and learning skills in a book on competency-based instruction demands some explanation. First, skills in these areas can be seen as functional to effective teaching in *any* kind of classroom. In this sense they can be seen as necessary entering skills for effective teaching in the competency-based classroom. Second, the skills we attempt to develop in the first two chapters are parallel to those used in formulating a competency-based curriculum. The teacher must first specify a desired outcome to a discipline or learning problem; he must then devise a strategy or strategies to achieve that outcome; and last, he must assess the success of those strategies in achieving the desired outcome. This approach can be seen as clearly analogous to the identification of objectives, selection of methodologies, and evaluation used in a competency-based curriculum. In using a reinforcement technique or in writing an objective, the approach is essentially the same.

Pretest

Having identified the focus of the chapters and the rationale for including them, the next step in the system is the building of a measurement device to assess the entering skills of students in the program. In a competency-based curriculum, the student cannot be legitimately told that because he is a senior or a fourth grader he must do certain tasks or demonstrate certain skills. If we are meaningfully to diagnose and individualize the needs of the student, we must indeed treat him as a person with particular skills and needs that are not necessarily the same as those of other entering students. We must comprehensively assess the student to determine his strengths and weaknesses, whether these be in arithmetic, music, or physical education.

How does the teacher go about making up a pretest? He starts by writing items and problems that evaluate those skills he thinks are important in his program. These skills, of course, have already been specified in his behavioral objectives. As in any evaluation instrument, he should put the least complex problems first and then proceed sequentially to include the higher-level skill problems. In some cases, pretests need to include items and problems that evaluate skills which are prerequisite to learning those skills in the learning unit. This is particularly true in the case of the teacher entering a situation in which he has little or no knowledge of the demonstrated skill level of the students. For example, if a teacher were preparing to teach a unit on multiplication to a group of students who were new to the school, he would do well to include addition and subtraction problems in his pretest. In this way he can get a broader diagnostic picture of the skill level of the students.

In our model, the student at this point takes the first pretest, the results of which determine the kind of program in which he will be involved. The pretest requires the student to demonstrate the skills specifically identified in the objectives of the chapter following it.[4] If a student demonstrates competence in all of the objectives for any of the five areas, the authors take the position that he should be directed to the next pretest to determine which of those skills he can demonstrate. When a student has demonstrated the skills required by each of the five chapters, he is directed to a field synthesis project. More will be addressed to this point later. For those students who do not "test out" of all the objectives in any of the areas, a diagnosis of pretest results identifies those skills in which the student needs additional work. Simply stated, students would be assigned responsibility for those objectives in which they have failed to demonstrate a satisfactory competence.

Instructional Processes

Students and teachers then involve themselves in the instructional-processes phase of the program. Each chapter is designed to facilitate the attainment of its behavioral objectives through involvement in learning activities. Such learning activities, of course, may vary with each student, but in any case they would need to be activities that enhance the development of the desired skills and require the student to demonstrate the behavioral objectives required in the chapter. We are interested in skills that the teacher and prospective teacher should be able to demonstrate in the classroom. Behavioral objectives in teacher education programs, in our view, ought to relate as closely as possible to the kind of behavioral skills teachers have to demonstrate in actual classroom situations. The closer behavioral simulations are to the actual conditions of the classroom, the better able the student will be to cope with the problems he actually will confront later. We are also arguing that confronting the teacher in training with simulated educational problems (rather than always having him face the problems only in real classrooms) is educationally functional. In the simulated behavioral problem, the teacher is better able to use his cognitive skills rationally if he is able to function in a climate which is not emotionally charged, as is the case in a classroom where he is confronting a discipline problem for the first time. Having used his cognitive skills to reach the behavioral objective involved in the simulated problem, he is better able to evoke these skills when he comes up against the real thing. We are not arguing that the real classroom should be avoided in teacher training. Far from it; we are simply saying that laying some intellectual grounding before confronting that environment is functional to coping more effectively with the problems that environment presents.

The classroom teacher's determination of the appropriate instructional process is generally consistent with these points, although it involves a great deal more complexity. Rather than deal with it superficially here, the reader is directed to the other sections of the book that deal with the problems of determining instructional processes, most of which are located in the chapter on building a curriculum.

Evaluation

When the student has completed the instructional-process phase, he is held responsible for demonstrating the appropriate objectives in the evaluation phase. He should be held responsible only for the skills that he has *not* already demonstrated on the pretest. This test, of course, must include only the skills that are specified in the required objectives. Modification of the objectives or throwing in some new ones at this point undermines the effectiveness of the total process. The results of this evaluation are assessed by the teacher to determine whether the student has satisfactorily demonstrated the required objectives. The skills necessary for building and assessing test instruments are developed in the chapter on evaluation.

A relevant point here is the relation of grades and evaluation in a competency-based approach. The nature of evaluation in such a program strongly suggests the need for a pass/no credit scheme. Because the student either demonstrates the skill satisfactorily or does not do this, imposing a gradation of A, B, C, D, and so on forces distinctions that are inappropriate in this kind of learning program. Rather than use these kinds of grades or rating systems, teachers should direct students who satisfactorily demonstrate basic objectives to more complex objectives in order that they might demonstrate their excellence on more demanding tasks. If grades *are* used with a competency-based curriculum, a higher grade should represent achievement of higher-level skills rather than merely completion of *more* lower-level skills (that is, *quality* rather than quantity distinctions).

Remediation

Some students will likely not have demonstrated at least some of those skills required. The teacher has the responsibility at this point to provide a remedial program that will facilitate the task of enabling those students to demonstrate successfully the requisite skills. Since we argue that it is educationally indefensible to send students on to multiplication if they are not proficient in addition, we cannot accept the idea that students should move on through the program to a more complex task if they have not demonstrated satisfactory skills in a prerequisite task. Such remediation or recycling programs usually need to involve a specific diagnosis of the learning difficulties and tutorial help with equivalent activities designed to develop the requisite skill. The essential point about this phase is that the student should *not* move on to a more complex phase until he has demonstrated the prerequisite skill.

Field Synthesis Project

Once the student has demonstrated these basic skills in the model program, he moves on to the field synthesis project. Since such a project requires the field application of many of the skills and cognitive understandings previously required, the clear need for minimal competency can be seen. The specific dimensions of such a project are detailed in the chapter on synthesis.

Reassessment

The process of reassessment needs to go on at every stage of the model. We must continually get feedback to assess student *and* teacher progress at all the steps on the way. Reassessment asks two central questions. First, to what extent has the operation of the model at each stage achieved the results it set out to achieve? Second, how might the operation of the model be changed to bring about an increase in learning? If particular areas in the evaluation have shown poor demonstration of the desired objectives, we need to reexamine the instructional processes related to those objectives to assess their relevancy to the objectives. If questions are raised pertaining to the diagnostic accuracy of the pretest, it must be examined as to its internal consistency and its external relationship to other available evidence. The original behavioral objectives also bear scrutiny. Has the pretest effectively measured them? Have the results of the evaluation shown that the objectives have effectively communicated their intended meaning to students? It is premature at this juncture to consider fully issues that will be dealt with more extensively in the evaluation chapter, but one central point should be emphasized. *A behavioral-objectives approach both facilitates and mandates a critical reexamination of its own efficiency of operation.* Sloppiness and failure cannot be easily hidden.

A critical point relating to the teacher training programs is in order at this juncture. In any endeavor related to the training or retraining of teachers for the classroom, all of those involved must continually bear in mind that *the ultimate test of effectiveness rests upon the actual performance of the teacher and the learning demonstrated by his students.* Any teacher training program must then examine its own products to see how they fare in the real classroom. If the ability to demonstrate cognitive objectives does not positively correlate with the demonstration of corresponding behaviors when the teacher functions in the classroom, then those cognitive objectives must be revised. We know that there is a positive relationship between being able to demonstrate learning in a simulated circumstance and being able to demonstrate it in the real circumstance.[5] This relationship, however, is a tentative one and can only be fully demonstrated by behavior in the classroom. Since the ultimate test of teacher training programs is the effectiveness of the teachers it trains, it follows that a teacher education program should include many opportunities for the candidate to practice and demonstrate the skills required in actual classroom settings. These experiences provide valuable behavioral evidence about teachers and teacher candidates, not only as to their cognitive skills but also in the domain of affective characteristics, which are almost impossible to measure reliably by other means.

THE USE OF THE MODEL IN OTHER CONTEXTS

While it is clear that this model has been explained primarily in relation to a teacher education context, the reader will perceive the functionality of its general characteristics when applied to an unlimited number of educational situations. Regardless of circumstance, the need for initial identification of educational goals is a fruitful step. Likewise, the use of pretesting to ascertain the entering skills of students can be defended in virtually all educational situations. Teachers in new positions are frequently faced with the dilemma of where to start at the beginning of the school year. What better criterion could they use than the present skill level of the student, as determined by a pretest? Behavioral objectives can be effectively used in virtually any learning situation. Evaluation and reassessment are likewise necessary steps in any functional learning program. Another of our components, the use of outside projects for high-skill individuals, is applicable to an almost unlimited number of circumstances. In sum, a competency-based curriculum has both adaptability and applicability to a broad variety of educational contexts.

RESPONDING TO SOME CRITICISMS

In spite of its obvious strengths, a behavioral-objectives approach has not escaped criticism from a variety of sources.[6] Perhaps the most comprehensive response to these criticisms has been made by Popham, who has tried to answer the eleven criticisms most commonly raised by his colleagues.[7] We have heard a few complaints from our colleagues and, in this discussion, shall attempt to amalgamate these with some of the criticisms that Popham identifies.

The first of these is the contention that behavioral objectives are often poorly stated and do not clarify the behavior or skill to be demonstrated. Behavioral objectives *are* often written sloppily. When they fail to meet the specifications demanded, objectives may actually increase educational ambiguity. For example, we cannot meaningfully relate to the objective, "The student will improve his citizenship," until we specify what student behaviors are involved in citizenship. Behavioral objectives must be explicitly written if they are to be evaluated effectively. Intellectual sloppiness and lack of effort are perhaps even more undermining to a behavioral-objectives approach than they are to other educational methods because they stand in stark contrast to the stated strengths of behavioral objectives; namely, clarity of goals and efficiency of learning. Rather than being hidden behind the teacher's closed door, poorly stated objectives serve to make the teacher's lack of explicitness more apparent to all. Hence an initial stimulus for change is provided by the fact that his poorly stated goals are at least open to scrutiny.

A second point of criticism is that behavioral objectives too often specify objectives which are intellectually trivial and inconsequential in nature. (For example: "List the twenty-four states west of the Mississippi River.") This kind of objective is not characteristic of a competency-based curriculum; it is simply an individual teacher fault. Because behavioral objectives involving simple recall or memorization are the *easiest* to write, teachers write them most often. This is no legitimate excuse, however, for retreating from more significant skills involving more sophisticated learning. Since the student is required to demonstrate more intellectual strength in meeting such higher-level objectives, the teacher must put forth more intellectual input in writing them. *Good* behavior objectives must meet *both* the criteria of objectives themselves *and* the criteria of significant learning. Rather than merely being asked to list or recall, the student should be asked to demonstrate significant skills requiring comprehension, application, and analysis.[8]

A third criticism we wish to examine is the belief that the use of behavioral objectives results necessarily in a "lockstepping" process, and that both teachers and students are forced into a conformity that inhibits learning. When behavioral objectives are at a trivial knowledge level, this statement carries much weight. Nonetheless, when we are dealing with higher-level skills, behavioral objectives force neither teacher nor student into a rigid conformity. The teacher may approach a learning goal with a variety of methods, judging the merits of each by the resulting consequences. The student can effectively cope with a behavioral objective at the analysis level through a variety of answers, not merely through *one* right one. In this case the *process* the student demonstrates is the behavioral product we are concerned with. Good behavioral objectives will serve to *promote* rather than impede open-ended inquiry in the classroom.

In the fourth critical theme (perhaps the most frequently heard), behavioral objectives are seen as "dehumanizing and undemocratic." "They deal with students mechanically, rather than treating them as people," is a commonly stated criticism. A proper response to this criticism would require that the critic supply explicit definitions of the terms "humanizing education" and "democratic education." Too often the first term involves condescension to students by refusing to evaluate them, and the second may involve leading students in a clandestine way to the teacher's "right" answer without the students' knowing it. There is little "humanity" in treating students the way they are treated in many classrooms: as masses who all must go through the same steps in order to complete the course. The use of behavioral objectives mandates the use of individual diagnosis in all phases, and does more, as we have already noted, to treat the student as a unique person ("humanize" if you will) than most educational approaches we have seen.

A fifth complaint argues that much that is gained in education cannot be covered by behavioral objectives; affective change cannot be effectively measured, nor can all cognitive gain be anticipated. It is certainly true that the broader gains of education are not easily well defined or measured in terms of behavior, but our skill in this area will not improve by avoiding the attempt to define and evaluate. And the fact remains that one type of such gain, attitudes, are only questionably meaningful if they do not manifest themselves somehow in actual behavior. In the meantime, while we are learning more about recognizing such manifestations, there is no reason to expect that omitting such gains from the stated objectives *prohibits* them from occurring. If some unanticipated cognitive skills of merit result from a specified unit, these skills can be incorporated into the unit in the future. The perfect set of behavioral objectives has yet to be written; unanticipated gains should be sought in all units and utilized in future planning. A curriculum based on behavioral objectives is an ever expanding one that is constantly examining its goals and looking for better ways to achieve those goals. Some have proposed that the use of objectives tends to promote the status quo;[9] far from this, they tend to promote a constant reassessment that forces change when the learning process is not producing its desired results.

A sixth criticism states that behavioral objectives foster mediocrity, pushing students only to minimal-level attainments. This is not the case if they are written to require varying levels of achievement. Minimal levels of competence need be set, but this does not preclude the use of additional behavioral objectives for students who can already cope with these minimal objectives. The use of a variety of behavioral objectives offers additional opportunities for individualization. The teacher who plans ahead will develop such objectives, sequencing them toward increasing degrees of complexity.

A final commonly stated criticism centers around the belief that some academic areas are not adaptable to the writing of meaningful behavioral objectives. "You just can't write usable objectives for creativity," an art teacher will say. Yet the same teacher will staunchly identify one student's work as creative and classify another's as lacking in creativity. If this difference is only the feeling the teacher has, evaluation is left to a sea of subjectivity that most art teachers are not willing to accept. When pressed on the point, however, most teachers are able to come up with at least some criteria that distinguish the creative from the uncreative. It's not an easy task; but if teachers are going to make differentiations with regard to the merit of a student's work, we have to come up with more than the nonanswer of "because it is, that's why!" This kind of response is neither fair nor functional to the promotion of improvements in students' work.

In reviewing these criticisms, we can draw several major inferences. First, to be effective, a behavioral-objectives approach is highly dependent on conscientious teacher effort, much like any other system. Second, setting higher-level cognitive skills as objectives is necessary for *significant* learning to take place. If these conditions are present, the use of behavioral objectives will furnish a clearer picture of whether or not learning has taken place. Above all else, a behavioral-objectives system focuses on the essential index of the educational enterprise: how much growth in skills the student has demonstrated.

IN CONCLUSION

To summarize and conclude what we have been saying, we can identify the following ten characteristics as essential to a fully functional competency-based curriculum.

1. Identification of Educational Objectives. *The teaching staff must initially identify the skills and behaviors they wish the student to demonstrate.*
2. Preassessment. *Prior to the learning program, the student should be assessed to determine which of these skills he can already demonstrate.*

3. Sequencing of Skills. *The skills the student does need to learn should be sequenced from lower-order complexity to higher-order complexity (e.g., from knowledge to comprehension, application, etc.)*

4. Continuous Progress. *The individual student should advance at his own pace through the learning program, moving on to subsequent skills as soon as he can demonstrate prerequisite ones.*

5. Optional Methodologies. *Neither the teacher nor the student should be tied to any one methodology; the development of new and varied learning methodologies is encouraged.*

6. Diversified Staffing. *The teaching staff should be organized to maximize the utilization of their specialized skills.*

7. Postassessment. *After he has completed his learning program, the student is assessed to determine which of the desired skills he can now demonstrate.*

8. Diagnostic Evaluation. *The evaluation of the individual student focuses on the skills which he can or cannot demonstrate, rather than ranking him in relation to some student norm group.*

9. Remediation Alternatives. *Alternative learning routes are made available to the student who cannot demonstrate the desired skills after completing the learning program. The student does not move on to the subsequent skill until he has demonstrated the prerequisite one.*

10. Continual Reassessment. *A competency-based curriculum must be subject to constant reexamination to determine which objectives, activities, sequencings, or evaluation procedures are in need of revision.*

A concluding point about the merits of utilizing objectives pertains to individualization. Assessing each student as an individual—not as a slow student, not as an underachiever, not as a senior—strikes us as being very close to what people imply when they refer to "humanizing" in education. This individual diagnosis and treatment is perhaps the most important element in a behavioral-objectives approach. We are concerned about *this* student's skills, strengths, weaknesses, and needs. To the extent that these are different from *that* student's, then his learning program ought to be different. This is the core of a behavioral-objectives approach: to diagnose individually, to treat individually, and to assess individually. We do not see this as limiting inquiry, precluding affective concerns, fostering conformity, inhibiting student freedom, intensifying anxiety in the classroom, or, in sum, as "dehumanizing" the student.[10]

NOTES AND REFERENCES

1. See, for example, Dan C. Lortie, "Teacher Socialization: The Robinson Crusoe Model," from "The Real World of the Beginning Teacher," *NCTEPS*, 1966, pp. 54–66.
2. Robert J. Kibler *et al.*, *Behavioral Objectives and Instruction* (Boston: Allyn and Bacon, 1970).

3. Adapted from and influenced by Kibler *et al.*, *op. cit.*, and George E. Dickson *et al.*, *Educational Specifications for a Comprehensive Elementary Teacher Education Program: Volume I, The Basic Report* (Toledo, Ohio: University of Toledo, 1968).
4. A sample pretest for each of the skill areas can be found at the beginning of each chapter.
5. Claude Mathis, John W. Cotton, and Lee Sechrest, *Psychological Foundations of Education* (New York: Academic Press, 1970), pp. 82–84.
6. See, for example, Robert J. Nash, "Commitment to Competency: The Net Fetishism in Teacher Education," *Phi Delta Kappan* 52, no. 4 (December 1970), 240–243. See also James B. MacDonald and Bernice J. Wolfson, "A Case Against Behavioral Objectives," *Elementary School Journal* 71, no. 3 (December 1970), pp. 119–127.
7. W. James Popham, "Probing the Validity of Arguments Against Behavioral Goals," in Kibler *et al.*, *Behavioral Objectives and Instruction*, pp. 115–124.
8. It is the authors' viewpoint that behavioral objectives should not be written without some reference to a taxonomy of learning, such as Benjamin Bloom's *Taxonomy of Educational Objectives; Handbook I: Cognitive Domain* (New York: David McKay, 1956).
9. Robert J. Nash and Russell M. Agne, "Competency in Teacher Education: A Prop for the Status Quo," *Journal of Teacher Education* 22, no. 2 (Summer 1971), pp. 147–156.
10. For an extension of these arguments see Robert Utz and Leo Leonard, "Are Behavioral Objectives Antithetical to a Humanistic Approach in Education?" *New Directions in Teaching* 4, no. 1 (Fall 1971), pp. 3–8.

SUGGESTED READINGS

Kibler, Robert, *et al. Behavioral Objectives and Instruction.* Boston: Allyn and Bacon, 1970.
>   *This book is an effective effort to orient the reader to a behavioral-objectives approach. The programmed approach utilized facilitates understanding of the process. See especially W. James Popham, "Probing the Validity of Arguments Against Behavioral Goals." Popham has declared war on those who deny the merit of behavioral objectives. His arguments effectively deal with many of the criticisms leveled against a behavioral objectives approach.*

National Commission on Teacher Education and Professional Standards. *The Real World of the Beginning Teacher.* Washington, D.C.: National Education Association, 1966.
>   *A number of authors have contributed articles to this enlightening volume on the beginning teacher.*

Olson, Arthur V., and Joe E. Richardson. *Accountability: Curriculum Applications.* Scranton, Penn.: Intext Educational Publishers, 1972.
>   *This volume contains a number of excellent articles pertaining to the development of competency-based educational accountability.*

Phi Delta Kappan 52, no. 4 (December 1970).
>   *The bulk of this periodical issue is devoted to various aspects of performance-based programs and accountability problems in education.*

Developing Student Self-Discipline

PRETEST

Note to teachers: These sample questions cover all of the objectives included in the chapter on developing student self-discipline. The teacher may wish to use a shorter pretest for a variety of reasons (for example, to test only the less complex objectives in the chapter, to exclude some because of personal preference, or simply to make a shorter test). Some of the questions may be seen as more appropriate for a take-home exercise rather than a classroom evaluation. Satisfactory sample answers to equivalent questions can be found in the following chapter.

1. *Examine the following paragraph describing the behavior of a pupil and (1) identify those portions of the statement that are not behaviorally stated, and (2) rewrite those portions to be behaviorally explicit.*

   Marilyn is a very intense fourth grade girl who tries very hard on her schoolwork but just can't seem to make the grade. In some ways she has a natural talent with words, but her work in math and science is not up to par. Her adding and subtraction skills are equal to the norm of the class, but her multiplication skills are limited to rote recall of the tables. She is rather popular with her group of friends, and this sometimes leads her into trouble. Last month two notes were sent home to her parents about her math difficulties and her poor behavior, but her mother did not contact the school as requested.

2. *In the following classroom incident, (1) identify the problem behavior and the behavior you wish to develop, and (2) identify and defend a strategy or strategies to lessen or eliminate the problem behavior and to promote the behavior you wish to develop.*

   John is a large and aggressive sixth grader who is bigger than all of the other boys in the class. He is of normal age and shows average achievement. Although he has limited his aggressiveness mostly to playground play and games, he has recently been seen to push several small boys in the hall and before class. One day during class, John was bringing a book back to the book cabinet and mildly pushed a boy out of the aisle. The other boy pushed him back with the same degree of force. John suddenly swung his fist at the boy, knocking him to the floor.

3. *In the following major classroom problem, (1) identify the major behavioral problems and the behaviors you wish to develop; and (2) identify and defend strategies to lessen or eliminate the problem behaviors and to promote the behaviors you wish to develop.*

Mrs. Antonelli teaches five tenth grade biology classes. Her first four classes in the day have shown excellent progress toward the skills she regards as important. The fact that the majority of these students are capable of managing their own behavior and schoolwork has enabled her to spend considerable time with the individual problems that have emerged.

Her last period class, however, has given her considerable trouble. The skill level shown by most of the students is markedly below that of the other classes. Work disruptions and extraneous noise have grown to equal those of the other four classes combined.

The class is made up of eighteen boys and twelve girls, whose grade averages range from B to D. Reading scores range from one year above the national norm to three years below. The principal stated to her on the first day of school, "There are a number of people we've had to put in there to fill out their schedule." About ten of the students were scheduled to go into the more practical general science course, but those classes were filled to capacity.

Most of the behavioral disruptions have occurred during the group work sessions, during which students are expected to solve workbook problems. These groups are made up of five or six students, each group consisting of all boys or all girls. One group of boys and one group of girls have been the groups that have caused the most class disruptions and shown the least work accomplished. Biology work problems that groups in other classes have solved in 20 minutes are not solved by these groups in the full 60-minute class period. Extraneous class noise and other disruptions have increased steadily since the class started two months ago.

Two weeks ago, Mrs. Antonelli attempted to remedy the situation by splitting the two groups up. While there was a slight lull in the problems at first, the last week has seen the behavioral disruptions and lack of work spread to four tables instead of the original two. Visits to the noisy work tables by Mrs. Antonelli result in a quieting and attention for only a few minutes. One day recently when she went to quiet one of the disruptive groups, one of the girls in the group responded, "Oh, why don't you leave us alone!" Mrs. Antonelli sent the girl to the detention office, but this resulted in a quieting effect only for the rest of that class. The disruptive groups were back to their same behavior pattern the next day.

INTRODUCTION

Before learning can take place in any kind of classroom, a positive climate must be initially present or
be developed. By a positive climate we mean a
classroom in which students can communicate with
each other and with the teacher. Screaming, physical aggression or other forms of chaos—whether
they be by teacher or student—do not make for the
positive climate that is necessary for learning to
occur. Before dealing with problems of learning
principles, curriculum development, or evaluation,
we shall focus on skills of classroom management
—which we see as leading to a greater development
of the student's self-discipline—because it is in this
area that many teachers have the most difficulty.

Within the domain of classroom management,
clichés abound. "A good lesson plan takes care of
all discipline problems." "Motivated children don't
cause problems in the classroom." "Lay out all the
rules early and later will take care of itself." These
bromides and others, with their partial truths and
oversimplifications, obscure the crucial need of
teachers for the development of specific skills for
classroom management. Time after time teachers
throw up their hands in frustration and say, "I
don't know how to handle that kid." The clichés
and ambiguous language that teachers fall back on
prevent the specific identification of what the problem is.

Any reservoir of strategies that is developed
seems to hold only two kinds of approaches: either
permissive strategies that see all children as in-
herently good and that reward any behavior regardless of its merits; or by contrast, strategies in

which the teacher invokes a total set of authoritarian rules to cover all possibilities.

This false dichotomy results in "murder" in the classroom. This murder is of two kinds. In the first variety, the teacher is the victim. Usually young and full of vigor, he enters teaching with some ill-defined notions about creating a "democratic classroom." Soon after the show gets on the road in September, the house begins to cave in, with students crawling up the walls in an infinite variety of ways. A typical exchange:

Teacher: Stop doing that and sit down!
Student: You never told us we couldn't do that!
Teacher: I'm telling you now!
Student: Jim Jones did it yesterday and he got away with it.
Teacher: I don't care what Jim Jones did yesterday! If you don't get into your seat in the next 5 seconds, you're going to get an F for the whole week!

In this brief exchange, the teacher has escalated the student-teacher war to the bluffing point, and the students will soon recognize it. Whether third grade or tenth, the war usually lingers for the rest of the year.

In the second variety of murder, the students are the victims. The assailants may well be the same teachers who took the permissive approach last year in their first year of teaching. Lacking any other alternative to the approach that failed last year, teachers pull out all the stops to explicitly define rules for *all* contingencies. Students are regimented into their seats with hands folded at a 45 degree angle. Students speak only when spoken to. This total behavior conformity usually extends to the intellectual domain; neither teachers nor pupils ask "why" kinds of questions, for these would open unpredictable kinds of responses. Physical punishment or a trip to the principal's office may well be in order for the slightest deviant behavior. This kind of murder is analogous to arsenic poisoning—slow but deadly— so that a dose over several years' time can reduce students to intellectual corpses.

Why does the teacher feel left with only the choice between these two ineffectual alternatives? The failure of teacher training and retraining programs cannot be denied. Finding the guilty parties, however, is far less important than identifying and training teachers in the specific skills that they can use to help students develop internalized discipline systems of their own. *This is the central focus of any long-term behavioral-control system: an evolving from a lesser reliance on external controls to a greater reliance on internal controls. The stu-*

dent behaviors that a competency-based classroom should promote are self-management behaviors.

SUGGESTED BEHAVIORAL OBJECTIVES

What skills do we see as important in the domain of classroom management? Here are three objectives designed to develop teacher skills in identifying problem behavior, changing immature classroom conduct, and fostering student self-discipline.

1. *Given a paragraph describing the behavior of a pupil, the student will (1) identify those portions of the statement that are not behaviorally stated, and (2) rewrite those portions to be behaviorally explicit.*
2. *Given the characteristics of a classroom behavioral incident, the student will (1) identify the problem behavior and the behavior he wishes to develop, and (2) identify and defend a strategy or strategies to lessen or eliminate the problem behavior and to promote the behavior he wishes to develop.*
3. *Given the characteristics of a major classroom behavioral problem, the student will (1) identify the major behavioral problems and the behaviors he wishes to develop, and (2) identify and defend strategies to lessen or eliminate the problem behaviors and to promote the behaviors he wishes to develop.*

IDENTIFICATION OF BEHAVIORAL PROBLEMS

A significant limitation in the way many teachers confront problems in the classroom is their inability to identify clearly what the problem is. Rather than specifically identify the problem behavior of the child, teachers often attempt to focus on the difficulty by using categorical and simplistic terminology. Rather than furnishing insights that can lead to a more effective coping with the child's problem, the simplistic approach (and the verbal description that accompanies it) tends to serve only as a reflection of the way the teacher views the world and the people in it. A language system expressing this outlook is largely categorical and labeling; a more useful perspective would be evidenced by a language system that is explicit about behavior.

Categorical and *labeling* are meant here to apply to language that fails to communicate a description of behavior which has meaning to all: terminology such as "troublemaker," "good kids," "underachievers," "a sweet child," or the classical "not motivated." *Behavioral language patterns* are meant to apply to language that explicitly states the educational problem under consideration. Examples would include "throws spitwads," "does class assignments," "does not use library," and "writes sloppily."

Questions could legitimately be asked at this point. "What is the use of such descriptive statements? Description does not help you to explain behaviors. Are we not primarily interested in analyzing behaviors rather than merely describing them?" Certainly we are interested in analyzing behaviors. But the primary function of analysis is not merely to gain greater understanding of the child, but to use that understanding to deal with the behavioral problem at hand (for example, to stop Johnny's throwing of spitballs and to produce more functional behavior). We can act upon behavioral descriptions and bring about the desired changes of behavior; we cannot act upon such terms as "underachievers" or "lacks motivation" because we do not know which behaviors we are trying to change. If someone tells us that we need to discipline the child, our legitimate response might be, "How are you defining discipline? What behaviors would you like the child to perform that he is not performing now?"

There are certain assumptions that must be made in such instances, of course. The first is that the teacher in question is more interested in coping with the individual child's problem than he is in "labeling" him. And secondly, we assume that the teacher is willing to analyze the problem in terms of its specific behavioral components and to develop strategies for behavioral change.

Why do we focus intently on this skill of recognizing and stating behavioral problems explicitly? First, it helps us to communicate explicitly to others—both students and other educators—what we are identifying as the problem and the suggested course of action. Second, it forces us to explicitly identify a strategy ourselves, rather than falling back on some ambiguously defined course of action that attempts to hide our inability to act effectively.

The need for this skill might be illustrated by the following example. You go to Miss Jones with your worst problem case, and she offers the following advice: "Persuade her to behave; she's really a good girl." Where does this statement leave us? About where we started. We certainly don't know what "persuade" means in terms of a specific strategy. Miss Jones may know, but she's hiding behing a semantic screen. When we tell the problem student, "Be good, Johnny; you know you can be," Johnny is very unlikely to know what behavior is expected of him. In total, everything is vague to everybody and the problem persists.

In the field of education we are particularly prone to the cliché and the ambiguous statement. Among suggested strategies, we often find these: "Meet their needs," "Motivate the child to work," "Let them know who's boss," "You need to rap with the students," and "Meet the student at his own level." Although some of these might have an explicit meaning in one teacher's mind, when he tries them out on the teacher across the hall or the student sitting next to him, he usually finds out that he had something quite different in mind. By the time this strategy gets to the students, it is an even more vague form. This is the worst limitation, because the student should receive the communication in its *most* explicit form.

Some additional examples will serve to clarify what we mean by behavioral explicitness. Rather than saying the child is "anxiety-prone," we would say that. he "refuses to stay in his seat," or "continually bites his fingernails." Instead of a "troublemaker," we would identify the student as "refuses to work with girls in a work group." Rather than suggesting that the teacher "persuade him to do it," we would suggest that the teacher give advice explicitly: "Talk to the child *alone* and tell him he must pay for any destroyed property." Each of these examples of a behavioral statement enables us to specifically identify a problem behavior or a course of action.

Do not mistake this skill for that of devising successful classroom strategies. But it *is* a functional and necessary starting point. If we can't explicitly state to ourselves and others where we are, we can't very well devise a successful strategy for behavioral change; in the same way, the strategy itself must be explicitly communicated to have a chance of success.

EVOLVING STRATEGIES FOR CHANGE

When the topic of classroom discipline is considered, most teacher attention seems to focus on the degree of authority that the teacher chooses to exercise in the classroom. Polarizations quickly emerge; teachers tend to be labeled either permissive (that is, "soft," "too easy," "lenient," etc.) or authoritarian (that is, "tough," "disciplinarian," "taskmaster," etc.). Most teachers, of course, are likely to fall on a continuum somewhere between these poles. The permissive teacher talks in terms of "failing to meet the child's needs" when a student deviates from socially accepted behavior. In contrast, the authoritarian is more likely to speak in terms of "troublemakers trying to put one over on me."

The functionality or dysfunctionality of each of these approaches bears examination. Of particular interest is the determination of their relevance to two questions. First, *what behaviors are we defining as requiring change?* Second, *what strategies have we devised in an attempt to change them?* To the permissivist, responses to these questions are likely to be global and lacking in specificity. When pressed, the permissive teacher might come up with some specific behaviors on the child's part that he regards as undesirable. The important question then is this: how might one change these behaviors? Meeting the child's needs does not do the job. Particularly in the demanding environment of a thirty-five-child classroom, the teacher can hope to deal with "causes" only to a limited extent; he must also deal with symptoms, if for no other reason than that failure to do so may lead to contagious effects among the class and the continuation of the individual child's undesired behavior. The terms put forth by the permissive teacher (for example, "needs," "problems," and "help") must be behaviorally defined before we can operationalize strategies for change.

How might the authoritarian respond to the questions about desired behavioral changes and strategies for effecting them? "Stop the behavior," he says. How? By "shutting them up," "kicking them out of class," or perhaps "whacking them" with the nearest available weapon. In a word, punishment. And if they keep it up, we punish them some more.

If we pursue our concern for behavioral implications, the authoritarian must face several questions. First, *are his primary goals to stop the undesired behavior and change it to a more socially acceptable form?* Second, if this is the purpose of punishment, *how do we determine whether the specific act of punishment* (for example, spanking the child) *has achieved its purpose?* His answer to the second might be, "because that's the way you stop kids from causing trouble."

How can we answer this second question until we follow up the behavior of the child? In essence, we are defining *punishment* as behavior by the teacher to lessen or eliminate undesired student behavior. If, after the administration of punishment by the teacher, there is not a change in the student's behavior, how can we define the teacher's act as punishment? Some might argue that you need more "spankings" to establish a stronger link between the undesired behavior and the punishment. If, after several more misbehaviors and a following "spanking," the undesired behavior still persists, how do we define the behavior of spanking the child?

Our conclusion is that it cannot be defined as punishment, but could be more justifiably defined as *reinforcement*, namely, behavior by the teacher that perpetuates or increases undesired student behavior. The critical point in this case is that the teacher's behavior (if we are primarily interested in its effects on students) *cannot* be meaningfully defined at the point of intervention; it can only be meaningfully defined after enough time has passed to examine effects. Thus, a child who is spanked each time after several instances of throwing spitballs in class is *not* being punished if he continues to throw spitballs.[1]

Focusing on behavioral factors has significant implications for interpersonal relations in the classroom. It means that the teacher will concentrate *both* on the formulation of strategies *and* the effects of those strategies. Unlike the permissivist, he is not lost in the quicksand of trying to deal with the total sphere of the child's social and psychological problems; unlike the authoritarian, he is not bound by the shortsighted strategies of classroom repression. The strategies of the more functional teacher, then, are subject to constant review and revision in order that they may attain the desired behavioral results. The strategies of the more functional teacher may take on a broad variety of alternatives, depending on the situation at hand and the behavioral goals desired.

The authoritarian and the permissivist fall short on another critical criterion, namely that of self-management. As we have already noted, a discipline system must meet the test of promoting an internally developed set of behavioral controls. Let us first examine the authoritarian on this criterion. Since such a system creates a highly structured environment for the child, the child cannot learn to cope with individual problems that he confronts by himself. When the child is on his own, he knows how to respond only to those situations that have been dealt with by his disciplinarian or that fall under the set of "rules" which have been introduced by the disciplinarian. Since a child (or an adult) is confronted by sets of circumstances that become continually more complex, he soon runs out of rules and must fall back on his own judgment. If, however, his own experiences have not forced him to solve problems in these kinds of circumstances, he will be ill-equipped to deal with decisions on behavior for which he is responsible.

An example here will perhaps clarify the dilemma of the "tough" discipline system:

> Mrs. Jones insists that her 15-year-old daughter call her when she arrives at the destination of her engagement. "I just feel better when I know where she is," says Mother. Daughter Mary says, "I feel like I'm being treated like a child."

What kind of responsibility is Mary developing? Eventually, when the ridicule of peers and other pressures become strong enough, she will develop means to beat the enforcement system (for example, by lying or other means of deceit). How then is a parent "to know where my child is," in the words of many concerned with the problem? Two means are available. The first is to follow her. A second, more feasible approach is to establish an internalized system of behavioral controls in which the individual assumes an increasingly larger portion of individual decisions. Such a system presumes open communication between parent and child, one in which rules are not evoked without reasons and an enforcement system in which the child plays a larger role.

The permissivist falls prey to some of the same criticisms. The most critical of these is the failure to supply the kinds of experiences that develop emotional resilience and a decision-making capacity. To "protect the child from failure" is to deny him the experience of building for future failures. Will he always experience failure with the comfort of a parent or teacher readily available? "Meeting the needs of the child" may take on the form of precluding the individual's chance for self-realization.

SOME SPECIFIC STRATEGIES

Redl and Wineman have identified a number of strategies for effectively dealing with the aggressive child. One of these they define as *planned ignoring.* This strategy is seen as dealing with the child's problem behavior by:

> . . . *limiting interference only to those behavioral trends [by the child] which carry too heavy an intensity charge and which would not stop from their own exhaustion unless directly interfered with.*[2]

Some problems, then, are dealt with by the *strategy* of ignoring. The technique of planned ignoring is difficult to envisage as an effective means of stopping behavior. Nonetheless, if we are primarily concerned with changing behavior (as contrasted with asserting the authority role of the teacher or parent), we should be open to that possibility. Many examples can be cited to illustrate its utility.

> *The students in Miss Brown's third grade class are working on their arithmetic exercises on the board. One of the boys (who has already completed his problem) has written a four-letter profanity on the blackboard.*

How should the teacher respond? Given the context of the classroom scene, the age of the child, and the potential contagion of the situation, ignoring the behavior is suggested as an effective strategy. We could not, of course, define the degree of effectiveness until future behavior can be assessed; yet we can suggest several factors that support its chances.

First, the most likely explanation is that the 8-year-old child does not know the meaning of the word and its implications; ignoring in this case serves the function of *not* focusing on an incident that is potentially highly contagious and explosive for future days in the classroom. If the child does know the meaning of the term and its implications, then it is likely that he is writing the word on the board for the effects it can produce, the most significant of which is the attention of the teacher. In this instance, ignoring as a strategy serves the function of denying the reinforcement the child is seeking by his behavior (that is, the attention of the teacher *and* its implications for greater prestige in the eyes of his classmates). In addition, it does not focus on the problem word and create additional problems with the other children, who likely do not know the meaning or implications of the word. Therefore, if we were to define *punishment* as "behavior by the teacher to stop or diminish undesired student behavior," and the child's behavior (in this case writing "dirty" words on the board) ceases or diminishes, then we may say for our purposes that the child has been punished. Here again the emphasis is on the consequences of the behavior rather than on the nature of the behavior itself.

Another example is perhaps worth noting. When a woman receives a crank phone call from a man who fills her ears with foul language, she is best advised to hang up. Why? Because this behavior is *least* likely to reinforce the behavior of the crank caller. He is "punished" by her hanging up. She is then less likely to get future calls from him. If, on the other hand, she reacts emotionally to such calls, she is more likely to get additional calls, and thus her reaction has become reinforcement. In this case, we are relying on vast evidence gathered by the phone companies.

In these cases, it is significant to note that understanding the use of words is at the heart of effectively coping with the problem; if the individual who is being "tested" persists in taking the meaning of words in a universal context, he may well be reinforcing behavior which he wishes to extinguish; by contrast, if he takes the meaning to be the response that the words evoke, then he will very likely more effectively cope with the behavioral problem such language poses.

Redl and Wineman suggest other techniques that bear fruitfully on the problem of classroom management. One is called "proximity and touch control," in which the adult calms the excited child by coming physically close to or touching him. This methodology is not meant to imply a threat of physical punishment to the child, but as Redl and Wineman point out, a "calming ego and superego-supportive device." This is another technique of utilizing the *minimal* amount of adult involvement to quell the child's antisocial behavior. The "dose" of the medicine is thus a critical factor; the use of "overkill" devices for minor problems not only creates psychological barriers between the adult and the child, but it also lessens the potential utility of such massive interference techniques when they do need to be invoked. The correct estimating of the minimal adult interference necessary also promotes greater individual autonomy (that is, behavior by the child that is not continually based on adult cues or the threat of adult interference).

At this point the question might well be asked, "You have suggested some techniques which may work some of the time, but what about the situation when the child gets really out of hand and is about to blow the room apart?" Obviously, limited interference techniques are sometimes inadequate to cope with the more dramatic events in the school environment. Consider for example the case of the fight that breaks out in the classroom. Limited interference techniques are inadequate to deal with the problem. How do we deal with an explosive incident of this kind? The suggestion offered here is to break up the fight immediately and to remove the students from the classroom.

"Kicking kids out of class" is repulsive to some teachers and perhaps more repulsive to some professors of education. Such action, they would say, attempts to cover up teacher inadequacies that are the root cause of such behavior. This may be a totally valid point. But we would argue that the more critical question is that, given the present set of circumstances, what action can the teacher take to stop or limit the behavioral problem at hand? A teacher error may unfortunately require what Redl and Wineman call an *antiseptic bouncing* of the child; it is not meant to cover up the guilt of the teacher, but rather to avoid worse errors that would result if such action were not taken. Failure to take such action potentially promotes two problems: first, an immediate contagion of the undesired behavior among the other students in the class; and second, reinforcement of such behavior in future instances of class turmoil.

Antiseptic bouncing necessarily introduces a consideration of the concepts of short-term and long-term strategies. In such problem cases, the short-term strategy of bouncing the student must be complemented by follow-up long-term strategy. Follow-up behavior should fulfill one or all of several functions: (1) explicitly connect the "punishment" (if it turns out to be that) with the antisocial behavior in question; (2) state to the child that the teacher's action is based on the student's antisocial behavior rather than being directed against the student personally (which needs to be reinforced by equal application of the behavioral standards to all students); (3) explain to the student that the failure to intervene might have resulted in more severe problems; and (4) state to the student what teacher actions will follow subsequent recurrences of the antisocial behavior. Teacher follow-up must indeed be that; it must not rest upon a verbal crutch. Students will usually respond favorably to a teacher's reward and punishment scale if it is made explicit, if it is followed up, and if it is administered with fairness to all students. To state it in its simplest form, what the teacher *does* is infinitely more important than what the teacher says.

More than limiting and eliminating disruptive behavior, the teacher should be trying to promote positive behavior on the part of the child. The continuation and growth of desirable behavior calls for specific strategies on the part of the teacher. Many of these strategies relate to the reinforcement of the disruptive child's positive behavior. For example, rather than concentrating on building a punishment strategy to eliminate Johnny's troublemaking, a more effective teacher strategy would be to search out those behaviors of Johnny that are functional to classroom processes and reward them as they occur. Instead of meandering among the short-term aspects of his problem, the teacher deals more effectively with Johnny's long-term problem: his identification with behaviors that are functional to himself and the class. In classroom discipline problems, more is necessary than the child's understanding of the range of tolerable behaviors; his existing positive behavior needs to be rewarded with the aim of expanding it.

The application of reinforcement in the problem classroom is by no means an easy task. "That's fine in theory," says the experienced teacher, "but what do you do when Johnny is threatening to hit Mary with a ruler or about to break an expensive piece of science equipment?" Obviously in these cases the teacher must intervene, even though he risks the chance of reinforcing Johnny by giving him the attention he wants. Physical danger to persons or property must take precedence. At the same time, the teacher should recognize that the behavior he is trying to develop on Johnny's part is civil behavior toward Mary and proper use of science equipment. When Johnny *is* performing these and other positive behaviors, the teacher should make special efforts to reinforce his behavior (for example, "That's the way to do it, Johnny!").

We hope that teachers will see these principles and strategies as applicable to a variety of classroom situations. Whether a teacher is operating in a conventional self-contained classroom or in an open classroom, a behavioral approach to developing self-discipline is functional. In many ways, the open classroom requires more effort by the teacher in developing internalized sets of controls. The student must demonstrate a variety of self-management skills to a greater degree than the child in the self-contained classroom. Setting up and using equipment, completing work tasks, and working cooperatively with other children in groups are but a few of these skills. The open classroom will likely do more for developing the child's self-management skills than will the self-contained one.

REVIEW OF BEHAVIORAL OBJECTIVES

Identifying and Writing Behavioral Statements

Having considered some concepts, strategies and rationale, let us now take on some sample problems and attempt to cope with them. A re-examination of the first behavioral objective in the chapter seems fruitful.

> 1. *Given a paragraph describing the behavior of a pupil, the student will (1) identify those portions of the statement which are not behaviorally stated, and (2) rewrite those portions to be behaviorally explicit.*

In light of this behavioral objective, examine the following paragraph describing a pupil.

> *Harry is always a problem in class. He is disrespectful, intolerant and just plain nasty. When talked to by teachers after school, he always says that he must leave immediately to go to work. In many ways he's a good boy, but he cannot seem to adjust to any class at school.*

Whether reading such a statement in a student's file or listening to a teacher describe him, we can see that such an ambiguous and cliché-filled statement gives us little to go on for devising a strategy for dealing with Harry's problems (whatever those problems are). When someone states that Harry is "a problem in class," "disrespectful, intolerant and just plain nasty," "a good boy," and "can't seem to adjust to any class in school," he is not explicitly communicating anything about Harry's behavior. The statement about Harry's having to go to work after school is the single example of explicit behavior. Let's rewrite the sample statement in a form that is behaviorally explicit:

> *Harry has been sent to the office by teachers for disruptive behavior seven times in the last three weeks. Teachers have reported that he swears at other students during class discussions, refuses to acknowledge that his opinion might be wrong, and has hit other students by throwing coins. When talked to by teachers after school, he always says that he must leave immediately to go to work. He is often helpful before and after class in setting up and taking down equipment; in all of his classes, however, he has at some point challenged the teacher's code of behavior and refused to comply with it.*

In this form the statement not only gives us a better understanding of Harry's problems; it also furnishes us with several possible starting points for devising a strategy to change Harry's behavior. We know, for example, that Harry values setting up class equipment (or else he wouldn't continue to do it), and this might be used as a reward to change some of his other behavior.

One more example relating to this objective will likely suffice to illustrate the skill of describing behavior explicitly.

> *Mary is a Mexican-American girl who is several inches shorter than any other girl in class. She is usually chosen last for games during recess. In class, she refuses to cooperate. It is apparent that she comes from a home with no standards. Mary's classwork is poor, and teacher attempts to help her haven't worked.*

In this case, "refuses to cooperate," "comes from a home with no standards," "poor classwork," and "teacher attempts to help her haven't worked," are all examples of vague and inexplicit description. Moreover, there appears to be an attempt to cast the child into the mold of an ethnic stereotype. In a behavioral form, a statement about Mary communicates much more effectively.

> *Mary is a Mexican-American girl who is several inches shorter than any other girl in the class. She is usually chosen last for games during recess. In class, she is unable to follow directions in carrying out assignments. Mary comes from a lower class home in which neither parent speaks English. Mary's classwork in English and arithmetic is almost never completed; her reading comprehension is two years below grade level. Teacher-aide tutorial help in reading last month did not significantly improve her reading scores.*

It should be apparent at this point that nonbehavioral statements describing students often reflect the teacher's lack of explicit information about the child. In order to describe a student's behavior explicitly, the teacher must make efforts to gain additional information about the child's problems. With this additional knowledge in hand, the likelihood of devising a successful strategy for behavioral change is greatly enhanced.

Dealing With Specific Behavioral Problems

Having dealt with the problem of stating problems behaviorally, we will now move on to a more complex task, that of identifying classroom problems and devising strategies for change. The next behavioral objective states the skills required of the student.

> 2. *Given the characteristics of a classroom behavioral incident, the student will (1) identify the problem behavior and the behavior he wishes to develop, and (2) identify and defend a strategy or strategies to lessen or eliminate the problem behavior and to promote the behavior he wishes to develop.*

This objective could be tested by the use of the following sample problem.

> *Duncan is a very active and outgoing first grader, with generally average academic abilities. When the teacher asks a question, Duncan will very often raise his hand and wave it wildly. When called on, however, he very seldom can make any response relevant to the question. When he is not called on, he will hiss and boo the teacher and the chosen pupil. Then, when the pupil answers correctly, Duncan will say, "That was easy —everybody knows that!"*

Having presented the behavioral objective and an incident that might serve as a means to evaluate a student's degree of attainment of that objective, let us examine two hypothetical student responses to the problem.

Student A's response:

> *It is obvious that Duncan's needs are not being met in the normal class- room activities. The key to this problem is Duncan's lack of motivation: it is the root cause of Duncan's problems in the class. As a short-term strategy the teacher needs to motivate Duncan in such a way as to pro- mote his responding in a desirable way and not to allow his responses to gain the attention of the teacher and his peers. The teacher also needs to make the material more interesting in order that Duncan might feel motivated to try to do better.*
>
> *If such short-term strategy fails, a follow-up strategy is required. In this case, taking Duncan away from the excitement of the classroom setting is best. The teacher should talk individually to Duncan and explain to him the limitations of his behavior; he should persuade Duncan that such actions may seem like fun now, but that they are hurting his chances of future success in school. Duncan needs to feel that he is part of the group and that he is making a contribution.*

Since we are oriented toward a behavioral point of view, this response must be examined in terms of (1) what problem behavior and desired behavior are identified with the child, and (2) the behavior suggested for the teacher to promote change in the child's behavior.

What behaviors are identified with Duncan?

> his *"needs are not being met"*
> his *"lack of motivation"*
> *"that Duncan might feel motivated to try to do better"*
> *"Duncan needs to feel that he is part of the group"*
> *"that he is making a contribution to the group"*

The problem is, of course, that these are not identifiable behaviors at all. They are inferences about Duncan that give us some general indication of what Student A sees to be the problem. Although it might be quite true that Duncan's needs are not being met, we cannot begin to meet his needs until we know which behaviors on his part must be changed in order to meet those needs. After reading this response, we perhaps have some understanding of Duncan's problems, but we have not the slightest idea about what behaviors on his part we wish to change nor do we know what the writer sees as desirable behavior on Duncan's part.

In Student A's response, what teacher behaviors are suggested to promote change in Duncan's behavior?

"the teacher needs to motivate Duncan"
"to promote his responding in a desirable way"
"not allow his responses to gain the attention of the teacher and his peers"
"needs to make the material more interesting"
"taking Duncan away from the excitement of the classroom"
"should talk individually to Duncan"
"should persuade Duncan"

These responses on the teacher's part suffer from essentially the same limitation as the set of descriptions; for the most part they do not identify behaviors that the teacher might take to stop or diminish the undesired behavior. Taking Duncan away from the excitement of the classroom and talking individually to Duncan are explicit behavioral steps; they do not, however, form more than a limited, piecemeal part of any overall strategy to act on the problem.

Overall, the response by Student A leaves us about where we started with regard to changing Duncan's behavior effectively. Evaluating the response in light of the behavioral objective, we can see that Student A has responded with the use of categorical and non-behavioral dimensions. Strategies to lessen or eliminate the undesired behavior and promote desired behavior have *not* been developed. Thus, Student A does *not* meet the requirements of the behavioral objective.

Student B's response:

Duncan's behavior indicates that he does not understand or care to abide by the teacher values of classroom propriety. The teacher's behavior may be reinforcing his antagonistic behavior; his calling on Duncan indiscriminately after he exercises antagonistic behavior toward the teacher and other pupils may well promote the behavior he is trying to eliminate. What behavior on the part of the child is he trying to promote? In this instance, it is reasonably assumed that he is seeking to promote responses in the classroom that are relevant to the questions posed. How might this be done?

First, he should ask questions of Duncan only when he is relatively sure that Duncan can supply the satisfactory answer. He should reinforce such behavior (e.g., "That's a good answer, Duncan."). This reinforcement potentially serves three functions: (1) it will lessen Duncan's undesirable behavior; (2) it serves to give him the recognition that he seeks by his current antisocial behavior; and (3) it does so within desired behavior limits, i.e., promotes responses acceptable to the classroom requirements. It is important that the teacher follow up his initial responses with continued reinforcement of the desired behavior, thus creating a clear association between Duncan's desired behavior and the teacher's reward.

Having analyzed the responses of Student A, let us now examine Student B's responses with the same approach. What behaviors on the child's part are identified?

"he does not understand or care to abide by the teacher's values"
"his antagonistic behavior toward the teacher and other pupils"
"responses in the classroom that are relevant to the question asked"
"he can supply a satisfactory answer"
"regardless of whether his hand is up"

Although they are not totally explicit, these responses more clearly identify the specific antagonistic behavior to which the student refers in Duncan's problem. It is also clear that "satisfactory answer" refers specifically to "responses . . . relevant to the questions posed." In the instance of student B, the response reflects a clearly adequate recognition of behavioral problems and identification of behavior desired.

How well has Student B identified teacher behaviors to change Duncan's behavior?

"the teacher's behavior may be reinforcing his antagonistic behavior"
"calling on Duncan indiscriminately"
"she is seeking to promote responses in the classroom"
"she should ask questions of Duncan"
"she should reinforce such behavior" (with an example given)
"she (should) follow-up her initial responses with continued reinforcement of the desired behavior"

These responses stand in clear contrast to Student A's; rather than lingering in a sea of generalities, they specifically focus on the behaviors to be taken by the teacher. Moreover, they lay out a strategy for specifically promoting the desired behavior by reinforcement tactics. Thus Student B's response, in clear contrast to that of Student A, meets the specifications of the behavioral objective.

A second sample problem relating to this objective offers a somewhat different challenge to the student:

Miss Gomez is a first-year teacher of a fifth grade class. At the suggestion of a veteran teacher, she adopted a no-gum-chewing policy in class.

"Those teachers here who allow it," she was told, "have all sorts of trouble." Three weeks after school opened, three girls who had demonstrated high achievement in class came and asked why they couldn't chew gum. Miss Gomez told them that gum chewing seems to lead to all sorts of messy disposal problems. The girls were dissatisfied with her response, and one of them said, "Those kinds of rules are unfair."

In this instance, the problem behavior is the *assumed* disposal of gum under chairs, on the floor, and without wrappers into the wastebasket. Indeed, this is the usual disposal process by students *and* adults, and the janitorial staff is unfairly asked to clean up the mess. The desired behavior on the students' part is *not* an absence of gum chewing; it is the proper disposal of gum *in* wrappers in the wastebasket. If a teacher states that students cannot chew gum because it is "unladylike," or "because I told you so," then he is invoking rules without a legitimate rationale, and students at all levels should rightly resent such action as arbitrary and authoritarian.

Is there a means by which the teacher can permit gum chewing and ensure that it is disposed of properly? A reasonable solution to this problem can be developed. Students can be allowed to chew gum in class as long as no gum is found on the floor, under chairs, or stuck to the wastebasket. If gum is improperly disposed of, student rights to gum chewing would be forfeited for a period of time and students would have to clean it up. This strategy offers several positive elements. First, it will assure students that the teacher is not arbitrary and unfair. Second, it will likely eliminate or lessen the undesirable disposal of gum by students. (Peer pressures will minimize the chance that even one or two students will break the rule; if that dilemma does develop, they alone should have to give up their gum chewing.) Last, and most important, it will invoke a discipline system which is in *the students' hands;* their behavior determines whether or not they can continue to chew gum. In this way they are assuming a responsibility and developing controls from within, rather than having them imposed arbitrarily from without.[3]

A third example with this objective illustrates still another kind of problem faced by the teacher.

You are a high school teacher and responsible for your homeroom students' behavior during school assemblies. Sitting in the balcony with your eleventh grade students, you notice that one of your students (from a middle class background) appears to be firing something with a rubber band toward the choir singing on the stage. On closer examination, you see that he is firing nails.

Without a doubt, the problem behavior in this instance is the firing of nails at people. The desired behavior is the student's attending to the program during assemblies. In this case, we must examine the reservoir of strategies that the teacher has at his disposal, given the nature of the problem behavior he is trying to change. He must, of course, in the immediate sense, remove the boy from the scene to ensure that no injury results. Beyond that obvious move, however, what can he do? The *severity* of this behavior should not be underestimated. A 16-year-old boy from a relatively affluent home is firing nails at people who do not even see him. He knows that he could cause permanent injury, perhaps to the eyes. Explanations from the teacher will tell him nothing that he does not already know. *An antisocial act of this severity should be seen as reflecting a mental health problem that is beyond the range of the classroom teacher's ability to effect change.* Unfortunately, heavy case loads may prevent this student from receiving psychological help for many months. This backlog of cases is often the result of teachers' being unable to distinguish the gum chewers, incessant talkers, and other minor problems from the "nail shooters" (that is, students with serious problems who need immediate help). These minor problems clogging the school psychologist's office clearly reflect the need for more careful teacher consideration of the severity of each student behavioral problem.

Major Classroom Problems

The third suggested behavioral objective in this chapter involves an even more complex set of behavioral problems.

3. *Given the characteristics of a major classroom behavioral problem, the student will (1) identify the major behavioral problems and the behaviors he wishes to develop, and (2) identify and defend strategies to lessen or eliminate the problem behaviors and to promote the behaviors he wishes to develop.*

With this behavioral objective in mind, consider the following major classroom problem.

> *Miss Jones, age 23, is in her first year of teaching at Jefferson Junior High School. Her teaching assignment consists of two "Core" classes (English–social studies combination) with eighth grade students. Both the morning and afternoon classes are 2 hours and 20 minutes in length, and each has a 15-minute break in the middle. Each class has thirty-three students. Her classroom is ample in size and facilities. At the beginning of the school year, the school principal, Mr. Hicks, identified the morning class as a "good group that does its work." He spoke of the afternoon class as a "more difficult challenge" because the majority of students had demonstrated emotional and/or learning problems in their earlier schooling. He stated that the Otis IQ range for the morning class was about 100 to 125 and for the afternoon class was about 85 to 115. (The*

classes were grouped on the basis of grades, IQ scores, and teacher recommendations.)

In the first several days of school, Miss Jones took time to talk to each class about what she expected of the pupils. She emphasized that she expected them to be orderly, to be courteous to others, and to make an effort to complete their assigned work.

Although the task requirements for the two classes were essentially the same, Miss Jones made attempts to differentiate her teaching in the afternoon class in two ways. First, she spent more time explaining the tasks to be done; second, the quantity of work done was not as great as that required of the morning class. Each day was divided evenly between social studies and English, with the general format being teacher explanation followed by student application on work tasks. Assignments were taken from texts, workbooks, and a weekly reader. In the first two months of school, several films were shown on both English and social studies topics.

After these first two months, however, trouble had developed for Miss Jones. In the first week or ten days, she noticed little difference in the effort and orderly behavior exercised by the two classes. Toward the end of the second week, she noted a general "sloppiness" to be more apparent in the work of the afternoon class. This was accompanied by increased student whispering, note passing, doodling and daydreaming. Persistent behavior of this kind was followed by teacher visits to the pupils' desks to point out that they should complete their assignments in order not "to get too far behind in their work." Students were also asking an increasing number of questions not immediately related to the assignments. Miss Jones responded that she would gladly answer such questions after school, but that at present these questions were interfering with their class work.

The success of her approach was limited to the individual case on a short-term basis; in the next two weeks, more overt challenges to her authority appeared. Incidents of horseplay began to appear more frequently and involved a wider circle of students. Two groups, one centered around a popular and athletically oriented boy and the other around a popular and physically mature girl, tended to be the source of much of the deviant behavior. During the first part of the fifth week, after numerous teacher warnings about troublemaking, two boys were sent to the principal's office for fighting in class.

The start of the next week witnessed a general decline in overt acts, but the extraneous noise level actually appeared greater. Moreover, an increasing number of students became involved in behaviors that hindered the completion of their work. The teacher's verbal appeals for quiet resulted in a noise decline only for a few minutes.

Her energies waning, Miss Jones took the approach of minimizing her class interference, thinking that her previous behavior might be reinforc-

ing their negative behavior. For several days she thought this approach might be having some success until she noticed that she could not communicate to a student above the noise without yelling. Beyond this, problems developed beyond the classroom limits; students who had been given library and rest room passes were found to be guilty of both forgery and property damage. By the end of the seventh week, most of the class time could be fairly described as chaotic. By Friday at the end of school, even the few students who had remained attentive were failing to do any of their class work. Just before the final bell rang, Miss Jones became enraged at several girls who were paying no attention to her verbal requests, rushed up to their desks, and physically shook them.

At the end of the school day, Miss Jones received a note from the principal requesting that she come in Monday to discuss "several classroom problems that have come to my attention."

Certainly Miss Jones or the teacher trying to effectively deal with a similar problem has no easy task. Her difficulties might indeed be classified as monumental. It is important to note that a diagnosis of her difficulties must take into account that it cannot be limited to what we have identified as the domain of developing self-discipline. Components of this problem are most legitimately associated with the curriculum and learning, supporting our original position that educational problems are not readily compartmentalized.

Examination of the case would seem to reveal two major problem areas of student behaviors needing change: (1) the students do not accept Miss Jones's definition of "proper" interpersonal relations in the classroom and engage in many disruptive activities (for example, note passing, extraneous noisemaking, fighting); and (2) the students do not accept the legitimacy of Miss Jones's learning activities, as evidenced by their increasing failure to complete her assigned task requirements.

A fruitful diagnosis of her problems might also consider some of the causes of the specific behaviors. Although it is difficult specifically to identify causal factors, a scrutiny of her classroom procedures reveals that some of her assumptions are on tenuous ground. With regard to the first problem area (disruptive activities), an examination of her behavior shows that she neither made explicit her criteria of behavioral expectations to the class nor reinforced behaviors that she regarded as desirable. Her irregular pattern of rule enforcement had the net effect of creating a large cloud of ambiguity in terms of behavioral expectations.

We can note several major problems relating to the students' lack of involvement in her learning activities. First, she has failed to consider the clearly different demonstrated skills and levels of awareness

of the children in the afternoon class (when compared with the morning class). She has fallen into the trap of making *quantitative* rather
than *qualitative* distinctions in her approach; instead of varying her
content and methodology, she has merely had them do five problems
rather than ten. Secondly, she is stultifying the classroom climate
with a narrow circular approach instead of utilizing one that attempts
to motivate by a wider variety of educational approaches. The latter
approach (for example, the use of many audiovisual materials), can
be assumed to be in order by the nature of the student characteristics
already known to her. These problems might be said to be mostly
curricular in nature rather than being primarily discipline matters. We
accept that argument, but the effects on the students' classroom behavior can be demonstrated by the use of varying curricular approaches.

Having identified the major problem behaviors, the central questions in this problem are now: (1) what behaviors on the students'
part do we wish to produce; and (2) what strategies might we invoke
to produce them? Let us presume in this case that the teacher elects to
produce two behaviors immediately related to the already identified
major problem areas: (1) behaviors on the students' part that demonstrate an acceptance of her code of classroom behavior (for example,
no note passing, no extraneous loud talking); and (2) behaviors that
demonstrate a commitment to the assigned class tasks (for example,
completion of assigned tasks by a majority of the students).

Many strategies can be legitimately suggested and defended; their
ultimate test, of course, must be their degree of attainment of the goal
behaviors that the teacher had identified. We will examine two. The
first of these relates to changing and utilizing the normative climate
of the classroom. Presently, it is working clearly against her, and it is
primarily a reinforcer of the deviant behaviors she wishes to change.
Given the degree of chaos that has developed in her classroom, she
needs to evolve a set of behavioral expectations (that is, a student
code) that is evolved with the full participation of the students themselves. It is now legitimate for her to put her own failure on the line
with a statement such as, "I haven't been very good at maintaining
a healthy class climate. Now how can we start to get along better in
here?" A student-involved code has the major advantage of having
the support of those with a major psychological investment in it;
namely, the students. Such a system can be made to involve the
leaders of the already existing social system in the classroom, in this
case the popular athletic boy and the physically mature girl. To the
extent that they can be involved in the creation and enforcement of
the code, they can have a contagious effect in the acceptance of the

code as normative student behavior. Such an approach will not work in all cases, but it has the advantage of some extensive social psychological research behind it.[4]

The second strategy is related to the teacher's discovery of the students' interests and level of awareness. She could do this in an almost infinite number of ways (for example, "Write a short statement about 'What I like to do most' "). With the results of such exercises in hand, she can start rebuilding her curriculum. Since it will be more directly related to the students' area of concern, it has a better chance of involving a wider classroom audience, thus making involvement and completion of classroom tasks normative rather than deviant behavior. Such strategies could be more expertly and explicitly developed. They are not meant to be the only or the best strategies to cope with this problem, but they give an indication of some fruitful directions the teacher might take.

The strategies suggested for these problems are not meant to be a "cookbook" approach to the problem; instead, we have taken some psychological and sociological concepts (reinforcement, norms, and so on) and applied them to this particular classroom problem. These concepts, if applicable at all, would require a different means of application in another situation. The student who asks for a single right answer to apply to all discipline problems is in for a disappointment. There is no ready-made recipe for success; we have only some principles that must be applied in different ways to new situations. The teacher must identify the behavioral aspects of the problem, determine the relevant psychological and sociological concepts involved, devise a strategy for change utilizing those concepts, and evaluate the effectiveness of that strategy in terms of its results.

The student can attempt such applications in the problems presented in the self-evaluation section.

SELF-EVALUATION ACTIVITIES

The following activities are equivalent to the problems given in the pretest and in the text of the chapter. The number of the question corresponds to the number of the objective in the chapter text.

1. *Consider the following descriptions of pupils in light of the first behavioral objective in this chapter.*

    a. Jane is a lively sixth grader who has made a name for herself at Lincoln School. She always completes homework assignments and work in class. She has a good personality that is admired by all in the class. She's always on the ball and is generally a lovely girl.

b. Don is nothing but a troublemaker in all of his classes. He is frequently cited by other teachers for hitting and running into other students. He is continually irritated by small things. Moreover, his school problems are intensified by the fact that he is not too bright. Overall, he is rather a peculiar person.

c. Larry has raised his achievement scores in math and reading to grade level in the last year. Generally, he is a good student. In spite of his difficulties in gaining friends, he seems to get along well with his teachers. Other boys in the class take advantage of his size, and this seems to frustrate Larry greatly at times.

d. Alice is such a nice girl that it's difficult to think of her as a problem. Her teacher and classmates just seem to love her. Her difficulty is that she's not motivated to work in any of her academic subjects. She loves gym, but this seems the only area in which her achievement is up to her measured potential ability. Boys sometimes make ridiculing remarks to her about her size, as she is about 25 pounds overweight.

Examine the responses you have written. Have you rewritten the ambiguous portions of these statements in a behaviorally explicit form?

2. *Develop solutions to the following problems as indicated in the second behavioral objective in this chapter.*

a. Bill is physically a very active seventh grader who is achieving at a level clearly below his average ability. He has just entered your class. His student file indicates that he has frequently been caught creating dangerous situations in the school (for example, placing tacks on other students' seats and making steps slippery with automotive oil). On the second day he is in your class, you see him sneaking into the supply closet in the rear of the school. Upon entering the closet, you see that he is setting fire to the paper in the wastebasket.

b. You are a teacher in a slum area junior high school and are supervising the playground before school. You look up to a first floor window and see a girl leaning out the window. She is not in your class. Suddenly you note that she is giving you the "finger."

c. On the day you start teaching a seventh grade class, one of the boy students markedly mispronounces your name ("Jive" instead of "Clive"). You pronounced your name and wrote it on the board at the beginning of class. About half the class modestly laughs at the mispronunciation.

d. You are confronted with a first grade girl of about average ability who cries or whines every time she answers a question incorrectly.

e. The tenth grade teacher had to step out of his geometry class to discuss an important message with another teacher. He told the students to do a problem in the text that he would explain when he came back. When he stepped back into the room about three minutes later, he found the class in chaos, with much yelling, books being thrown, students hitting others, and so on.

f. Mary is a bright third grader who does well in most of her schoolwork. She has the habit, however, of frequently borrowing other people's things (pencils, crayons, rulers, etc.) and failing to return them until she has been reminded of it. Miss Green, Mary's teacher, has warned Mary several times that she cannot continually borrow from people and should remember to bring back her own supplies when she takes them home. The warnings, however, have not changed Mary's behavior.

In dealing with these problems, have you clearly identified the problem behavior you wish to change? Will your strategy for change both lessen the undesirable behavior and promote the desirable one?

3. *Examine this major classroom problem with regard to the third behavioral objective.*

Mr. Brown has been assigned to teach geography this semester at Cloverdale High School. While he has a number of background courses in geography and related areas, he has never taught the subject before. The course is an elective, open to sophomores, juniors and seniors. The word in the teacher's room is that the course is a "tough one to teach because you get a lot of flunkees and troublemakers in there."

Mr. Brown, in his third year of teaching at the school, makes considerable effort in preparation to teach the course. He builds a series of units on the basic principles of geography and the different sections of the world. These units include films, filmstrips, and materials for bulletin board displays. Unit tests are also constructed.

On the first day of class, Mr. Brown notes the makeup of his class of thirty (twenty boys and ten girls, and about an equal number of seniors, juniors and sophomores). The information sheets returned by the students show a great disparity in the writing skills displayed. Mr. Brown hands out texts, a syllabus of study, and a set of rules for behavior.

These rules consists of five points:

a. Be on time. Students are expected to be in the class when the bell rings.
b. Treat your fellow classmates as you would like them to treat you.
c. All assignments should be handed in on time. One full grade will be subtracted for each day late.
d. Students who damage school materials are financially responsible. Books should show no more than normal wear.
e. Students who disrupt the learning process in the classroom will be sent to the detention hall.

Mr. Brown immediately notices varying responses on the first assignments. Some students (mostly girls) do complete and careful work; others do very sloppy work or nothing at all. This pattern continues up through the time of the first test. During the same period, discipline problems emerge. Boy students immediately try to test Mr. Brown's will by throwing spitwads, answering questions with half-crude language, and generally refusing to participate in classroom activities. Not to be intimidated, Mr. Brown soon begins to throw students out of class. This action, however, does not seem to lessen disruptive behavior or increase work output. In some ways, getting thrown out of class appears to become a game with the boy students. Attempts at curriculum variation result in little improvement; when films are shown, boys make a game out of hitting friends with spitwads in the dark.

Mr. Brown decides he will show the students how much academic trouble they are in. He makes up a tough test (instead of using the unit test already made), and it does result in a marked display of poor grades. Two-thirds of the class get Ds and Fs; no student gets an A and only five get Bs. When he goes over the test in class several days later, much classroom disruption occurs; students who received poor grades make jokes on many points, and the hard-working students who failed to get A's complain because the test was unfair. "What's the use of doing all that work?" says one of the girls.

At the end of the day, Mr. Brown stops by the counselor's office to get some information on the nature of his students. He finds that about half of his pupils are ordinarily assigned to slow sections in other courses. Many of the boy students with academic problems have a long history of discipline referrals. Few of these students expect to go to college. They have been put into geography because "there wasn't any other course they could take." On the other hand, seven of the remaining students (mostly girls) are high achievers, expect to go to college, and have elected geography because of an interest in the subject.

In your response to this problem, have you identified the major behavioral problems and the behaviors you wish to promote? Do your strategies for change direct themselves toward eliminating the problem behaviors and promoting the behaviors you wish to develop?

NOTES AND REFERENCES

1. The concepts of reinforcement and punishment are introduced with some brevity here. Their use and effects will be examined in more depth in the next chapter.
2. Fritz Redl and David Wineman, *Controls From Within: Techniques for the Treatment of the Aggressive Child* (New York: The Free Press, 1952), p. 158.
3. This can be recognized as a use of contingency management principles, which will be discussed in more detail in the next chapter.

4. See Bernard Berelson and Gary A. Steiner, *Human Behavior: An Inventory of Scientific Findings* (New York: Harcourt, Brace and World, 1964), for an extensive review of relevant social science findings.

SUGGESTED READINGS

Jackson, J. M. "Structural Characteristics of Norms," in National Society for the Study of Education Yearbook, *The Dynamics of Instructional Groups*. Chicago: University of Chicago Press, 1960.
   This article presents an interesting conceptual model for understanding the normative aspects of behavior problems in the classroom.

Madsen, C. H., Jr. and Clifford K. Madsen. *Teaching/Discipline: Behavioral Principles Towards a Positive Approach*. Boston: Allyn and Bacon, 1970.
   The authors have built a useful manual demonstrating the use of contractual reinforcement techniques in changing undesirable behavior in the classroom.

Meacham, Merle L., and Allen E. Wiesen. *Changing Classroom Behavior: A Manual for Precision Teaching*. Scranton, Penn.: International Textbook, 1969.
   In developing perhaps the best practical book on the use of reinforcement techniques, the authors amply illustrate a variety of techniques for eliminating undesirable classroom behavior and for promoting student self-management skills.

Redl, Fritz, and David Wineman. *Controls from Within: Techniques for the Treatment of the Aggressive Child*. New York: The Free Press, 1952.
   This study deals with children with demonstrated aggressive behavior problems. It suggests many techniques that can be effectively used by the classroom teacher.

Redl, Fritz. "Aggression in the Classroom," *Today's Education* 58, no. 6 (September 1969), pp. 30–32.
   This short article contains a few of the concepts and techniques developed in the volume above.

Smith, Louis M., and William Geoffrey. *The Complexities of an Urban Classroom*. New York: Holt, Rinehart and Winston, 1968.
   This intensive longitudinal examination of the single classroom furnishes the teacher with valuable insights relating to the development of a student behavior code.

Applying Learning Concepts

Note to teachers: These sample questions cover all of the objectives included in the chapter on applying learning concepts. The teacher may wish to use a shorter pretest for a variety of reasons (for example, to test only the less complex objectives in the chapter, to exclude some because of personal preference, or simply to make a shorter test). Some of the questions may be seen as more appropriate for a take-home exercise rather than a classroom evaluation. Satisfactory sample answers to equivalent questions can be found in the following chapter.

1. *Read the following description of a classroom situation, and do the following:*
   a. *Identify the pupil behaviors reflecting artificial learning.*
   b. *Identify the teacher behaviors promoting artificial learning.*
   c. *State an alternative set of teacher behaviors designed to produce real learning.*
   d. *Identify a consequent set of pupil behaviors that would reflect real learning.*

   Mrs. O'Hara uses a point system designed to motivate her seventh grade math class. Students are given points for each right answer they supply, whether it is in class exercises, homework, or tests. During class exercises, Mrs. O'Hara goes alphabetically through her roll book, calling on each student to solve a problem. If the student furnishes the right answer, he receives a point. Any wrong answer receives no points (nor is any partial credit given for any kind of work). Homework is handled the same way, with students asked to turn in only the answers to the problems, double-spaced on the front of a white, lined piece of paper. If any homework problems are wrong, the student is asked to do them over again and hand them in the next day. Tests are taken every Friday, with the major difference being that each problem counts three points instead of one. Mrs. O'Hara takes all the test problems from the book, changing only some of the numbers in the word problems. Since all but five members of the class have scored over 225 out of a possible 250 points, Mrs. O'Hara has indicated that she is well satisfied with the students' rate of learning.

2. *Examine the following behaviors of an "un-motivated" child, and do the following:*
   a. *Rank them for their priority of treatment according to Maslow's hierarchy of needs.*
   b. *Furnish supportive rationale for your rankings.*

   (1) The student never volunteers for any classroom activities.
   (2) The child several times has been physically intimidated into giving his lunch money to other boys.
   (3) The child exhibits little or no interest in schoolwork, completing only the minimum of assignments.
   (4) The child is markedly underweight for his height and age group.

3. *In the following description of teacher-pupil interaction in the classroom, identify the teacher behaviors that are positive reinforcers and those that are some form of punishment.*

   In Miss Johnson's fifth grade class, the students are working on some paintings with watercolors. The teacher is walking from desk to desk, observing each child's work. Johnny is painting a tiger in the jungle. "That's very good!" Miss Johnson comments. Johnny continues to work at his painting. She stops at Henry's desk because he is looking out the window and not painting. "Let's get started, Henry." Henry picks up his brush, but puts it down and continues to look out the window when Miss Johnson goes on to the next desk. Toward the end of the period, the noise level in the class begins to rise. "Let's keep the noise down, class," she says. The noise level does not subside and actually increases after several minutes.

4. Read the following description of a student unmotivated to perform a school task and do the following:
   a. Identify the reinforcement factors operating.
   b. Identify and defend a positive reinforcement strategy designed to produce pupil involvement in learning.

Bill is a physically active fifth grader who shows little or no interest in reading. Occasionally he will pick up a sports book and look at it, but he refuses to read in front of the class and never picks any books from the open leisure-reading shelf. Nonetheless, his reading scores are average for his grade level. Attempts to get at the cause by asking Bill, his student peers, and his mother have provided little in the way of helpful information. His schoolwork indicates average work in most other areas, with strong interest shown only in playground games and automobiles.

INTRODUCTION

The effective application of learning concepts has been an illusive target for many classroom teachers. The body of knowledge and concepts accumulated in the field of educational psychology has been frequently seen as an abstraction not applicable to the real world of the school classroom. Theories of learning, motivation, and reinforcement have been traditionally viewed as facts and theories to be memorized, applicable only to animals in a controlled laboratory situation. The failure of teacher training programs to require candidates to *apply* these concepts to classroom learning problems (both simulated and real) has helped build and reinforce the belief that such concepts cannot be utilized effectively. Indeed, many teacher training courses fail to practice many of the learning principles they are attempting to teach. (A colleague has reminded us of a graduate course in motivation in which most of the students received incompletes.) The purpose of this chapter is to develop greater skills in the comprehension and application of a few of these learning concepts, skills intended to increase the teacher's effectiveness in a performance-based classroom.

We will first clarify our meaning of several key concepts. The first of these is the term *learning* itself. What do we mean by it? Certainly it has been defined in an almost unlimited number of ways. Some think of it as "training in specific skills"; others see learning as a more global "maturation of intellectual capacities." Since our approach is essentially a behavioral one, we shall focus on learning as being demonstrated by a desired *change in behavior on the part of the learner.* At the risk of redundancy, we shall repeat some points made in reference to viewing learning as a change in behavior: (1) all changes of behavior are not necessarily demonstrations of learning; (2) attempts at assessing changes of behavior should require the desired change of behavior to be demonstrated; (3) it is neither practical nor feasible that all changes in behavior (learning) be planned. Some unanticipated behavioral changes will accompany all learning situations.

In this chapter we will borrow from the concepts of John Holt and distinguish between *real* and *artificial* learning.[1] Thus learning as a change in behavior can be seen in several ways: if it is short-term memorization and cannot be applied outside the immediate context of the learning situation, then it is *artificial*; if it is long-term learning and can be transferred and applied to a variety of new educational tasks, then it is *real* learning. Such distinctions, of course, greatly effect both the learning process and the teaching process. These implications will be more closely examined later.

Our examination of motivation will consider Maslow's hierarchy of needs as it applies to motivational problems in the classroom. Since children with learning problems often give evidence of a variety of behaviors, it is important for the teacher to recognize the order in which these needs can most effectively be met. A last focus of this chapter will center on two skills relating to reinforcement. The first skill relates to the ability to recognize instances of positive reinforcement and punishment; the second involves devising teacher reward strategies to increase a student's desired learning behavior.

Having briefly laid the skeletal groundwork for our critical concepts, we shall now state the suggested behavioral objectives of this chapter.

1. *Given the description of a classroom situation involving artificial learning, the student will (1) identify the pupil behaviors reflecting artificial learning; (2) identify the teacher behaviors promoting artificial learning; (3) state an alternative set of teacher behaviors designed to produce real learning; (4) identify a consequent set of pupil behaviors that would reflect real learning.*
2. *Given a list of behaviors of an "unmotivated" child, the student will (1) correctly rank these for their priority of treatment according to Maslow's hierarchy of needs; (2) furnish supportive rationale for these rankings.*
3. *Given a behavioral description of teacher-pupil interaction in the classroom, the student will identify the teacher behaviors that are positive reinforcers and those that are some form of punishment.*
4. *Given the description of a pupil unmotivated to perform a school task, the student will (1) identify the reinforcement factors operating; (2)*

*identify and defend a positive reinforcement strategy designed to pro-
duce pupil involvement in the learning task.*

REAL VERSUS ARTIFICIAL LEARNING

A central focus of John Holt's *How Children Fail* is to distinguish
between *real* and *artificial* learning. Holt, as we have noted, sees
artificial learning as short-term, involving only recall processes, and
meaningless to the child; *real learning,* by contrast, is long-term, involves higher-order cognitive processes, and has meaning to the child.
Holt's position is that the bulk of teacher and student activity in the
classroom is largely of an artificial nature. The basic causes for this
condition are seen as the school's "cover the material" mentality, and
teacher and student acceptance of the appropriate behaviors for such
a mentality. Holt cites the numerous games and roles employed by
both teachers and students that mask the realities of classroom
processes.

The term *artificial* means "giving the appearance of something
without being the real thing." Such is artificial learning. Examined
more extensively, artificial learning may be seen as dysfunctional in
terms of learning criteria generally. To say that it is product-oriented,
as opposed to process-oriented, minimizes its limitation. The child
dominated by rote learning not only fails to understand the process
by which he arrived at the right answer; he also quickly forgets his
memorized product because it has no more meaning to him than a
memorized nonsense syllable. The "right answer" mentality harbors
a number of delusions for both student and teacher. Students are
often deluded because artificial learning gives them a packaged set of
answers to make them secure. Such packaged sets of answers, of
course, involve less need for thought on their part; as such, they are
cherished much as a shortsighted young child cherishes an excess of
candy. Teachers are often deluded by students' getting the right
answer; rather than risk finding out that a student doesn't understand
what he has done, they usually ask no more questions. A right-
answer mentality, after all, is an easy way to teach; a teaching
process with a prepackaged set of right answers involves fewer complexities and is likely to produce high student scores (thus reinforcing the efforts of the teacher). The critical test, however, is not
whether the student gets a high percentage of right answers. The key
question is whether or not the student can take the knowledge, concepts, and so on, learned in the unit and apply them in a context outside the familiar framework of the prepackaged lesson. The artificial
learner, of course, will fail woefully on this criterion.

A word of warning that we have echoed before on behavioral objectives. Behavioral objectives, no matter how well they are written, can easily fall into the category that Holt legitimately labels as artificial learning. If the teacher's unit consists of behavioral objectives that require only recall and memorization processes, he is guilty of taking the easy road to a short-term gain. Such routes cannot lead to meaningful learning on the part of children.

Real learning, in Holt's perspective, is evidenced by the child's being able to take his skill, concept, and so forth, and *apply* it in a new environment outside the familiar confines of the learning situation. In terms of the cognitive taxonomy, what Holt calls real learning, then, precludes knowledge-level material (involving only recall and memorization) and limits the inclusion of understanding-level material. For the most part, he sees application and higher levels of the taxonomy as relevant to real learning. Real learning also relates to the principle of retention. The student who *can* apply the concept he has learned outside the original learning climate will retain that application skill better than the student who has merely gone through the motions of memorizing it.[2] Both student and teacher can easily be threatened by the mentality and behavior that real learning requires. The student is threatened because he has fewer right answers that he knows represent sure rewards; he must also do more thinking. The teacher is threatened by the increasing complexities of concentrating on processes and products that are open-ended; he is in no position to anticipate all the consequences and will very likely get some questions that he has not had to face before. Teachers must, nonetheless, ultimately face the question of how long they can accept short-term learning as a legitimate goal; sooner or later, the student is going to find out that the world is a complex one and requires that education deal with real learning problems. When the student eventually awakes to this realization, he will likely take part of his wrath out on the teacher facing him.

CONSIDERATION OF MOTIVATION CONCEPTS

Few would argue about the critical relationship of motivation to learning. Yet when teachers attempt to assess the problem, often they come up only with a statement like "Mary is motivated and Jean isn't, but I certainly don't know why." Rather than attempt a conceptual approach to coping with such problems, we will try to use concepts in terms of their behavioral implications. In essence, our consideration of motivation will center on the question, "What do the observable behaviors of the student reflect about the state of his motivation?"

From the authors' viewpoint, a particularly useful motivational theory is Maslow's hierarchy of needs,[3] shown in Figure 2. This conceptualization represents an attempt to build a taxonomy of motivation and is divided into two domains: biological and psychological.

This taxonomy may be viewed as sequential, starting from the bottom of the diagram. Thus each level of the hierarchy needs to be minimally satisfied before the next higher level is dealt with. First in priority are physiological needs, such as hunger and thirst. The other category within the biological domain, safety needs, relates to health and physical safety needs, and in children, needs pertaining to a sense of order and protection by elders.

If these biological needs are minimally met, Maslow predicts that individuals will behave in a way to satisfy their needs at the higher levels in the psychological domain. Thus people then seek to fulfill love and belonging needs; logically enough, these usually involve parents, children, spouse, and friends. The next step up the hierarchy is esteem, which entails both self-esteem and the esteem of others. Having satisfied these levels, the individual would move to the highest levels of self-actualization and the desires to know and understand. Self-actualization involves doing what one is suited for; the desires to know and understand relate to the attainment of both intellectual and aesthetic satisfaction.

Although at present full empirical support for this need theory is lacking, Maslow cites clinical evidence and historical case studies as evidence supporting its general validity at all levels. The sequence of the lower levels of the hierarchy has greater research support than the higher levels; it can be more legitimately argued that physiological and then safety needs must be minimally satisfied before the individual is motivated to deal with his psychological needs.[4] At the higher levels of the hierarchy, the sequential order is more subject to question; for example, certain people could clearly be seen as seeking esteem from others before their needs for love and belonging are minimally satisfied.[5]

Given these limitations, Maslow's hierarchy is useful in formulating teacher strategies to cope with learning problems. It is of particular relevance when one considers the number of educational decisions that presume that the child is ready to learn when even the simplest examination of his circumstances would reveal that he is not (for example, the child who has had no breakfast and does not complete his arithmetic assignment). If some kind of motivation needs to precede learning, then we fairly assume that the environmental factors which affect the child's motivational characteristics need to be considered when the teacher formulates his learning strategies for that child.

FIGURE 2

Maslow's Hierarchy of Needs

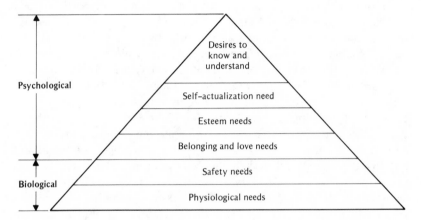

IDENTIFYING REINFORCEMENT AND PUNISHMENT

Evidence accumulated over many years involving a multitude of studies has shown the effectiveness of reinforcement techniques in improving learning. Our concerns here shall focus on identifying and distinguishing between examples of positive reinforcement and punishment, and on the use of techniques associated with operant conditioning. Our key question in this area is what kind of reward strategies can be utilized more efficiently to effect learning (that is, the desired changes in behavior). Although a number of the issues and concepts we are emphasizing were also expressed in the last chapter, our emphasis here will center around recognizing and reflecting changes in behavior relating to academic accomplishment, rather than the changing of disruptive behavior, which was predominant in the chapter on developing student self-discipline.

Our first concern in this area relates to amplifying our meaning of some key terms introduced in the previous chapter. In this book *reinforcement* (unless otherwise noted) shall imply *positive* reinforcement; that is, an environmental event which increases the likelihood that the preceding student behavior will continue or recur.[6] By contrast, our use of the word *punishment* refers to an environmental event which decreases the likelihood that the preceding student behavior will continue or recur. Reinforcement and punishment take on a variety of forms, both verbal and nonverbal. Examples of verbalizations that are usually reinforcers are "Good work!" "That's an excellent answer," and "You'll do even better next time."[7] Examples of nonverbal reinforcers might be material rewards, extra time for recess, or merely a teacher's smile. Punishment could be demonstrated verbally by use of such phrases as "Work faster," "You're on the wrong page," or "That's not right." Examples of nonverbal punishment might be use of spanking, isolating a student, or requiring extra homework. Many behaviors (such as a teacher's glance or the teacher's standing at a pupil's desk) could be seen as possible reinforcers or punishments, depending on the situation. In different instances, the same teacher behavior might serve to perpetuate a desired behavior *or* reduce an undesired one. In all cases possible, we should not rely on the *likely* results of the reinforcer to serve as our evidence; we should make every effort to follow up the treatment to see what the behavioral consequences are.

An example in a classroom context will perhaps clarify this point. When Johnny is refusing to participate in the laboratory experiment in science class, Miss Smith might be tempted to say, "Johnny, would you please get to work!" Is this an example of a reinforcer or a punishment? As in the case of the use of physical punishment in the chapter on developing student self-discipline, we do not know with certainty until we look at the following behavior. If Johnny continues to sit inactively at his desk, then we may see it as reinforcing his inactivity. If he starts working on the problem, the same statement must be viewed as punishment (since his inactivity has ended). In most cases, however, because of past experience, we have general ideas of which teacher behavior will tend to produce what kind of results. Both the teacher's knowledge of the behavioral sciences and his past experience can furnish help in the selection of appropriate reinforcers.

Since we have defined both reinforcers and punishments as being *environmental events* that increase or decrease the likelihood of the future occurrence of behaviors, we should also point out that a *variety* of factors can serve as reinforcers in the school setting. Beyond any action taken by the teacher, reactions by student peers almost always serve as a potentially strong influence of behavior. Additionally, reinforcers and punishments introduced by parents are of substantial influence. Beyond these, each individual school setting should be examined for the many other factors that serve to influence behavior.

Let us now review some of the basic research findings in the area of reinforcement.[8] First, we know that when a child's response is followed by a reinforcement, the likelihood of the recurrence of that response increases. Reinforcing by reward after each occurrence of the desired behavior will more effectively promote the development of the behavior than reinforcement given intermittently. Thus, the child who is given a star after each correct response will more likely give a correct response than a child who is given a star after every ten correct responses. Relevant to this point, the likelihood of a correct response will *diminish* more quickly after the removal of total reinforcement as opposed to less frequent reward.

Conversely, when physical punishment is used, we have another set of findings to examine. When a child's behavior is followed by punishment—in this case, we refer to behaviors such as paddling that *usually* diminish the undesired behavior—the likelihood of the recurrence of that behavior is lessened. It is of particular significance to note that punishment tends *not* to deplete the reservoir of undesired behavior. When the physical punishment is discontinued, the child's total number of undesired responses will tend to catch up with those of the child whose responses were *extinguished* by the absence of any overt reinforcement. Evidence suggests that the use of traditional punishment does not reduce the number of undesired behaviors, but rather delays them or defers them to another time or place.[9] The punished student may not change his undesired behavior; he may simply learn to avoid the punishment.

At this point, it should be noted that the extinction strategy has been shown to be an effective strategy to change behavior. In the case of extinction, the withholding of reinforcement lessens the likelihood that the behavior will continue or recur. From *our* viewpoint, the extinction strategy might easily be seen as a form of punishment. A teacher who ignores a student's undesirable behavior can often successfully extinguish such behavior. The student, denied the "reward" of the teacher's attention, demonstrates the effectiveness of the method by stopping the undesired behavior.

Reinforcement through the use of rewards has a number of different potential applications. Not only can we increase the likelihood of Johnny's solving the next math problem by reinforcing his preceding correct responses; we can also increase the likelihood of his correct response *on the first trial* by promising a reward to follow. In the latter case, of course, the reward must consistently follow. Linking the two in the child's mind sets up the effective future use of the technique.

THE USE OF REINFORCEMENT TECHNIQUES

The use of rewards obviously is relevant to formulating strategies to cope with problems of motivation. Many times in educational settings we hear the statement, "The student is not motivated." Does the person really mean that? From a behavioral point of view, one might infer that the student who is not motivated has no behavior at all. What the person usually means by the statement is that the student is not motivated to conform to the requirements of his particular classroom. The existing academic reward system does not motivate the student. He does demonstrate behavior; unfortunately, that behavior does not comply with the teacher's set of values. The student has responded, not to the reward systems of the academic setting, but rather to some other reward system external to the classroom. Teachers must be open to a broad variety of reinforcement techniques if they expect to deal effectively with the "unmotivated" child.

In this context we shall consider behavior modification through the use of contingency management techniques. This concept involves the application of the Premack principle, which makes a more likely behavior (for example, the child's taking a reward) contingent upon the completion of a less likely behavior (such as the child's completing a work assignment). For example, if the child gets all ten problems correct, he gets an extra ten minutes of recess. If he gets the work done by Tuesday, he gets a free meal. If he finishes his homework, he can go get an ice cream soda. Note that the contingency requires that the student demonstrate some performance in order to get his reward. That performance should involve real and not artificial learning tasks. The contingency should not involve taking away existing possessions or privileges or the passive stand of merely staying out of trouble. The student must connect the task completion with the reception of the reward. These strategies have shown a marked effectiveness in producing desired changes in a variety of behavioral circumstances.[10]

Behavior modification has also fallen prey to certain pointed criticisms, notably that it reflects a manipulation of the child's behavior and that it introduces an excessive degree of materialism (and even bribery!) to the classroom context. These criticisms merit response. First of all, the charge of manipulation implies the absence of reinforcing agents when such manipulation is not present; in this instance, the child is seen as free to develop in his own creative way. This observation ignores the diverse and numerous reinforcement factors present in any environment (such as peers). We would argue that a selective set of reinforcements is more functional than an eclectic set of reinforcements.

As to the charge of materialism and bribery, we should bear in mind that the entire educational enterprise can be seen as guilty of encouraging individuals to continue their education for those very reasons. In this framework, we may fruitfully examine the concepts of immediate and deferred gratification. These concepts are germane to dealing with reinforcement in different social class contexts. For example, the evidence shows that immediate material gratification tends to be more successful among children from lower class and/or minority group backgrounds. By contrast, middle class individuals tend to be motivated to a greater extent by deferred gratification.[11] Many middle class youth, accepting the merit of deferred gratification and all that it implies, do not have a great need for immediate and continual classroom rewards. They will get their rewards after they get out of college or medical school. By contrast, many lower class youth do not perceive the merits of deferred gratification and have a great need for such rewards, although they usually get fewer of them than middle class children do. Setting one set of rewards above another rests solely on the acceptance of one set of class values as better than those of another social class. This strikes us as an arbitrary imposition of values; our view is that if immediate rewards can produce the desired changes in behavior, they are a legitimate educational technique.

The use of contingency management techniques also calls forth criticisms that it inhibits the development of "intrinsic" motivation, or learning "for its own sake," untarnished by the presence of material reward. Such criticism can be seen as vulnerable on several points. First, there is often a false dichotomy made between behavior that is motivated by material rewards and behavior that is not. Can materially rewarded behavior be seen as undesirable when compared to the behavior of a student who is motivated to learn more so he can put down other classmates? Second, is not the use of material rewards often the only way to motivate persons whose focus of interest is limited to only a few topics? How can such an individual get out of his myopic state except by being materially motivated to consider a greater variety of subjects? Such rewards can start the child toward the desired goal of valuing learning experiences in themselves.

An example will clarify several of these points, along with demonstrating a use of the contingency management technique. This example is hardly new, and may echo something said at grandmother's house, but it effectively illustrates the points we are emphasizing.

Six-year-old Tommy eats in an irregular pattern. He seldom eats a balanced diet. Following the advice of several magazine articles, Mother put all portions of the meal (vegetables, meat and dessert) on the table at the same time, allowing Tommy to eat what he wished. In this way she hoped that special foods (such as dessert) would not take on any significance and that Tommy would eat a balanced diet. Almost always, however, Tommy ate little meat and vegetables but did finish his dessert.

The presumption in this case is that the dessert does not take on a reward status if the parent doesn't make a big issue of it. But can the adult control the reward status of the dessert by this approach? Not likely, because the reward status of the dessert will very likely be already established. The preference for the sweet dessert can be shown in children who are only a few months old. If this is not enough, the constant barrage from adults and peers and the unending messages from the communications media will solidify the reward status of desserts. The child *knows* desserts are best, regardless of what you say, and he demonstrates this by his behavior.

The contingency management technique takes a different route. In this case, what is the less likely behavior? Clearly it is his eating the meat and vegetables. What is the more likely behavior? Again clearly, it is his eating the dessert. Applying the Premack principle (and perhaps grandmother's advice) we say to Tommy, "You can have your dessert when you finish your meat and vegetables." By utilizing this technique we are helping the child to develop his *own sense* of responsibility. He will soon learn to take only as much as he can eat, thus avoiding the waste of food. Second, he learns that he must perform certain necessary tasks (eating the foods that ensure a balanced diet) before he will receive the reward of dessert. An additional value is the child's coming into contact with a greater variety of meats, vegetables, and food generally; the breadth of his horizon is widened. Some might see this as tyranny, but to allow the child to eat as his whim directs allows the child himself to be the tyrant. Sooner or later, the child is faced with the responsibilities of self-management. Learning them at an early age is easier than at a later age.

REVIEW OF BEHAVIORAL OBJECTIVES

Identifying and Developing Real Learning

Having considered some concepts related to learning, we will now reexamine the behavioral objectives for this chapter. The first of these deals with skills concerning real and artificial learning.

1. *Given the description of a classroom situation involving artificial learning, the student will (1) identify the pupil behaviors reflecting artificial learning; (2) identify the teacher behaviors promoting artificial learning; (3) state an alternative set of teacher behaviors designed to produce real learning; (4) identify a consequent set of pupil behaviors that would reflect real learning.*

Here is an appropriate question testing this objective:

> Camp Runamuck runs a two-week orientation session for its new camp counselors during the winter preceding its summer camp season. The sessions are necessarily held at the local YMCA. One unit (involving two classes) deals with planning and organizing a campsite during campouts. The stated goals of the unit are to:
>
> 1. Develop ability to pick appropriate campsites and allot space properly (for sleeping, eating, storage, etc.).
> 2. Ensure that minimal safety standards are met with regard to use of water.
> 3. Promote maximum efficiency in food preparation and consumption.

The following behaviors are observed:

> During the first class the teacher gave the students a pamphlet entitled *Camping Out* and told the students to read it for the next class. He then talked to the students about "the needs of kids" and how camp experiences helped them achieve their needs. The teacher then went through the 25-page pamphlet, pointing out what the students should know for the short test next week. In the next session, he organized the counselors into groups and told them "to rap about

problems they might have on campouts." He was out of the room during these group discussions. During the last part of this class, he gave them a short true–false, fill-in test on the pamphlet.

During the teacher presentation on the "needs of kids," most students laughed at the teacher's jokes and nodded agreement with the teacher after several points. All students opened up their pamphlets when the teacher pointed out the important points. While the students were in their discussion groups during the second session, most students talked about their childhood experiences at camp. On the test over the pamphlet, the mean score was 90 with a range of 75 to 100.

In this case, what student behaviors reflect artificial learning? The laughing and the nodding are suggestive first symptoms. It is significant to note that, in the teacher's absence, the students reverted to a bull session in the group discussion. They grabbed at the chance to get right answers when the teacher went through the pamphlet; on the test relating to this material, they went through the mechanical process of memorizing the desired information, scoring high on the simple recall test. All of these behaviors reflect artificial learning.

The teacher behaviors promoting artificial learning are also clear. The teacher elicits laughing and nodding heads rather than demonstrations of student competency. His handing out of the right answers ensures that student performance will reflect learning (and supposedly good teaching). Unfortunately, this learning is of the most trivial kind, in no way requiring the students to apply their knowledge and understanding. In addition, he fails to follow up the student discussion groups to see that they relate their discussion to its stated goal.

The teacher could take many steps to promote real learning. We shall suggest several. Appropriately, the steps start with the goals of the program. If the student is to demonstrate real learning, he should be able to apply what he has learned. Here are three problem tasks that would be given either to groups or individuals. They relate to the three goals of the group and require that the student *apply* his knowledge and understanding.

1. *Give students appropriate photographs or drawings of potential camp-sites and require that they evaluate them with regard to their suitability.*
2. *On a map with a river, require the students to devise a plan for proper water utilization.*
3. *Give the students the components of the problem (number of campers, equipment, and available menus), and require them to organize personnel around necessary tasks.*

Students would demonstrate real learning by being able to demonstrate the application skills required above. Rather than laughing and nodding, they would perform. They would ask questions that demonstrate reflection on real camping problems, rather than asking questions about what answers they have to memorize. There should be real rather than artificial involvement in these problem-solving sessions; if, for example, the teacher leaves the room, students would reflect real learning by continuing seriously to pursue with their task.

A second example deals with artificial learning in a different context.

Almost all the members of Miss Green's third grade class complete their arithmetic assignments during the time allotted in class. Students are given one point for each correct answer (10 points equals one silver star on the achievement progress board; 100 points equals one gold star). The students are given a variety of different arithmetic problems to solve. Here is a sample of a typical class math assignment:

46	78	41	32	102	146
$+72$	-22	$+33$	-21	$+35$	-35

$7 \times 1 =$ _____ $7 \times 2 =$ _____ $7 \times 3 =$ _____
$7 \times 4 =$ _____ $7 \times 5 =$ _____ $7 \times 6 =$ _____
$7 \times 7 =$ _____ $7 \times 8 =$ _____ $7 \times 9 =$ _____

Miss Green is very proud of her children, who get a higher percentage of right answers on math exercises than students in the other two third grade classes. She is particularly pleased with the students' learning of multiplication tables. "We drill together on this every morning," she says. "Emphasis on these basic skills is important because these are the skills the children need in later life."

In this case the students are responding to a teacher's reward system, but an examination of the circumstances reveals that their responses do not constitute real learning. They grope for points and get a high percentage of right answers, but there is no evidence that they understand the mathematical operations they are performing. The responsibility for the students' artificial learning can be laid almost totally at the door of the teacher. No part of her program can be seen as promoting real learning on the part of the students. The two-digit addition problems are misleading, since in none of them is the student required to carry or borrow. Consciously or unconsciously, she wishes to give the appearance that the students possess a more complex skill than they actually do. In the multiplication problems, the student is asked to demonstrate only rote responses. These simplistic problems are not even mixed up for variety; the student can actually come to the correct answer by adding rather than multiplying. The teacher's reward system serves as the carrot for the students' rote responses. At no point are the students asked to apply the skills of addition and multiplication to a real learning situation, problems that would require them to demonstrate skills that they *do* need in later life.

A variety of options are open to the teacher for producing conditions more conducive to real learning. She should first structure her addition problems to require carrying and borrowing. The low-level multiplication problems should be mixed up and varied in order that the student would have to solve them individually (such as 7 × 3, 6 × 7, 9 × 5). Beyond these basic changes, the teacher should include problems that require the student to apply addition and multiplication principles in a different context. Word problems, puzzles and analogies are only a few ways in which this could be done. Any reward used should be structured to reward only real learning on the part of students.

Students would demonstrate real learning by being able to solve such problems correctly, at the same time being able to explain the steps followed in reaching their solutions. Their understanding of the problem-solving process is more important than supplying the correct answer. Questions and class responses that demonstrate such understanding are additional evidence of potential real learning. Students should respond to a reward system that rewards analysis rather than demands points and credit for only the right answers they provide.

Handling Motivation Problems

The second behavioral objective in this chapter requires the determination of a student's motivational needs.

2. *Given a list of behaviors of an "unmotivated" child, the student will (1) correctly rank these for their priority of treatment according to Maslow's hierarchy of needs; (2) furnish supportive rationale for these rankings.*

Consider now a problem that implements this objective:

Assume that you are a teacher aide and that you have been asked by the fourth grade teacher to help improve Johnny's involvement in the morning arithmetic period. You have noted the following behaviors on Johnny's part:

1. He usually sleeps at his desk for part of the morning.
2. He often does not start and almost never completes his arithmetic assignment.
3. He is often bullied by other students on the playground.
4. He is always the last child chosen on teams for classroom games.

Applying Maslow's hierarchy, we can see that the behaviors listed do fall into a sequence with regard to priority. The first and third behaviors fall in the biological domain and therefore need to be attacked first. Since the sleeping problem can be placed at the physiological level, it would take the highest priority. It might be argued that the sleeping behavior is a symptom of disinterest rather than representative of a physical need (thus making a lower-level priority). Perhaps this is the case; but in such an instance of doubt, we would first investigate its possible higher-priority level in order to ensure that we do not fail to identify a higher-priority need. If investigation were to reveal that the behavior were symptomatic of a lower-priority need (such as disinterest), then it could be dealt with in its proper sequence.

The third behavior reflects a threat to the child's safety needs and would be next on the list of priorities. The fourth behavior, if it reflects the child's lack of esteem among his peers, would be seen by Maslow as the next need. Last on the list would be the behavior relating to his lack of work completion; this reflects his lack of desire to know and understand (at least within this learning climate).

Although it is beyond the scope of this particular behavior objective, some preliminary consideration of strategies for change seems relevant at this juncture. The initial problem of probing the cause of the child's sleeping requires home investigation; if evidence indicates that the child is not getting sufficient rest, home cooperation in supplying basic conditions to meet this need is mandatory. Dealing with the safety needs of the child in this case probably involves two sets of strategies: a first set limiting the kind of hostile environment currently threatening the child, and a second positive set reinforcing the children who display cooperative (as opposed to aggressive) behavior toward Johnny. This latter strategy relates closely to a possible strategy for coping with the esteem needs of the child. In this case, we would hope to supplement the teacher's positive reinforcement of Johnny with positive reinforcement of children who deal cooperatively with him. Having dealt with the three lower-level needs, we are in a position to say that Johnny is now in a position to cope better with his need to know and understand. The latter need, of course, may involve a number of factors relating to curriculum, such as the child's perception of the relevance of this work to his vocational or intellectual goals.

One additional point on this subject: it is foolhardy to presume that a single classroom teacher *by himself* can meet the needs of thirty-five children. The teacher must get help, in the form of teacher aides, administrative support, and services supplied by psychological personnel. Application of Maslow's hierarchy presumes a school climate and available facilities that afford minimal levels of these kinds of supplementary services.

A second problem concerning motivation reveals some different elements.

Thirteen-year-old Billy exhibits the following characteristics:

1. He seldom shows interest in any schoolwork.
2. He has been "beaten up" at least twice by three of the larger boys in the class on the way home from school.
3. Some girls refuse to dance with him during square dancing.
4. He is very much underweight and under height for his age group.

As in the previous case, we must seek as much additional information as is obtainable and make our interpretations cautiously. First of all, the cause of Billy's small size should be probed to determine if some physiological need must be met. If this can be traced to a cause such as inadequate diet, then this need should be met first. If it cannot be laid to physiological causes, then this problem should be explored as one relating to Billy's self-esteem. A self-preservation safety need also emerges in this case. A further examination of Billy's behavior may show additional evidence that he fears for his safety because of the physical threat of other boys. If this is the case, then this need could be seen as the second priority. The third behavior might be considered next, as one relating to either a need for love and belonging or a need for self-esteem. Several points of information are needed for legitimate conclusions on this point. Is Johnny rejected by the boys in the group? Does his behavior reflect a need for some kind of acceptance by girls? If neither is the case, then we might not see this behavior as reflecting a need at all. Lastly, we might consider the needs relating to his lack of schoolwork and what specific behavioral problems are involved here. If the other behaviors reflect the needs suggested, then this would still be seen as of last priority in the Maslow hierarchy.

Recognizing Reinforcers and Punishments

The third behavioral objective relates to principles and reinforcement. Initially we are concerned about the skills of identifying examples of reinforcers and punishments.

3. *Given a behavioral description of teacher-pupil interaction in the classroom, the student will identify the teacher behaviors that are positive reinforcers and those that are some form of punishment.*

Here is a sample problem to test the preceding objective.

The setting is a fourth grade class, and the students are currently doing math problems individually at their desks. Miss Jones, the teacher, is going to each desk to check on the work of pupils. Stopping at Johnny's desk, she says, "That's good work." Johnny continues working at the problems. She hears some extraneous noise at the rear of the class. "Be quiet in the back. I'll be by to check your work in a minute," she warns. The boys making the noise become quiet. In her next action she goes over to check on the work of Mary. Mary works at the problems and continues to do this after Miss Jones leaves her desk.

The teacher's initial verbal statement to Johnny might be seen as a likely reinforcer, and indeed it is; Johnny continues working at his problems. Her admonishing language directed to the noisy students in the back of the class appears to be a punishment (that is, designed to lessen the undesired noise). Since the noise from the boys ceases, we may again presume that the initial assumption is correct. In this instance, we should be careful to check if the students' extraneous noise gets channeled to another undesired outlet. In her last interaction we do not know initially whether to classify it as a reinforcer or punishment. Since Mary continues to work after Miss Jones leaves her desk, we may infer that the teacher's action has served to reinforce Mary's work on the problems.

A second problem in this area involves a description with some more complex elements.

In a ninth-grade geography class, the students are engaged in making relief maps with putty and cardboard materials. Mr. Kerkorian, the teacher, moves around the room to the different tables to help students clarify any problems they are having with the task. At the first desk, the students are working on the map but are having trouble interpreting the meaning of several contour lines in their atlas. Mr. Kerkorian stops to clarify their meaning. After he leaves their desk, they proceed with their map building. At the second table, the four boys are either sleeping or reading car magazines. Mr. Kerkorian takes about five minutes to give them a pep talk on the virtues of geography and on the importance of being able to read maps. He also briefly explains the task to be done and promises each of them ten bonus points if they get the map done correctly. The boys get out their materials, but several minutes later, when Mr. Kerkorian is out of the immediate area, they revert to their former behavior. At the third desk, Mr. Kerkorian finds that the three students building the map have inverted the meaning of two different map symbols. Since this type of error has been made twice recently by this group, Mr. Kerkorian expresses considerable dissatisfaction with their work. He spends several minutes telling them there is no excuse for their sloppy work and that they can do excellent work. He also tells them that he will have to take a full grade off their work on the map because of their sloppiness. After he leaves their desk, the students make considerable effort to correct their mistakes and by the end of the period have a finished product that meets the specifications of the assignment. Mr. Kerkorian is on his way to the fourth table when he is called to the door to clarify a school problem with another teacher. The fourth table continues their work on the map.

In the instance of the first table we have a clear case of simple reinforcement, with the students continuing their work at the assigned task. Can Mr. Kerkorian's behavior at the second table be taken as reinforcing or punishing? From the evidence given, it is difficult to see what behavior he is trying to reinforce. If his behavior is punishment, then we must expect to see a diminishing of the undesired behavior. But this happens only for a short time, after which the students revert to their former behaviors. Since he has clearly intervened at this table, we must interpret his intervention as *reinforcing* the behavior which he is trying to eliminate. Although this cannot be identified as the sole reinforcer of this behavior, we have no evidence that it has served as anything more than a brief deterrent to the undesirable behavior. In the case of the third table, his behavior may be interpreted as punishment, and the undesirable learning behavior is diminished or stopped. Beyond this, we might note, the students proceed to accomplish the assigned task without any further teacher intervention. Because of this we may infer that other reinforcing factors beyond those described were in operation. In analyzing such classroom problems, we must be careful to consider the total environment, rather than letting our attention be monopolized by student–teacher interaction. Additionally, we should note a strategy may have different effects on different students.

Applying Reinforcement Strategies

The fourth and last behavioral objective relates to reinforcement.

4. *Given the description of a pupil unmotivated to perform a school task, the student will (1) identify the reinforcement factors operating; (2) identify and defend a positive reinforcement strategy designed to produce pupil involvement in the learning task.*

Relate this objective to the following question:

John is in your fourth grade class and seldom works at the assigned individual class tasks or the cooperative group projects. His interests seem to be largely monopolized by outdoor activities (for example, he spends a great deal of time daydreaming or working up plans of his own for games to play after school and at recess). His active involvement in class learning is usually limited to geography, in which he is fascinated by map work. His intelligence test results are average, but his achievement pattern is below average. The problem has worsened over the present school year; his narrow interests have further lessened his school learning activities, which, in turn, have further lessened his achievement. Conferences with his parents indicate that they also see this behavior pattern.

What reinforcement factors can we identify here? While John seems reluctant to do some tasks, he does do a few things. We should try to take advantage of these. We can see that John in some way is reinforced by his involvement in geography. John is also reinforced by planning for his play activities. Beyond these more obvious factors, however, we should note several others. First, we can legitimately assume that John's "planning" is reinforced by the actual playing itself that he can carry out on the playground. Second, John's rewards are not dependent upon his performance of a minimal number of tasks in class; instead, he is reinforced (for example, being allowed each recess) for whatever behavior he demonstrates. In contingency management terms, his less likely behaviors are doing class tasks (other than geography), and his more likely behaviors are activities during recess, games, and geography.

We shall suggest several behavior-modification techniques to bring about changes in John's behavior, specifically to increase John's participation in classroom learning activities. First, it is necessary to break the reinforcement of John's nonperformance of tasks. What about the denial of recess until minimal performance standards are met? This raises a touchy point; since children see recess as a normal part of the school day, its denial would be interpreted by most children as an infliction of punishment rather than the denial of a reward. Thus, even though it can be seen as reinforcing undesirable behavior, we would argue that denial of recess in this case stands to lose more than it would gain in changing the child's behavior. Clearly identified privileges (such as extra recess and special fun tasks) should not be given to John until he does meet minimal performance standards. In carrying out this strategy, the teacher should be sure to (1) make clear to the student what these performance standards are, and (2) set performance standards that realistically relate to the child's learning capacities. This strategy would implement contingency management techniques; the student would be working toward the achievement of reward, knowing that the reward was contingent upon his performance. Such contingencies could be broadened to take advantage of other potential factors. Extra games and tasks in geography could be made contingent upon his performance of other desired skills. A second reinforcement strategy could take advantage of his existing interest in and demonstration of geography skills. The teacher should continually reinforce John when he performs well in this domain. When the teacher perceives behaviors in other skill areas resembling those demonstrated by John in geography, he should make efforts to reinforce these behaviors by word, gesture, evaluation, and special privileges. In this way, the teacher invokes strategies that attempt continually to broaden the extent of John's desirable behavior.

A second case relating to this objective calls for somewhat different kinds of reinforcement strategies.

Malcolm is a bright eighth grader in Miss Green's class. When class assignments in English grammar are given, Malcolm is always able to finish before other students. Previously he handed in assignments and then pulled out comic books to read. Finally Miss Green said, "No comic books can be read in class." Malcolm then brought in such pulp magazines as Western Adventure *and* American Indian. *Miss Green is upset with Malcolm's reading tastes. Several times she has encouraged him to read "better" literature (such as* A Tale of Two Cities, *but he has shown no interest. She finally decided to prohibit his reading of the pulp magazines in case he set a bad example for the other students. Malcolm now reads his magazines behind the cover of his notebook and refuses to do his grammar assignments.*

The reinforcers operating here are more complex than those in the previous problem. Malcolm is obviously reinforced by his continued activities in reading different forms of literature. Miss Green is not making a conscious attempt to reinforce Malcolm, and yet she may be doing this inadvertently. She has arbitrarily forced her own standards of literature on Malcolm. Her attempts at punishment (prohibiting comic books and pulp magazines) have not lessened his "undesirable" reading. Since his reading continues, we may conclude that Miss Green's prohibitions have only served to reinforce the behavior she is trying to eliminate. The net result of her actions has been to eliminate one of Malcolm's activities that she considers positive (doing the grammar assignments).

What strategies, then, might Miss Green invoke in order to involve Malcolm both in the grammar work and in more ambitious outside reading? Again, a contingency contract may well be in order. In this case, the less likely behavior now is his doing the grammar exercises, and the more likely behavior is his reading in his area of interest. When Malcolm completes his grammar work (which he has clearly demonstrated he can do), he would be given the option of reading from a variety of sources supplied by the teacher. Such options should be varied enough to appeal to the variety of interests sure to be present in any class. In Malcolm's case, pictorial histories of the American West and Zane Grey novels might be two potential starting points. If this strategy proves successful, Miss Green might make available such books as Howard Fast's *The Last Frontier* or one of Oliver LaFarge's many books on the American Indian. The important point here is that the options available should be perceived by Malcolm as close enough to what he has been reading to be regarded as rewards. Nonetheless, they can be seen as escalating the sophistication of Malcolm's reading level. By evoking such a strategy, it can be seen that the teaching is changing from an authoritarian approach to one that emphasizes self-determination and reward for performance at the same time that it broadens the scope of Malcolm's reading.

In each of these objectives, we have asked the student to consider learning concepts to some educational problems. In this way, we have shown that dealing with these problems requires real learning to be demonstrated by the student. The self-evaluation activities that follow illustrate examples of additional problems requiring such application skills on the part of the reader.

SELF-EVALUATION ACTIVITIES

The following learning problems are equivalent to those supplied in the pretest and chapter text.

1. *Examine and respond to the following problems, which require the skills of the first behavioral objective in the chapter.*

    a. Mr. Brown gives an extra fifty points in his eleventh grade American history class for any student who can correctly memorize the Declaration of Independence. Fifteen of thirty students attempt to perform this task; eleven succeed in earning the fifty-point bonus.

(1) *Identify the pupil behaviors reflecting artificial learning.*

(2) *Identify the teacher behaviors promoting artificial learning.*

(3) *State an alternative set of teacher behaviors designed to produce real learning.*

(4) *Identify a following set of pupil behaviors that would reflect real learning.*

    b. Mrs. Smith's suburban fifth grade class has been studying rivers and lakes in geography. Students have been learning the names of the largest rivers and lakes in the county, state, country, and world. Mrs. Smith has supplied information as to the length, width, and depth of these bodies of water. Pictures and slides have been shown depicting the great rivers and lakes of the world. Scrapbooks have been kept by the students. Mrs. Smith has built up a reward system to help students learn the material. Students are given ten points credit for each page of their scrapbook they fill with pictures and articles. Students are also rewarded for knowing the names and dimensions of rivers and lakes on their examination. Beyond this, each student can earn an extra hundred points by memorizing the twenty-four major cities located along the Mississippi River. Mrs. Smith is very pleased with the work of her students. All those in the class complete at least five pages in their scrapbooks and score at least 80 on the unit examination. Almost two-thirds successfully memorize the names of the twenty-four cities.

Have you identified all the factors required (as listed below question a)? Do the new learning exercises require that the students apply their knowledge in a new context?

2. *Develop responses for the following motivation problems relating to the second behavioral objective.*

    a. If you were the teacher of a ninth grade pupil who demonstrated the following characteristics, in what order would you attempt to deal with them (accepting the Maslow hierarchy)? Explain your choices.

    (1) He has no parents and he resides in a children's home.
    (2) He almost never volunteers answers in class.
    (3) He never has enough money to buy lunch at school, nor does he bring one.
    (4) His intelligence test scores reflect average ability, but his school performance is clearly below average.

    b. If Maslow were confronted with an "unmotivated" 10-year-old child who exhibited the following behaviors, in what order would he "attack" them? Defend your choices.

    (1) The child seldom does his homework.
    (2) The child is the last one picked for games on the playground.
    (3) The child seldom eats breakfast.
    (4) The child says he has no idea of what he wants to be in life.

Have you related your rankings in these cases to Maslow's scale? Have you specified the additional information necessary? Does your rationale contain the specific conditions that you perceive to be operating?

3. *Identifying instances of reinforcement and punishment is the focus of the third behavioral objective. Consider the following description in light of that objective.*

    a. Mr. Wall's ninth grade civics class is particularly troublesome today. He comes into class late and finds the class in turmoil; the noise level prohibits communication. He stands in front of the class for several minutes waiting for the noise to subside, but it continues at a loud level. Finally, Mr. Wall asks the students to get out their government game kits. After receiving their assignments with the kits, the students participate fully in the designated activities. During the last part of the class, several boys become involved in a wrestling match and refuse to stop when asked by the teacher. Mr. Wall asks them to go down to the principal's office. The same boys have been sent to the office three times in the last two weeks.

    b. When her afternoon kindergarten class is engaged in painting animals, Mrs. Novakowski goes from desk to desk, giving each child a verbal compliment. Many children ask her to look at their pictures. When all students have finished their paintings, she says to them, "As soon as we all put away our painting equipment, we can go out to recess." All students quickly put away their own equipment. After recess and during music time, Harry takes his cymbal and starts banging it on his table. This behavior goes on for several minutes, with Harry looking up to see if Mrs. Novakowski is watching. She hears him, but then chooses to ignore him. After several more minutes, he ceases to bang the cymbals.

Can you support your identifications of reinforcers and punishments? Does the following behavior support your choice? Are there any examples of punishment by extinction?

4. *The fourth behavioral objective involves more complex skills of reinforcement. The following items illustrate related sample problems.*

   a. In Mr. O'Hara's ninth grade algebra class, one of the requirements is that students turn in homework daily. Mr. O'Hara believes that such a requirement ensures that students will stay up with the work. One student refuses to turn in any, saying that it doesn't do him any good. Moreover, he is able to make As on all the tests. Even though the student has been warned that he will get a C on his report card, the student continues not to hand in homework.

   b. Jane is an above-average achiever in the sixth grade. Her only academic problem is in the area of arithmetic, in which she has had a history of poor achievement. At present she is unwilling even to try to work on problems, saying that she knows the answer will be wrong. Her behavior in other academic areas demonstrates a strong desire for perfection in her work. It is also apparent that she most enjoys English and social studies.

Have you identified the reinforcement factors in operation? Does your strategy contain positive reinforcers rather than punishment? Is it specifically directed at the problem of involvement in the learning activity?

NOTES AND REFERENCES

1. John Holt, *How Children Fail* (New York: Dell Publishing Co., 1964).
2. R. W. Tyler, "Permanence of Learning," *Journal of Higher Education* 4 (1933), pp. 203–204.
3. See A. H. Maslow, *Motivation and Personality* (New York: Harper & Row, 1970).
4. C. N. Cofer and M. H. Appley, *Motivation: Theory and Research* (New York: John Wiley and Sons, 1964).
5. Maslow, *op. cit.*, pp. 52–53.
6. Negative reinforcement pertains to a situation in which only *removal* of a stimulus from the environment is likely to increase the behavior that precedes it (e.g., "If you don't finish your dinner, I'm going to spank you."). In this case it is hoped that the child will clean his plate to promote the removal of the unpleasant stimulus. Note that the child is working to avoid punishment rather than *for* a reward.

7. Reinforcers are the specific events or rewards that serve to strengthen the reinforced behavior. For a more extended discussion of these and other related terms, see Merle L. Meacham and Allen E. Wiesen's *Changing Classroom Behavior* (Scranton, Penn.: International Textbook Company, 1969).
8. Bernard Berlson and Gary Steiner, *Human Behavior: An Inventory of Scientific Findings* (New York: Harcourt, Brace, and World, 1964), pp. 136–168.
9. Robert R. Sears, Eleanor E. Maccoby, and Harry Levin, *Patterns of Child Rearing* (New York: Harper & Row, 1957).
10. Glen Terrel, Kathryn Durkin, and Melvin Wiesley, "Social Class and the Nature of the Incentive in Discrimination Learning," *Journal of Abnormal and Social Psychology* 59 (1959), pp. 270–272.
11. Lloyd Homme, *Contingency Management* (Albuquerque, N. Mex.: Westinghouse Laboratory, Behavioral Technology Department, 1966).

SUGGESTED READINGS

Gagne, Robert. *The Conditions of Learning.* New York: Holt, Rinehart and Winston, 1970.

The author clearly explains eight kinds of learning and relates them to decision-making in education.

Holt, John. *How Children Fail.* New York: Dell Publishing Co., 1964.

Reflecting on his experiences as an elementary math teacher, Holt effectively analyzes his experiences with regard to their influence on real learning.

Homme, Lloyd, et al., *How to Use Contingency Contracting in the Classroom.* Champaign, Ill.: Research Press, 1970.

Homme's book clearly explains this contractual reinforcement technique by taking the reader through a programmed learning experience. The skills developed range from simple reinforcing to classroom organization strategies.

Keller, Fred S. *Learning: Reinforcement Theory.* Garden City, N.Y.: Doubleday, 1954.

The work offers a well-stated explanation of reinforcement theory, furnishing numerous examples in the process.

Maslow, A. H. *Motivation and Personality.* New York: Harper & Row, 1970.

Here is a thorough explanation of Maslow's theories and research.

McDonald, Frederick J. *Educational Psychology.* Belmont, Cal.: Wadsworth Publishing Company, 1965.

This is one of the better texts in educational psychology and includes extensive sections on both cognitive and affective learning.

Mink, Oscar G. *The Behavior Change Process.* New York: Harper & Row, 1970.

Mink has developed an excellent self-instructional programmed text to build skills in the use of reinforcement techniques as tools to change behavior.

Taxonomy of Learning and Educational Objectives

Note to teachers: These sample questions cover all of the objectives included in the chapter on taxonomy of learning and educational objectives. The teacher may wish to use a shorter pretest for a variety of reasons (for example, to test only the less complex objectives in the chapter, to exclude some because of personal preference, or simply to make a shorter test). Some of the questions may be more appropriate for a take-home exercise than a classroom evaluation. Sample answers to equivalent questions can be found in the following chapter.

1. *State at least two arguments used by Benjamin Bloom and David Krathwohl* (Taxonomies of Educational Objectives) *supporting the cognitive ordering of learning goals and explain how such goals may be used in planning and evaluation, based on the Bloom-Krathwohl model.*

2a. *Examine the following list of statements and state whether each is a goal or behavioral objective.*

   (1) To gain an increased understanding of the Constitution.
   (2) From a list of twenty arithmetic word problems involving addition, subtraction, and multiplication, the student will pick fifteen and correctly solve at least ten of these.
   (3) The student will increase his knowledge and understanding of the solar system.
   (4) The student will correctly list at least five out of the last six Presidents of the United States.

2b. *Examine the following list and determine whether each statement is a correctly or incorrectly stated behavioral objective.*

   (1) Given fifteen sentences that each contain an example of a dangling participle, the student will (a) correctly identify a minimum of

twelve of the dangling participles, and (b) rewrite at least ten of these in a manner that demonstrates correct English usage.

(2) Given the opportunity in class discussion, the student will demonstrate his increased understanding of the American character and its relationship to the American dream.

(3) From a list of forty given biology terms, the student will select five and explore the meaning of those terms as they relate to the first two chapters of the text.

(4) In a 25-yard pool without competition, the student will swim 50 yards freestyle in less than 40 seconds.

2c. *Examine the following behavioral objectives and determine at which level of the cognitive taxonomy they fall.*

(1) After reading a passage on supply and demand, the student will correctly translate it into lay terminology.

(2) The student will translate a list of annual unemployment data to a bar graph that correctly represents a 10-year period.

(3) The student will correctly list at least six of the causes of the Civil War given in class.

(4) Given two passages relating to the causes of the 1929 crash, the student will identify (a) points of agreement in the two passages; (b) points of disagreement in the two passages; (c) points addressed by one author and not the other.

3. *From the following learning goal, write three related behavioral objectives, all at different levels of the cognitive domain.*

To increase the student's skill in using the dictionary.

4. *Examine the following four behavioral objectives in English and place them in the correct sequential order.*

a. The student will correctly identify at least eight of the subjects in the given sentences.

b. Given a list of five sentence components, the student will compose five original sentences demonstrating their correct usage.

c. The student will list at least five of the possible parts of a sentence.
d. Given a two-page reading followed by twenty statements related to the reading, the student will correctly identify in at least fifteen cases whether the language use in each sentence is (a) supported by the rationale of the reading, (b) refuted by the rationale of the reading, or (c) irrelevant to the rationale of the reading.

INTRODUCTION

The first purpose of this chapter is to explain Bloom's and Krathwohl's taxonomies of educational objectives and show how they relate to student learning.[1] The second purpose is to see how the taxonomies can be used for curriculum planning, especially the planning and evaluation of a teacher's learning goals and objectives for his students. The merits of behavioral objectives in writing lesson plans and units will also be discussed. A number of examples and opportunities will be provided to give the reader practice in recognizing, writing, and sequencing objectives.

Ideas regarding educational taxonomies and techniques for writing objectives have been borrowed from a number of writers. The abstraction of essential ideas from these sources, combined in a simplified manner, provides an approach that is brief and useful. In contrast to the usual approach of texts that make lengthy distinctions between types of behavioral objectives by labeling some *process, student, teacher,* or *terminal,* the objectives in this book are merely *behavioral objectives* that are written in terms of what the teacher wants the student to perform. Furthermore, it is necessary for the teacher to prepare the behavioral objectives at the beginning of a unit or lesson so that the objectives can later serve as the basis on which students will be evaluated.

A taxonomy is essentially a hierarchical *ranking of elements.* A taxonomy designates the complexity and differences between these elements. There have been many different taxonomies developed in education, but the Bloom and Krathwohl handbooks on the taxonomy of educational objectives have had the greatest impact of any single model of education in the last decade. As originally defined by Bloom and Krathwohl, the taxonomy was an attempt to catalog, in both sequential and cumulative order, the stages of learning from the most elementary to the most complex.

This hierarchy of learning was developed for both the cognitive (intellectual) and affective (emotional) domains. The cognitive domain increases in levels of complexity through the following categories: knowledge, comprehension, application, analysis, synthesis, and evaluation. The affective domain categories are receiving, responding, valuing, organization of values, and development of a set of values.[2] These two domains, while separated for the purpose of considering specific educational planning, are interrelated. To illustrate, assume an individual has just learned something new. This learning came into the individual's nervous system through one of the five senses. The information was subsequently analyzed and channeled to various places in the individual's mind. To move from lower to higher centers of the brain, the information must go through the person's levels of awareness. If the learning seems relevant, the individual continues to use the information; if the stimulus seems inappropriate, the information is stored. The first stage in learning involves the affective domain. The second stage—that of making a decision of whether and how to use the information—is a cognitive process. If the individual associates the new learning with previously acquired information and decides to react to this new learning, the psychomotor or physical domain comes into the picture.

The concern of this chapter is not with the actual tracing of information through the individual or with measuring learning in the psychomotor domain. Rather the specific concern is with providing learning situations in which the learning of a specific written instructional objective can be measured by the psychomotor response demonstrated by the student. If the student does not demonstrate the psychomotor response specified by the objective, the teacher assumes he has not learned. The objectives may occasionally be concerned with the student's awareness, or at other times, with how the student analyzes information. In either case the psychomotor domain is the vehicle that allows the student to show the teacher that he has met the objectives at the various levels of the cognitive and affective domains.

In short, the authors of the taxonomy believe that learning is at least a two-fold task that requires the learner to involve himself to some degree in the cognitive and affective domains during any given exercise. These operations are often complex, but they are *observable, measurable,* and *definable.*[3]

Not all learning situations employ all steps in each domain. Recent research questions whether learning is as distinct as the steps in each of the domains would indicate.[4] Whether a student, for example, begins to analyze before he comprehends all of the knowledge taught or whether he begins to value before he has applied the knowledge are important aspects of curriculum planning. Whether or not the taxonomy is entirely accurate, it is a logical tool for planning lessons. The taxonomy can show the theme of the lesson the teacher is presenting as well as the primary behavioral objectives and activities that the student is being asked to perform. This is not to say that the student may not on his own go beyond the objectives of the lesson. Indeed, students may be working at several levels of the taxonomy almost simultaneously. The higher-level skills, while important and necessary, are not basic to the actual lesson being given. Subsequent objectives and evaluations may test for these acquired skills somewhat later. For the lesson being given, the only skills the teacher is concerned with teaching are those that have been planned for, using the taxonomy and related materials.

Although the objectives of a lesson may be geared to one or more levels in the domains, the learning process is so dynamic that there is almost constant interplay of these domains in any classroom situation. When any material is presented, the student's cognitive learning will be initially influenced by the degree to which the student is aware (an affective domain classification), his willingness to receive the material (an affective domain classification), and his willingness to respond (an affective domain classification).

For example, listening to a lecture in biology in which the instructor is classifying animals according to phylum, class, order, family, genus, species, scientific name, and common name might represent a lesson organized only at the lowest level of the learning taxonomy. However, both the teacher and student might be comparing and contrasting the knowledge-level information in this lesson with material learned from previous experiences. As this comparison and evaluation is taking place, the student is synthesizing this material into some meaningful pattern, perhaps placing it in some kind of priority, and putting some value on the information. In the case of a student performing all these skills, the learning taking place taxonomically exceeds the requirements of the class. The minimal requirement of learning the biological orderings is still the skill for which the student will be graded. This case reiterates the point made earlier that new learning considered relevant by the learner is associated with prior learning and formed into some type of pattern. It would be practically impossible for a teacher to attempt to write objectives that would test every association pattern for every student in the class. The concern should be to write instructional objectives that test initially for very simple skills and learning responses. Later the teacher should provide objectives, lessons, and learning opportunities in which students can demonstrate some of the more important higher-level association skills, such as analysis, synthesis, and evaluation.

By using the taxonomy, the teacher can decide the appropriateness of a particular lesson or set of objectives and their placement in a unit plan. In the biology class example, this lesson might best be placed toward the beginning of the unit because the lesson required no application, analysis, or interpretation of information skills. The lesson asked the students to classify, a knowledge-level function.

SUGGESTED BEHAVIORAL OBJECTIVES

The behavioral objectives for this chapter are as follows:

1. *The student will state in writing at least two of the four reasons contained in Bloom and Krathwohl's rationale for organizing a taxonomy of learning and describe how it is used in planning and evaluating courses of instruction.*
2. *Given a series of statements, the student will be able to*
   (a) *identify the statements that are objectives and those that are goals;*
   (b) *distinguish between correctly and incorrectly stated behavioral objectives;*
   (c) *identify the taxonomic level of each objective.*
3. *Given a learning goal, the student will be asked to write three behavioral objectives, all at different levels of the cognitive domain.*
4. *Given a set of objectives, the student will place them in sequential order from the lowest to highest order of learning according to the Bloom–Krathwohl model.*

RATIONALE FOR BLOOM AND KRATHWOHL'S
EDUCATIONAL OBJECTIVES

Before further discussion, let us view a condensed version of the cognitive and affective learning domains as developed by Bloom, Krathwohl, and their associates. In the following model, each term or category is defined and some corresponding pupil behaviors are listed.

The Cognitive Domain

Definition of Major Learning Steps	*Corresponding Pupil Behaviors*
Knowledge: This is defined as remembering facts and information. It involves recall. This level does not presuppose any prior understanding. Bloom classifies this memory-level operation as the lowest step of his taxonomy.	Recalls, labels, identifies, matches, selects.
Comprehension: This refers to the ability of the student to interpret and make sample predictions based on earlier learned material. To Bloom, this is the next step beyond simple recall.	Defines, paraphrases, rewrites, summarizes, gives examples.
Application: This is the ability to solve new problems using the previously learned material. At this level is the application of theories, rules, and principles to a concrete situation.	Computes, modifies, relates, solves.
Analysis: This is the ability to identify the component parts of a given problem, determine their relationships, distinguish relevant from irrelevant material, and recognize the underlying theory involved in all of the components.	Distinguishes, discriminates, outlines, separates, diagrams.
Synthesis: This refers to the ability to put together all the elements or components to form a new and complete whole. This might be a musical composition, a research design, or a letter. In a broad sense, it refers to creativity or at least critical thinking.	Designs, rearranges, creates, composes, compiles.
Evaluation: This is the ability to make judgments based on a set of criteria. Evaluation determines the value one places on the material based on its consistency of organization and purpose.	Criticizes, concludes, justifies.

The Affective Domain

Definition of Major Learning Steps	*Corresponding Pupil Behaviors*
Receiving: This means an awareness or attention on the part of the student toward the material being presented.	Describes, identifies, listens, sits erect.
Responding: The student not only attends but reacts. According to Bloom, a willingness or satisfaction in responding can be termed as representing a student's interest.	Answers, reads, greets, performs.
Valuing: This suggests a commitment and a worth a student places on a particular object, material, or behavior. It is difficult to identify a student's values or appreciations. However, some clues to an individual's values might be obtained from the examples of the corresponding pupil behavior.	Completes, invites, charts, explains, justifies.

Organization: This refers to the ability to bring together different values and build a value system.	Alters, arranges, combines, generalizes, organizes.
Characterization of a Value Complex: This level is concerned with developing a life style that covers a broad range of activities but that is consistent.	Performs, qualifies, questions, influences.

Note: Both the differences between the steps in the domains and the examples of corresponding pupil behaviors are not inclusive. However, further study of the behaviors will show a repetition of terms both between and across domains. This can help to illustrate that as one moves up through analysis in the cognitive domain, he is displaying a valuing and organization in the affective domain. When a student reviews a poem, he not only uses cognitive analytical skills but also gives his valuing and organization of values by the selection of certain skills and the insistence upon a set of criteria in evaluating and ranking the poem and poet.

This condensed version of the taxonomy and examples of corresponding pupil behaviors serves only as a rough working model. In order to achieve the objectives of this chapter, it would be helpful to look at other materials. It might be useful to review the Bloom and Krathwohl books of the *Taxonomy of Educational Objectives: Handbook I: Cognitive Domain* and *Handbook II: Affective Domain*. Another good reference is Norman E. Gronlund's *Stating Behavioral Objectives for Classroom Instruction*. Also a useful source is H. H. McAshan's *Writing Behavioral Objectives: A New Approach*. Complete references to these and other sources are made at the conclusion of the chapter under Suggested Readings. Because of the broader scope of this book, no attempt is made to duplicate the excellent work of these writers. The taxonomy is simplified here to make it quickly and efficiently applicable to instructional planning. Illustrations and learning problems will use the terms listed in this condensed version of the taxonomy. The reader may wish to refer to these charts when solving some of the sample problems.

Having viewed these charts that describe the learning steps and pupil behaviors appropriate to each level of the cognitive and affective domains, let us consider in more detail why Bloom and Krathwohl suggested such an explicit approach in planning and evaluating the curriculum and the learner.

From a careful analysis of the preceding charts, it is obvious that the underlying premise of Bloom and Krathwohl's philosophy of education is behavioristic. They would not deny that, although the student may make a large number of learning associations in the classroom, many of which possibly exceed the requirements of the particular lesson, there can be no evidence that the individual is actually performing these functions until he has demonstrated a portion of this learning so the teacher can see that something has happened to the student. The teacher's task is to plan for learning experiences which are observable and measurable in terms of student behavior.

Through behavioral objectives, the teacher plans the instruction so he can teach specific kinds of responses that the students can demonstrate, showing that they have acquired a new skill. The charts show that these behaviors may range from recall to justification, or description to creativity. An objective could be written that would allow any overt response on the part of a pupil. Objectives could be developed to allow a student to pursue intuitive and inquiry approaches to learning, and objectives could be written by pupils illustrating how they might apply and integrate previously learned skills in new and imaginative synthesis projects. In a broad sense, objectives provide a way for students and teacher to plan and evaluate a course of action. Although it is impossible to plan and assess all learning, it is possible for students and teacher to develop objectives and evaluation of certain basic skills. The teacher's role is to develop specific activities and evaluation opportunities that directly implement the skills and responses called for by the objective.

Let's look at a case that shows how these points in Bloom's rationale come into play. In the biology class example, it was suggested that a given student might be operating in more than one domain at a given time. In contrast, other students during the same lesson may not be achieving any of the objectives and may have completely "turned off" any kind of measurable learning. If the biology teacher had developed some specific objectives for the lesson and developed pretests and posttests, we could conclude that he had accepted the premise of Bloom and Krathwohl and that he wanted to be able to define and measure what minimal learning was or was not taking place in his classroom. Thus, in succeeding weeks, more complex information about biology could be provided to the students. As the amount of information and skills increased, the biology teacher could increase the level of learning by asking the students to apply the skills in problem solving and analyze a given set of problems using the previously learned information.

If a teacher recognizes that there are degrees of complexity in learning, he can plan his instruction so that he does not overemphasize any one of the categories or begin instruction on too high a level. We are all familiar with the teacher who spends most of his time at the knowledge level, recounting facts and data on his favorite topic and never allowing the students an opportunity to do more than recall this information on an objective test. Another common problem is initiating a unit of instruction by having the students analyze or synthesize data before they comprehend the meaning of the material. A social studies teacher who spends his entire two-week unit merely giving the battle statistics of the Civil War is an example of the first problem. The second problem is exemplified by the English teacher who asks the students to analyze a poem and the poet without first establishing the criteria. These examples represent failures to recognize some basic concepts of learning. Not only is this unethical for the student, but it also violates the teacher's own terminal objective of having the students fully "appreciate and value" the subject matter.

These examples reinforce the argument of Bloom and Krathwohl that one should *build skills from the simple to the complex, test only for those skills that have been taught, and be sure that the activities and methods used in the course of instruction implement the objectives.*

Taxonomy: A Descriptive Classification System

The third point of Bloom and Krathwohl's rationale for a taxonomy is that it is a descriptive device to be used in planning ever increasingly complex learning. By assessing previously learned student skills, the teacher plans to gear the instruction so as to take advantage of these skills and apply them in new and more challenging ways. Because the taxonomy is only a descriptive device, this presents some difficulties. Bloom and Krathwohl make the point that their classifications are descriptive and the choice of such terms as *analysis* or *application* is the result of a desire to use educational terms with which most teachers would be familiar. They did not intend to indicate the value or quality of one classification as compared to another or to specify which category or level is appropriate for various lessons. These judgments are left to the teacher. In developing the classification system, Bloom asserts that in any given learning situation, behaviors may be taking place beyond those intentionally being taught. A student's interest or experience may allow him, as suggested earlier, to go beyond the objectives of the class while others view even the simple knowledge-level classification of data as irrelevant or beyond their comprehension. Nevertheless, Bloom takes a position that is entirely consistent with what we know about psychology. A course of instruction should have a number of objectives, some of which contain the *minimum skill* required to complete the task successfully—objectives that all students must achieve. Other objectives with increasingly higher-level skills allow some students to move to more complex skills. In all cases, the teacher wants to set a minimum level of behavioral change, and this change can be assumed to have taken place when at least the minimal objectives of the course of instruction have been attained by the student as measured on a posttest evaluation. The taxonomy helps the teacher promote at least minimal behavioral change by taking such complex terms as synthesis and analysis and separating them into simple classifications and definitions. The simple classifications can in turn be guides for writing simple behavioral objectives to meet the minimum skill levels.

The Taxonomy: A Tool for Planning

The final point made by Bloom and Krathwohl in their rationale is that the taxonomy should be used as a tool. Throughout our discussion, certain limitations of the taxonomy are pointed out. Nevertheless, the taxonomy is a very functional tool for curriculum planning. This is exemplified by the use of the taxonomic classification system in planning for kinds of goals and experiences that the teacher wants to take place in the classroom. But beyond planning, the taxonomy has even more immediate usefulness in focusing the teacher's evaluation of the curriculum units and lesson plans that he has already prepared. Suppose an elementary science teacher wants to plan a two-week unit on the topic of volcanoes. Perhaps science is not his strongest subject, and he is perplexed about the proper content of the unit. An acceptable solution is to adapt or to rely on prepackaged curriculum materials for which the goals have already been worked out on the basis of the taxonomy. Although this may solve the immediate problem, there are potential dangers we will discuss below and in the chapters on curriculum and evaluation.

Let us assume for the sake of the illustration that the teacher must rely on his own ingenuity, the taxonomy, and whatever material resources are available in the school. The search for resources produces an old college textbook, a few pamphlets, and a filmstrip. Now the question is how to use the taxonomy to put these materials in their proper perspective so that his general goal of having the students understand volcanoes is achieved. This goal is actually too broad to be workable, and it should be restated in behavioral terms so that specific methods can be developed and explicit student responses can be determined. When using the taxonomy, the teacher must first examine all the materials and see which relate to the lowest levels of the taxonomic classification system. In other words, the first task is to define what is meant by "volcano." The second task is to give some facts about volcanoes and explain how they are related. Then the teacher might spend several days of instruction covering such topics as heat within the earth, magma, volcanic eruptions, and materials ejected by volcanoes.

The unit to this point is confined to the knowledge level of learning. The teacher wants the students to define the terms, identify the phenomena (such as magma) from examples shown to them, and recall these items on some kind of test. Remembering that the goal was for the students to understand, the teacher may not feel that the goal has been achieved.

Although the taxonomy was used in planning the unit, the teacher has not gone very far toward providing the students with learning experiences that will give them a more complex view of the topic. To move to higher levels of the taxonomy, the teacher should first determine whether the students have comprehended the knowledge on volcanoes already given them. After giving the students further instruction on the types of volcanic cones and conditions that create volcanic activity, the teacher may plan subsequent lessons where students have an opportunity to select potential volcanic eruption areas and to defend their predictions. According to the taxonomy, if the proper activities are coordinated (a point discussed in the curriculum chapter), the students are working through the application level. If these skills are wholly consistent with what the teacher meant by the term "understand," then the goal has been accomplished. However, if he wants to redefine his goal in more behavioral terms, he might consider either rewriting the goal for this unit or providing different learning activities that would fulfill his definition of "understanding."

Let's review the first objective of this chapter.

1. *The student will state in writing at least two of the four reasons contained in Bloom and Krathwohl's rationale for organizing a taxonomy of learning and describe how it is used in planning and evaluating courses of instruction.*

The discussion in the preceding section should prepare the reader to fulfill the objective. If not, it may be necessary for him to reread this section and look at further exercises presented later in the chapter and in the Suggested Readings.

OBJECTIVES AND THEIR RECOGNITION

Every teacher has some kind of goal or objective for his instruction. These goals may come from a variety of sources: the teacher's own philosophy; state, district, or school requirements; stated desires and interests of the students; or community needs and pressures. Most teachers want their students to have values consistent with the broadly defined democratic way of life and the Judeo-Christian ethic. In this context, the teacher may plan his lessons so that each achievement is a building block in the final development of a participating, democratic citizen. Behavioral objectives can be used to operationalize these broad goals. If learning produces change, it logically follows that accomplishment of the terminal outcome of citizenship begins with a course of instruction based on very specific objectives that the student should accomplish.

A common problem is the failure to distinguish between broad, long-range goals and specific, immediate objectives. For the purposes of this distinction, we will use *goal* whenever we refer to broader, longer-range ends and *objective* whenever we refer to more specific and more immediate ends. *Goal* and *objective* are nevertheless relative terms; within the context of a whole curriculum, the teacher's goals for each course could be considered objectives of the curriculum. In a shorter unit of instruction, the teacher's goal might be "to improve the softball skills of second-grade girls," and one of the specific objectives might be "given one week's instruction on batting form, the student will be able to demonstrate proper batting technique as measured on an evaluation at the end of the unit."

Even though a teacher can list his goals, how does he know which objectives are appropriate to meeting his learning goals? To answer the first part of the question, it is necessary to determine whether or not his goals are feasible as a result of the course of instruction. Are the goals so complex that their achievement—although desirable—cannot be achieved within the planned course of instruction? If the goals are so complex or vague that they cannot readily be used in planning an instructional program, they must be rewritten so that they are so concise that a series of behavioral objectives may be developed from them.

Goals have two purposes. One purpose is to help teachers put concepts into writing and specifically designate what the student must know at the end of the course of instruction (terminal goals). The second purpose of a goal is to help the teacher bridge the gap between the abstract nature of a goal and the precise written specifications of a behavioral objective. Often curriculum guides list a number of incompletely stated objectives so vague that they are really goals. In such a situation, the teacher must consider how he can restate these goals in terms of behavioral objectives so that he can plan the course of instruction and assess the student's achievement. The key is that *objectives are a clear guide to achieving the goals*. Although goals and objectives can be written for both the affective and cognitive domains, objectives are only as good as the amount of effort the teacher puts into their development. The real quest is for the teacher to write objectives skillfully, plan activities to implement the objectives, and constantly evaluate the objectives to be sure they point the way to the intended learning goals.

A number of writers other than Bloom have developed some kind of learning–thinking taxonomy. Gagne, Taba, and Gilford are three examples.[5] Bloom has been used here because his taxonomy is more comprehensive and appropriate for writing behavioral objectives. The same can be said for the use of Robert Mager's approach to writing behavioral objectives, and a number of authors, such as McAshan, Gronlund, and Kibler, have developed forms for writing behavioral objectives.[6] It is highly recommended that every teacher building a competency-based curriculum consider these materials and adapt them to his use.

Below are listed *the four important elements of any behavioral objective.*

1. *A behavioral objective should be stated in terms of desired* student *behavior.*
2. *The objective should state the* behavior *we want the student to perform.*
3. *The objective should state the* conditions *under which the student will perform the behavior.*
4. *The objective should list the* criteria *that will be used to judge whether the student has successfully completed the behavior.*

If we wanted to write a behavioral objective that measured a student's performance in a swimming course using a particular stroke, we might write the objective in the following manner: "The student will swim 200 yards within 10 minutes using the crawl stroke." The term "10 minutes" gives the criterion for successful completion. All objectives that a teacher writes should contain the four elements listed above. If this is done, lesson planning is simplified. The teacher can then determine whether his planned activities for the students actually help them move toward the learning goals he has previously established. The behaviors and conditions stated in the objective give the teacher guidelines for the activities he needs to provide. The criteria give him the necessary materials when building tests and evaluation items for measuring student performance.

The following example of an objective contains the four elements:

> *The student will be able to complete a 100-item multiple-choice examination on the topic of nineteenth-century American literature. The lower limit of acceptable performance will be 70 correct answers within an examination period of 90 minutes.*

The objective is correctly written because it is stated in terms of the student and his desired behavior, which is to complete the examination. The conditions are the 100-item test and the 90-minute time limit. The criterion is 70 correct answers. It should be remembered that behavioral objectives can be stated in more than one sentence. When establishing the criteria for successful completion, the teacher should make a careful study of evaluation techniques and procedures. The choice of using 70 out of 100 items as the minimal correct number is not the result of random selection. This point is discussed more completely in the evaluation chapter.

Let's look briefly at two more examples to determine whether they are goals or objectives and see if they are stated correctly.

> *By the end of the course, the student will appreciate the contributions that the Baroque composers made to the development of musical history.*

From our definition, this is obviously a goal to be achieved at the end of the course. It seems entirely appropriate as a goal. It is *not* an objective, but a number of good behavioral objectives could be developed from it. The teacher's obligation is to begin breaking this goal into its elements and planning a number of objectives to achieve the desired goal.

Try this one:

> *To be able to understand the theory of relativity as evidenced on a written essay examination.*

It is difficult to recognize what this is, but it seems to fit best into the category of a behavioral objective. However, it is not complete. Who is to perform the task? The objective should have been stated in terms of the student. The word "understand" is *not* a behavior. If the word had been "match," "compute," "define," or "judge," then it would be possible to determine what kind of learning skill is required of the student. Using the term "essay examination" fulfills very minimally the requirement that a behavioral objective must state the conditions. How long does the student have to complete the essay? Are there any other specific instructions the student must follow to accomplish the objective? Where are the criteria to evaluate the student's final product? What must the student do in order to receive a passing grade? In order to qualify as a behavioral objective, a statement must include the four elements listed above and relate to some learning–thinking process that is classified in the taxonomy. The objective must give direction to the teacher and the student and be concerned with what is to take place in the instructional lesson. Once an objective is complete, the teacher should share it with the students so that *they will know what is expected of them.*

When writing these behavioral objectives, the teacher uses the taxonomy to select the desired learning level and match it with an appropriate word that describes the behavior. In other words, if a teacher wants a student to analyze, he can look at the taxonomy and choose a word such as "diagrams," "relates," "discriminates," "selects," or "compares." This word is then used in the behavioral objective.

On the basis of our definitions of the terms *goal* and *objective* a question might be raised: How do goals and objectives tie into the taxonomy? Throughout the discussion, it has been suggested that the taxonomy defines learning levels and that objectives show exactly at what learning level the teacher wants the students to perform. It follows that once the objectives have been written, they can be measured against the definition contained in the taxonomy to see whether the desired learning levels have been achieved.

The teacher also uses the taxonomy when he looks at learning goals that he has formulated to determine the levels of learning to be used for achieving the goal. After he has written the objectives, he can check whether his objectives and the accompanying activities appear to be appropriate to accomplish the goal. This procedure often causes a teacher to rewrite or eliminate some of the objectives he intended to use in the lesson or to create new ones.

The experienced teacher can use the taxonomy to evaluate existing lesson plans. This, of course, becomes a more difficult situation if the teacher has not specifically listed the objectives and goals he has in mind. Nevertheless, an analysis of the text, reading materials, films, tapes, and other instructional resources that are used may be most helpful in determining the level of instruction. Much of the research, unfortunately, indicates that most teaching is primarily at the knowledge and comprehension levels.[7]

Before leaving this section, try to determine the level of the following two objectives:

> *The student will define the term "fiscal year" as measured on a 20-minute test to be given at the end of the course of study. Included in the definition must be all the points discussed in class.*

> *The student will be able to match pictures of festivities and celebrations in other lands by naming the lands depicted as provided on an end-of-course examination. Students must correctly name all the lands for the examples given.*

As suggested earlier, the key to using the taxonomy in evaluating or writing objectives is in looking at the behavioral word and seeing where it falls within the taxonomy. In the first objective listed above, the term "define" was used. According to the corresponding pupil behavior accompanying the taxonomy, the word "define" is classified as a word illustrating knowledge-level behavior. In the second objective, the behavioral word is "match." This objective probably falls within the knowledge or perhaps comprehension levels.

These sample objectives also show that it may be very difficult to determine the *precise* level of an objective. As a rule of thumb, one should give them the highest possible ranking. This is especially true when the objective contains several sentences and specifies several behaviors.

Consider this last example:

> The student, involved in a conflict situation within his classroom, will modify and reorganize his position so that a resolution can be reached.

In this case, only one behavior is indicated by the word "modify." According to the taxonomy, this behavior might be at several levels. The highest level would be synthesis; the lowest, application. Using the rule of thumb, we would place it at the synthesis level. This points to a significant fact about objectives. Although it is possible to have a general indication of where they fall in the taxonomy, it is difficult to be precise without knowledge of the instruction that immediately preceded the objective.

Suppose the preceding lessons provided opportunities for the students to practice application skills. Then this objective might appropriately be placed at the application level. Unless one actually views the lesson for which this objective is intended, it is sometimes difficult to determine whether the objective requires application or synthesis-level response. The immediate task for the teacher is to begin to translate his instruction into goals and attempt to place them in some kind of order. Only constant evaluation and revision can provide precise answers. The real task is to begin writing objectives for the units of instruction.

WRITING OBJECTIVES

Achieving the third objective of this chapter requires practice. Keep in mind that objectives are developed from educational goals and that objectives should be written in terms of desired student behavior which is consistent with these goals.

Before actually writing objectives, let us perform a prerequisite activity to see whether educational goals based on learning needs can be written. We shall examine some instructional needs and develop the goals and then the behavioral objectives. In an advanced music course concerned with orchestra conducting, the teacher has assessed a need for the students to learn to group a symphony orchestra so that the sounds from the various sections are balanced. This need is written into the following goal: "The student will learn how to balance the sound of a symphony orchestra." Such a goal appears to be an honest attempt to operationalize the need. However, it is still quite vague because it does not suggest a way in which it can be achieved. To do this, a behavioral objective is written to outline the specific behavior the student is to perform, the conditions of the performance, and the criteria that the performance is to satisfy.

After thinking about the behaviors that are necessary to achieve the goal, the teacher might develop several objectives. One of them might read as follows:

> *The student will devise a plan for seating the members of a symphony orchestra so that no one section will predominate in sound when all the sections are playing together. The student may follow the examples of balancing previously demonstrated to the class. This task is to be accomplished during a symphony practice session.*

Now it is possible to get a clear indication of what is expected from the students and what the teacher must do to help the students achieve the objective. In other words, the task the students are to perform is both *observable* and *measurable*. It is *not* possible to measure the term "learn." However, it *is* possible to observe and measure whether a student is able to seat an orchestra so that the sections are balanced in the sound that is produced. In this case, the criterion is complete mastery of the skill.

Remember that a complete behavioral objective must contain the four elements discussed earlier. The objective must be stated in terms of the *student*, the *behavior* desired, the *conditions* under which the task is to be performed, and the *criteria* for success. The teacher and the students should be aware of these elements. The condition and the behavior indicate to the teacher what methods can best be used to instruct the students. The criteria suggest the evaluation that is used to assess the student's performance. Since the student is being measured on this performance, it is important for him to know what is expected. The criteria of the objective provide him with that information. If the minimum pass is five correct items of ten given in an examination, the student should know this information at the beginning of a course of instruction. This information makes it perfectly clear what level of performance he must achieve in order to succeed.

When objectives are written to operationalize higher levels of the taxonomy, it is often difficult to specify precisely the conditions and criteria. A good example of this situation is in the case in which the student is asked to balance the sounds of the orchestra. It would be very difficult to state in quantifiable terms what constitutes balance among the sections of the orchestra. In an objective of this kind, the conditions and criteria can best be handled by providing the student with an example of what is expected of him. The teacher, for example, has previously illustrated orchestras in which the sections were balanced. In this objective, the student is to duplicate the sound in his orchestra. Whether the objective specifies the conditions and criteria in quantifiable terms or asks the student to duplicate something previously illustrated, the need always remains to make the objectives as clear as possible so the student will know what is expected of him.

Behavioral Objectives and Evaluation

There is an interesting relationship between behavioral objectives and student evaluation. Two kinds of pass levels have been shown in the behavioral objectives of the preceding examples in this chapter. Sometimes the criteria have been written in terms of minimal levels; at other times the criteria were in terms of absolute or 100 percent perfect performance. Before discussing how a teacher translates these criteria into letter grades, let us first consider briefly how a teacher decides whether an objective should require minimum or absolute performance on the part of the student.

In most cases, the decision is arbitrary. There is very little "hard" research to suggest how much a student must know about a given topic in order to be considered minimally competent. For example, how many mistakes can a student make on a set of simple three-digit addition problems and still be said to have achieved an understanding of the concept of three-digit addition? A similar dilemma arises in every subject matter. Only within the last few years has there been any attempt to field-test and evaluate criteria standards. For years teachers have established criteria, but these standards represent each teacher's perceptions, which may or may not be valid.

The evidence now beginning to appear suggests that a teacher should divide his behavioral objectives into three groups. The first group contains objectives that quite clearly designate *total mastery* performance. The second group contains objectives that indicate *minimal* pass levels. The third group consists of objectives that do not fall into either of the other two groups. Only experimenting by the teacher and constant assessment can help determine the criteria for passing the objectives in this third group. In the meantime, the teacher needs to make a *successive approximation,* or rough estimate, of the appropriate performance level.

With lower-order basic skills, perfect or nearly perfect performance is required of the students. In learning the alphabet, students must master all twenty-six letters. When learning multiplication tables and other basic skills in any subject area, all students must master the skill perfectly. This does not mean that higher-level skills necessarily allow more options in establishing criteria. Minimum and maximum criteria depend upon the importance of the skill. Because student capabilities and learning rates are different, teachers in any course of instruction should attempt to provide a large number of objectives that contain minimally stated criteria. This is especially helpful when student performance must be translated to letter grades.

Consider how a teacher could evaluate the students who were given this behavioral objective:

The student will recall in writing a minimum of sixteen out of the thirty-two presidents of the country of Quandaria.

The behavior requires recall and writing skills. The criterion for minimal passing is sixteen out of thirty-two. Obviously the student is aware of the skills and level of performance needed to pass this section of the course work. Evaluating the student is simple. The test item will contain thirty-two possible presidents, and listing sixteen out of thirty-two means the student has passed the test. The objective could have been written to read that twenty out of thirty-two would be an average passing score, while more than twenty correct responses would be a high passing score. For reasons discussed in the evaluation chapter, this pass level of 50 percent, or sixteen out of thirty-two correct, is a bit low. A rule of thumb is that minimal pass level should be 70 percent. If the teacher was working with a pass/no credit system for student grades, the criterion for minimal could be rewritten to read twenty-two out of thirty-two as necessary for pass. If the teacher is forced to work with a grade scale or normative evaluation system, the objective could be rewritten to read twenty-two out of thirty-two as lowest acceptable pass, equaling a grade of C; twenty-seven out of thirty-two representing a higher pass, equaling the grade of B; and twenty-eight to thirty-two out of thirty-two representing the highest pass, equaling the grade of A.

Try this objective:

The student will swim 200 yards in 10 minutes using the crawl stroke.

The evaluation scheme must test whether or not the student can swim 200 yards in the alloted time. The minimum pass is swimming the 200 yards. The student who stops swimming at 199 yards fails the evaluation. At this point the student either ends the swimming program or is rechanneled for further attempts.

In both of these examples it is easy to see that the objective and the evaluation are identical. *The accomplishment of the objective is the test.* Students who perform the terminal behavior have accomplished the objective.

Translating Performance to Grades

After the teacher has decided on the level of performance to be stated in the behavioral objective that the student must achieve, the final task remains of translating this performance into grades. The evaluation chapter will deal with this problem more completely.

Behavioral objectives imply a criteria-referenced evaluation system, one in which the students pass or do not pass a given objective. This is true whether minimal or higher levels of performance are established. In terms of grades, this means that all or none of the students may pass. A *pass/no pass* or *pass/no credit* option is not the rule in most school systems. This means that in order to use behavioral objectives, it is necessary to translate performance levels into some kind of system in which letter grades can be given. (All students may receive As, Bs, or failures.) There are two means by which teachers may translate performance levels into letter grades. The first is to translate higher-level skills to higher grades. In this case, the student demonstrating application-level skills might receive an A, whereas a student demonstrating only knowledge-level skills would receive a C. The second means is to make a quantitative distinction between performances. For example, in an objective in which a student must correctly answer 70 out of 100 items on an examination, a minimal acceptance level is 70. This could be translated to the grade of D; 80 might represent C; 90, B; and 95, A. Both of these methods, however, should be seen as only necessary compromises until a pass/no credit system is implemented.

SEQUENCING BEHAVIORAL OBJECTIVES

Objectives should be sequenced. Since learning should move from the simple to the complex in accordance with the taxonomic levels, objectives should also move from the simple to the complex.

For example, one goal for a given unit might be stated:

The student, at the conclusion of the unit on map reading, will be able to recognize differences in elevations.

Let us assume that this is an appropriate goal. Now look at some possible objectives to implement it:

1. *The student will identify color codes used in distinguishing different elevations on a map, as measured on an end-of-course exam, matching the appropriate color with the appropriate elevation level, without error.*
2. *Given a map showing elevation differences, the student on an end-of-course exam will, using the color coding previously taught, match the appropriate color to the appropriate elevation level, without error.*

These objectives are sequenced taxonomically. The first objective requires knowledge-level skills. The second requires comprehension-level skills. If the second objective had read that the student "will demonstrate his understanding of scale by measuring distances on a map," the conclusion would have been that the teacher was probably introducing an objective that was not appropriate to the goal or sequenced from the first objective.

Sequencing objectives is one of the most crucial skills a teacher can develop. For example, it would be wrong for the teacher to ask students to perform more than they are capable of doing. This does not mean that every lesson must begin at the knowledge level. What it does mean is that the teacher should pretest the students to determine the skills they already possess before planning the unit of instruction. Then the teacher can use this pretest information to build and sequence the objectives.

There are packaged curriculum materials that try to avoid student boredom and cue their motivation by asking the students in the first lessons of a unit to perform at a high skill level. Even though the students are usually unable to perform the assignment, they are often interested in knowing what information and prerequisite skills they must have in order to perform at the higher level. A typical example of this approach is the Oliver-Shaver controversial issues materials.[8] The students are provided with case studies. They are asked to give their analysis of the situation. It becomes evident from the first group discussion that most students are merely providing their opinions— opinions seldom based on accurate fact. In order to tackle the problem properly, the students must then return to lower-level tasks and complete them before resolving the basic question first presented to them.

Sequencing objectives helps teachers avoid too much knowledge-level teaching, a problem of some traditional instruction. Sequencing helps the teacher provide opportunities for students to attain higher-level skills. When teachers are reminded of the existence of analysis, synthesis, and evaluation skills, they usually make an effort to focus more instruction at these levels.

REVIEW OF BEHAVIORAL OBJECTIVES

A Rationale for Bloom's Taxonomy

Another look at the suggested behavioral objectives of this chapter is now in order. Let's reeaxmine the first one.

1. *The student will state in writing at least two of the four reasons contained in Bloom and Krathwohl's rationale for organizing a taxonomy of learning and describe how it is used in planning and evaluating courses of instruction.*

To achieve this objective, it may be necessary to reread the section of this chapter entitled "A Rationale for Bloom and Krathwohl's Educational Objectives."

The four points are as follows:

1. *Learning is sequential and moves from the* simple *to the complex.*
2. *Learning is observable and* measurable *in terms of student behavior.*
3. *Instruction should be geared to take advantage of a student's previously learned skills and build them to ever increasing degrees of complexity for both the intellectual and emotional domains.*
4. *The taxonomy should be used as a tool for planning instructional goals and objectives and evaluating lesson plans and units of instruction.*

Recognizing Correct and Incorrect Behavioral Objectives and Placing Them in the Proper Level and Domain

The second objective for this chapter reads as follows:

2. *Given a series of statements, the student will be able to*
   (a) *identify the statements that are objectives and those that are goals;*
   (b) *distinguish between correctly and incorrectly stated behavioral objectives;*
   (c) *identify the taxonomic level of each objective.*

Which of the following are objectives and which are goals?

1. Trigonometry students will learn the functions for specific arcs.
2. The student will answer correctly a minimum of 75 items out of 100 on a test of analysis of variance within a 4-hour time period.
3. The student must give the formal and informal names of all fifteen birds presented to him.
4. To develop solutions for everyday problems.
5. Given a set of capital cities and countries, the student will be able to match the appropriate capital city with the appropriate country.
6. To understand competency-based instruction.

The first statement is a goal. It lacks the precise behavioral requirement of the student and also does not state specifically the conditions and criteria. The next two statements are both correctly stated objectives. Item 4 is a goal but is so vague and general that its purpose is unclear. It would be hard to develop objectives for such a goal. Item 5 is an objective. Item 6 must be a goal since it is unclear who is to achieve the task. No criteria, specific behavior, or conditions have been specified. As with all goals, the task is to use them in writing objectives.

Distinguish between these correctly and incorrectly stated objectives:

1. The student will make a chart illustrating the advantages and disadvantages of a monopoly, using at least two-thirds of the criteria previously discussed in the course of instruction. The chart is to be turned in by the end of the unit on monopoly and will constitute half the final grade for the course.
2. The student will use one of the following statements and be able to defend his choice:
   a. America *is* a melting pot of many different races and nationalities.
   b. America is *not* a melting pot but a conglomeration of many cultural, racial, and ethnic groups.
   The student will be able to evaluate his own success in incorporating the information from previous class sessions and logically argue his position.
3. The student will select from a given list of nations at least four that participated in World War II and defend these nations' involvement, using materials found in at least three references.
4. Following a course of study, a student will be evaluated as to his commitment and interest in musical performance by his choice, given an opportunity, to become involved in one of the school music groups:
   a. Record Club
   b. Band
   c. Choir

The first example is correctly stated. It meets all four requirements that have been outlined. It is stated in terms of the student, and it clearly states the behavior to be performed. It lists the conditions to be met in making the chart, and it illustrates the criteria by which the student will be evaluated. The second item is not complete. Although it is stated in terms of the student, it is not clear just what behavior the student is to perform. The student must be able to defend one of the two statements given, but it is not clear how or when this is to be done. In short, the conditions and the criteria are too vague. It would be very difficult to evaluate the student on the basis of this objective. The third statement is not correctly stated because both the conditions and the criteria for passing are not specifically outlined. The behaviors "select" and "defend" by themselves do not tell us whether this is to be done orally, in writing, in small groups, or individually. This objective needs considerable revision. The last item is correctly stated. Not only is it stated in terms of the student, but the behavior, conditions, and criteria for successful completion are clearly given.

This section provides practice for the third part of the second objective. At what levels of the cognitive domain are the following objectives? As a general rule, remember to place the objective at the highest possible level.

1. The student will list the first ten Presidents of the United States.
2. The student will write an essay employing the three types of paragraph organization given in class.
3. The student will design a building according to unfamiliar specifications and restrictions.
4. The student will compare parts of speech in six sentences, using concepts learned in previous sessions.
5. Given a series of problems, the student will compute rational numbers and work correctly 25 out of 35 problems given.

Using the taxonomy and the corresponding pupil behaviors, it is possible to predict that the first objective is at the knowledge level. The second sample appears to be at the application level. The student is applying the skill of paragraph organization previously learned. The third example seems to be at the synthesis level. Application-level skills are called into use in designing the building. Analysis skills are involved in considering the problem of planning the building with new specifications and instructions. The ability actually to design the building according to the new specifications calls for creativity on the part of the student and therefore falls into the synthesis category. The behavioral word "compare" in the fourth example falls within the category of analysis. In the fifth example, the behavioral word is "compute." This seems to fall at the application level.

The preceding samples dealt with the cognitive domain. Here are some for the affective domain.

1. *The student teacher will demonstrate his preference (value) for one of a number of previously acquired teaching styles by performing that style during his student teaching experience without being asked to do so. The prospective teacher will be asked to justify that style by clarifying verbally the reasons why this style is consistent with his teaching philosophy.*
2. *The student will demonstrate his awareness and willingness to respond to teacher directions by following all the directions correctly during a practice session on the school's fire drill regulations.*

The first objective asks the student to choose a teaching style and defend it. As indicated in the objective, this is asking the student to demonstrate his values regarding teaching styles. The second objective is primarily concerned with having the student demonstrate the lowest two orders in the affective domain. One of the problems in writing objectives in the affective domain is that it is virtually impossible to put the criteria and conditions into quantifiable form. The kinds of questions that are appropriate in this domain test whether a student demonstrates his awareness or responsiveness, has or has not developed values on the topic, or has changed that value on the basis of a course of instruction. This problem is considered in more detail in the evaluation chapter.

The key to planning objectives or evaluating already existing ones is to scrutinize carefully the behaviors and the conditions under which the student is to perform. The *behaviors* and *conditions* will give the best indication of the level and domain of the objective. Like any task, skill in writing and recognizing proper objectives requires practice. Further activities are found at the conclusion of this chapter.

Writing Objectives from Goals

3. Given a learning goal, the student will be asked to write three behavioral objectives, all at different levels of the cognitive domain.

The assumption is made that writing objectives in the cognitive domain is initially a simpler task than writing ones for the affective domain. This is particularly true if consideration is given only to the lower levels of the cognitive domain such as knowledge, comprehension, and application. Assuming that this is one of the first experiences a reader has had in writing objectives, the focus of this section is only upon the cognitive domain.

To fulfill the requirements of this objective, it is not necessary to sequence the behavioral objectives as they are developed from the given learning goal. However, it is a good idea to attempt this skill since it is part of the task of the next chapter objective. The concern here is simply to write an objective that contains all four elements and evolves from the stated goal. Although the objective does not need to be entirely appropriate or educationally sound, it is wise to make the objective as realistic and valid as possible.

Consider this goal and its three objectives:

The students will be able to write a good, persuasive English letter.

1. The student will be pretested for his ability to write English as measured by the Ohio English Achievement and Composition Inventory. A passing score of 150 out of 200 will be the minimal acceptance level for admittance to this course.

2. The student will demonstrate his memory skills by listing in writing all the steps to be followed when writing a "persuasion letter" as contained in the course textbook on business communication.
3. The student will write five sample letters, each of which illustrates all the components for persuasive requests as discussed in class.

In operationalizing this goal there is a great deal of flexibility about the objectives that might be developed. The task requires the students to write, and all objectives written from this goal must somehow relate to the students' ability to write letters in English. The requirement is that they must somehow be "persuasive" and "good." The use of the vague term "good" allows the flexibility seen in the objectives. In the first objective, a pretest is to be given to see whether the student can write English. The second objective is at the knowledge level, which tests the student's recall of the elements contained in a persuasive letter. In the third objective, an application-level requirement has been written asking the student to apply his skills in the actual formulation of a letter.

The first objective determines the skill of the student, which is necessary in order to perform the next two objectives. Before the third could be performed, the first two were necessary prerequisites. Referring to the taxonomy, objectives should be sequenced from the knowledge level through evaluation in the cognitive domain. Many objectives at each level of the domain can be achieved before completion of the course. The key to sequencing is this: do not assume that a student can perform evaluation-level exercises until he has mastered the prerequisite skills of comprehension, application, analysis, and synthesis.

Assume you have been given instructions by your school principal to teach a lesson by operationalizing the following goal:

The students should recognize and know the roles of the school nurse, office secretary, school counselor, and building principal.

1. The student will be able to list the functions of the school nurse, office secretary, school counselor, and building principal as measured by an end-of-course examination. The student must give correctly all the functions for each job as presented in class.
2. After a course of instruction, the student will be able to select from a given set of school situations the proper school authority from whom to seek help.
3. During a career day seminar, the student will choose which of the following school personnel positions he would prefer to fill:
   a. Nurse
   b. Secretary
   c. Teacher
   d. Principal

The student will orally defend his position, using the description of the job roles in his argument.

This goal was written in such a broad and general way that considerable leeway is provided in determining which objectives seem appropriate. The first objective is at the knowledge level; the second, at the application level; and the third can be considered to be at the value level of the affective domain. As a rule, goals should be more specific if a teacher is actually expected to operationalize them for classroom instruction. The more concisely and directively a goal is written, the easier it is to develop consistent objectives.

Sequencing Objectives

The fourth behavioral objective for this chapter is as follows:

4. *Given a set of objectives, the student will place them in sequential order from the lowest to highest order of learning according to the Bloom–Krathwohl model.*

Before determining the sequential order of the following examples, remember that the rule is to place the objective at the *highest possible level* indicated by the behavior and conditions in the objective.

Place the following objectives in sequential order:

1. *Given paper, paste, scissors, and yarn, the student will create a border design by pasting yarn in straight, curved, and jagged lines on a strip of colored paper.*
2. *The student will be able to identify three types of lines, the straight, curved, and jagged used in the masterpiece of Joan Miró,* Through the Window.
3. *Given a pile of cards having a number of straight, jagged and curved lines, the student will be able to sort all cards into these three categories.*
4. *The student will demonstrate his ability to illustrate on the chalkboard one object having straight lines, one object having curved lines, and one object having jagged lines.*

The objective that should be written first is the one asking the student to illustrate on the chalkboard the straight, curved, and jagged lines because it represents the lowest level of the taxonomy, a knowledge-level activity. The next objective in the sequential order is the third, which asks the student to sort cards into categories. This is probably a comprehension objective testing the student's skills as taught in the previous objective.

The application-level objective is the second, in which the students are to recognize the three types of lines in the masterpiece by Joan Miró. The final objective should be the first, in which the student is asked to create a border design. In spite of the use of the term "create," this objective would appear to be at the application level. It is of a higher order, however, than the task required of the student in the previous objective.

Try this set of objectives:

1. Students will compare and/or contrast in writing two values and two institutions of rural and urban living in each of three countries, within a 30-minute testing period.
2. In a 30-minute testing period, students will describe in writing the characteristics of primary and secondary groups in three societies showing how they
   (a) interact with one another,
   (b) are interdependent,
   (c) share common goals, and
   (d) believe in common values; students are to cite two or more examples of each of the four points above.
3. Students will analyze orally in five minutes how the values of a particular society relate to its institutions by citing at least three examples.
4. Given the problem of starting a new country, students in small groups will, within a one-hour work period, construct a flow chart of
   (a) primary and secondary groups to be planned for,
   (b) new institutions to be established, and
   (c) goals to be attained.

The first objective should be the second one listed, in which the student is asked to describe the characteristics of groups. This would appear to be a knowledge-level skill. The next two objectives both require analytical skills. After close examination, the objective requiring the least skill is the one in which the student is asked to compare and contrast in writing two values on institutions and countries. The most difficult of the analysis-level skills, and the one that should be ranked third, is the one in which the student is asked to respond orally about values of a particular society and its institutions. Most complex, and therefore placed last, is the objective asking the students to construct a flow chart. Based on the immediately preceding objective, this one most likely ranks on the synthesis level in the cognitive domain.

SELF-EVALUATION ACTIVITIES

This section of the chapter provides an opportunity for a self-test to see if the concepts, practices, and examples contained in each behavioral objective in this chapter have been comprehended and can now be applied by writing the correct answer to the following problems.

If the reader is not sure of the proper answers, he should refer to the discussion and examples given earlier in the chapter. The number of each question corresponds to the number of the behavioral objective for the chapter.

1. *State in writing at least two of the four reasons contained in Bloom and Krathwohl's rationale for organizing a taxonomy of learning, and describe how it is used in planning and evaluating courses of instruction.*

2. *Examine the following statements.*

    a. *Identify the statements that are objectives and those that are goals.*

    (1) To improve golf skills in college women's freshmen physical education classes.

    (2) The student will appreciate and accept the new foreign student in the school.

    (3) Given ten sentences, each containing possessives, the student will be able at the end of the course of study to circle the possessives with 90 percent accuracy.

    (4) The student enrolled in a general mathematics course will improve his comprehension of computation skills as measured by the arithmetic computation section of the Stanford Achievement Test.

    b. *Distinguish between correctly and incorrectly stated behavioral objectives.*

    (1) Each student will list in writing at least six of nine agencies of consumer protection that exist in his own city; these must include a brief description of the actual job each agency performs.

    (2) To develop the understanding and ability of students studying in a foreign language as shown by their ability to translate words in a paragraph prepared by the classroom teacher.

    (3) To develop typewriting skills of vocational office education students as determined by the standard civil service typewriting test.

    (4) Each student will recall by listing in writing the names of at least two publications he could refer to for information about a product he wishes to purchase.

    c. *Identify the taxonomic level of each of these objectives:*

    (1) After reading a poem, the student will be able to recite the poem in three minutes and make no more than three errors.

    (2) The student will be able to take shorthand dictation for three minutes at 80 words per minute with no more than four errors.

    (3) During the class period the student will create a poem on a topic of his choice that is at least 20 lines long.

    (4) Given a list of states and state capitals, the student will use the class period to match the capital to the appropriate state, making no errors.

3. *From the following learning goal, write three related behavioral objectives, all at different levels of the cognitive domain.*

    To introduce the student to basic skills in reading map symbols.

4. *The final objective of this chapter requires a student to place objectives in sequential order. Try these five:*

    a. Given a list of twenty nouns, the student will form the plural by adding *s* with at least 90 percent accuracy.

    b. The student will explain orally and in writing the term "singular" as meaning "one" and the term "plural" as meaning "more than one" and give at least three examples of each.

    c. By looking up the plural forms of designated words in the dictionary, the student will discover and write the principle that nouns ending in *s, ss, x, z, ch,* and *sh* add *es* to form the plural.

    d. Given a newspaper article, the student will be able to list the nouns that are in singular form and rewrite them in plural form.

    e. The student will make a chart explaining that nouns ending in *s, ss, x, z, ch,* and *sh* add *es* to form the plural.

Now try this set:

    a. The student will write an original paragraph in which he uses at least five possessives correctly.

    b. Given ten sentences containing plural possessives, with the apostrophe and *s* or apostrophe missing, the student will correct the sentences with 90 percent accuracy.

    c. Given a list of ten phrases such as "the winter coat of my mother," the student will correctly convert the phrases into the possessive form with 90 percent accuracy.

    d. Given ten sentences, each containing a possessive, the student will circle the possessives with 90 percent accuracy.

    e. Given twenty plural nouns, singular possessives, and plural possessives, the student will sort the words into three appropriate columns.

NOTES AND REFERENCES

1. Benjamin S. Bloom, ed., *Taxonomy of Educational Objectives, Handbook I: Cognitive Domain* (New York: David McKay Company, 1956); and David R. Krathwohl, *et al., Taxonomy of Educational Objectives, Handbook II: Affective Domain* (New York: David McKay Company, 1956).

2. *Ibid.*

3. *Ibid.*

4. George F. Madaus, Ronald L. Nuttall, and Elinor M. Woods, "A Causal Model Analysis Suggests Modification of the Cumulative Hierarchical Structure Assumed in Bloom's Taxonomy of the Cognitive Domain" (unpublished paper read at American Educational Research Association Annual Meeting, New York, February 6, 1971).

5. Robert J. Kibler, Larry L. Barker, and David T. Miles, *Behavioral Objectives and Instruction* (Boston: Allyn and Bacon, 1970); Hilda Taba, *Teachers' Handbook for Elementary Social Studies* (Reading, Mass.: Addison-Wesley Publishing Co., 1967).

6. H. H. McAshan, *Writing Behavioral Objectives: A New Approach* (New York:

Harper & Row Publishers, 1970); Norman E. Gronlund, *Stating Behavioral Objectives for Classroom Instruction* (New York: The Macmillan Company, 1970); Kibler, Barker, and Miles, *op. cit.*; and Robert F. Mager, *Preparing Instructional Objectives* (Palo Alto, Calif.: Fearon Publishers, 1962).
7. Robert J. Armstrong, *et al.*, *The Development and Evaluation of Behavioral Objectives* (Worthington, Ohio: Charles A. Jones Publishing Co., 1970).
8. Donald Oliver and James P. Shaver, *Teaching Public Issues in the High School* (Boston: Houghton-Mifflin Co., 1965).

SUGGESTED READINGS

Armstrong, Robert J., *et al.*, *The Development and Evaluation of Behavioral Objectives.* Worthington, Ohio: Charles A. Jones Publishing Co., 1970.
   This provides a readable text on a rationale for objectives and how they can be used in evaluating student achievement.
Bloom, Benjamin S. *Taxonomy of Educational Objectives, Handbook I: Cognitive Domain.* New York: David McKay Company, 1956.
Gronlund, Norman E. *Stating Behavioral Objectives for Classroom Instruction.* New York: The Macmillan Company, 1970.
   This book is a must for every teacher who writes behavioral objectives. Gronlund's sections on the taxonomic categories with the illustrative instructional objectives and accompanying student behaviors is extremely helpful for writing objectives. The book is inexpensive—an added inducement.
Krathwohl, David. "Educational Goals," in *Conceptual Models in Teacher Education.* Wash., D.C.: Association For Supervision and Curriculum Development, 1967.
   This article discusses the direct relationship between the theoretical structuring of goals on one hand and their translation into a plausible system of teachable and testable goals on the other hand.
Krathwohl, David R. *Taxonomy of Educational Objectives, Handbook II: Affective Domain.* New York: David McKay Company, 1956.
   The Bloom and Krathwohl volumes provide the reasons for writing a taxonomy of learning. Ample illustrations are provided for each domain and the types of learning that take place within each category of the domain. While lengthy and at times difficult to comprehend, these books are highly recommended, particularly for the teacher wanting to delve into the logical construct of organizing learning into measurable categories.
Mager, Robert F. *Preparing Instructional Objectives.* Palo Alto, Cal.: Fearon Publishers, 1962.
   Although the book does not go into the detail and distinctions given by other writers, its simplicity and correctness probably makes it the most preferred book for the beginner.
McAshan, H. H. *Writing Behavioral Objectives: A New Approach.* New York: Harper & Row Publishers, 1970.
   The merit of this book is in developing within the teacher the ability

to clarify his instructional ideas into curriculum goals and behavioral objectives. The book provides the reader with the basic writing skills for behavioral objectives.

Vargas, Julie. *Writing Worthwhile Behavioral Objectives.* New York: Harper & Row Publishers, 1972.

This book is one of the most recent on the market. It is precise, is easy to comprehend, and makes an excellent companion source for this book.

Building A Curriculum

Note to teachers: These sample questions cover the objectives included in the chapter on building a curriculum. The teacher may wish to use a shorter pretest for a variety of reasons (for example, to test only the less complex objectives in the chapter, to exclude some because of personal preference, or simply to make a shorter test). To pretest fairly for the skills below, it is advisable for the teacher to give this task to students as a take-home assignment. Sample answers to equivalent questions can be found in the following chapter.

1. *Develop one analogous and one equivalent activity for the following behavioral objective.*

   Given the specifications of finances, family size, food costs, and other incidental expenses, the student will plan a week's menu to comply with the quantity and quality dietary criteria as stated in the *Healthful Eating* handbook.

2. *From a subject area of your choice: (a) select one generalization, and (b) write appropriate accompanying concepts, subconcepts, goals, behavioral objectives, activities, and evaluation items.*

INTRODUCTION

Curriculum is more than the more formalized learning of the subject matter. It involves all the learning that takes place in a school. It represents the learning climate, interpersonal relationships, and subject matter materials and their incorporation by the student into his cognitive and affective development. This view of curriculum agrees with that of Fred Wilhelms, who says that "curriculum is not so much the stuff to be taught but the stuff to be *used*."[1]

Although it is not within the scope of this book to plan or measure goals and behavioral change in each of these areas, it is important to recognize that personality, behavior, learning, and the classroom climate have direct bearing on the course of instruction. In order to achieve instructional objectives, the skilled teacher must be able to recognize and effectively deal with these factors. He must be able to redirect and modify behavior, emphasize appropriate interpersonal relationships, recognize learning difficulties, and develop appropriate solutions in order to maximize the possibility that all students will be able to achieve the objectives of the course. The teacher should view curriculum in this broad way. Unless the teacher is able to develop skill in dealing with the many influences that affect the course of instruction, the successful implementation of the subject matter may be seriously compromised.

In the taxonomy chapter, it was pointed out that instructional objectives are confined to those relating to subject matter. This was done in full awareness of the larger conception of curriculum.

Most of the objectives teachers will be dealing with relate to their subject matter and the various methods and activities for implementing these objectives. Once skill has been developed in this area, it is wise for the teacher to broaden his curricular development. He might plan objectives within a course of study that relate to improving peer and student–teacher relationships, enhancing the opportunity for the student to develop positive attitudes toward learning, and providing experiences that reinforce his socially acceptable behavior. Obviously it is very difficult to plan curricula in this area, because the teacher usually views learning difficulties and discipline problems as something outside his primary area of concern for student skill development in the subject matter being taught. The teacher may focus his attention on behavior difficulties only when they begin to interfere with the subject matter lessons. This book does not make a comprehensive attempt to provide objectives in the interpersonal realm. However, it should be remembered that by using the competency-based model developed in this chapter as a framework for curriculum planning, there are possibilities for objectives, activities, and evaluation *beyond those that merely plan for subject matter programs.*

The intent of this chapter is to develop skills in formulating appropriate objectives and activities for subject matter instruction. For this purpose, the objectives given demonstrate how the skills of developing objectives and related activities can be incorporated within the lesson modules and curriculum units when a competency-based model is used.

A competency-based curriculum is a skeletal outline that provides a teacher with a system for *sequentially* and *specifically* developing the learning to be accomplished during the course of instruction. Usually this learning is confined to cognitive skills directly relating to the subject matter, although, as mentioned above, other learning opportunities can be offered. *Competency-based instruction is not a method of teaching* like self-discovery learning, programmed texts, or inquiry processes. In a competency-based curriculum, the teacher chooses the method he considers most effective to fulfill the requirements of the objective. In its simplest form, competency-based instruction involves the development of behavioral objectives, appropriate activities to implement these objectives, and precise evaluation measures to assess the student's achievement of the objectives.

SUGGESTED BEHAVIORAL OBJECTIVES

The objectives for this chapter are listed below. As discussed in the introduction, these objectives relate to the development of a competency-based curriculum.

1. *The student will write appropriate generalizations, concepts, subconcepts, and goals and objectives from a subject matter area of his choice. The objectives must directly relate to the concepts and generalizations. The objectives must be measurable and organized so that they can be used in planning subsequent appropriate activities.*
2. *The student will write appropriate analogous and equivalent activities for a set of behavioral objectives that he is given.*
3. *The student will write a learning module that includes objectives, appropriate activities, evaluation items, and other components illustrated in the chapter. The student will be able to define and defend his use of competency-based skills in curriculum planning.*
4. *Given a set of modules, the student will sequence them from the simple to the complex. This is to be done by referring to the behaviors contained in the objectives of each module. The student will supply his rationale for ranking the modules.*

DEVELOPMENT OF GENERALIZATIONS, CONCEPTS, AND OBJECTIVES

Fred Wilhelms said that curriculum is what a teacher *uses* when he teaches students.[2] The real question of instruction is just *what* to use. There is no consensus on this question. Many teachers are primarily concerned with the subject matter. Others focus on creativity. Others propose that students should learn to develop skills in asking questions. Others want students to develop inquiry or analytical skills (in which students investigate data, analyze its possible significance and meaning, and form conclusions about how it relates to the topic under investigation). Some suggest doing away with the more formalized cognitive concerns and providing a series of experiences and personal contacts from which the student can draw his own conclusions. Which of these approaches the teacher sees as most relevant depends largely upon his philosophy of learning. Once a teacher has decided on his course of instruction and what he wants to teach, a competency-based curriculum provides a *comprehensive way of organizing his curriculum* into sequential components. Later in the chapter, when the requirements of the third chapter objective are being discussed, a more thorough picture will be shown of the unique components of competency-based curriculum.

A competency-based curriculum places some limitations on the philosophical viewpoints mentioned above. An integral component of a competency-based curriculum is the statement of behavioral objectives that are geared toward student performance—performance that is both *observable* and *measurable*. The objectives are written to contain skills in the cognitive, affective, and psychomotor domains. This means that what the teacher uses and does in the classroom must help the student change his behavior in measurable and observable ways, beginning with simple, and moving to complex ways. Ideas and concepts grouped into subject matter disciplines is one convenient way of beginning this learning-teaching process.

The teacher who views learning solely as acquisition of subject matter content may have difficulty in planning student learning above the comprehension level. Mere recall skills do not by themselves directly change a student's values or analytical capabilities. Consider the case of the history teacher who has the students recall facts and dates, presents both sides of an argument, and asks the students to record this information on an end-of-course examination. This teacher has not adequately provided for necessary learning at the higher levels of the cognitive and affective domain.

The teacher who views instruction solely as having students create must recognize that creativity is more than random activity and is the result of thorough and consistent instruction in the acquisition of skills within the domains of learning. In other words, to create a musical composition, the student must be well versed in both the techniques and range of possibilities open to him. It is admitted that all learning is not always sequential or the result of careful planning. On the other hand, it is a mistake to assume that without careful planning students will automatically possess or develop high-level cognitive skills and adequate value systems. If high-level skills in both domains could be achieved without the benefit of instruction, our language would not contain such terms as "ignorance" or "prejudice."

Instruction centered on the students' performing inquiry and analysis must also provide the students with opportunities for being evaluated for their perception of the facts and the application of these facts to other learning situations. The inquiry activities should not force a student to form conclusions before he is capable of doing so. Furthermore, the student should not feel that the particular inquiry approach being used is the only way of looking at the facts; teachers should provide more than one way of looking at data. Asking students to analyze, to form conclusions, or to create before they learn the prerequisite skills assumes that all students have equal capabilities, skills, and educational sophistication. This view of learning needs considerable revision to be consistent with what is known about psychological development and learning.[3] To use a competency-based model, the various philosophies mentioned above must recognize the components in the psychology of learning and see how subject matter can be a vehicle for implementing a variety of learning opportunities.

Now we can focus directly upon the first objective for this chapter. The first step is to decide what is to be taught and state it in the form of generalizations. Subsequently these generalizations are used to form concepts, subconcepts, goals, and behavioral objectives.

Generalization: *This is a universal application statement at the highest level of abstraction relevant to time (or stated times) about man engaging in a basic human activity.*

Concept: *This is a clarification of a generalization and represents a class or group of things that have common characteristics. A concept helps an individual make meaning of the things he experiences. It helps him classify experience. Concepts are subject to revision as an individual's experiences accumulate.*

Subconcept: *This is a more specific statement of one of the ideas contained in the major concept.*

Goal: *This is a statement of the concepts in a form that can later be translated into behavioral objectives requiring specific action on the part of the student.*

Behavioral Objective: *This is a statement of intent written in performance terms to describe the skills the student is to achieve and be evaluated on at the end of a course of instruction.*

These terms are difficult to comprehend at first. It is even harder to use these classifications in developing subject matter to be taught in the classroom. However, the initial difficulties surrounding the use of generalizations and concepts should not prevent their use in instructional planning.

Let us start by illustrating the definitions of these terms and show how a teacher can begin to build a competency-based curriculum. Suppose a social studies teacher decides to teach a course of instruction on the idea that events are usually caused by more than one factor or incident. (This decision is a result of influences from the community, subject matter, and student sources.) In short, the instruction must show how to deal with the idea of "multiple causation." In a competency-based curriculum, the teacher's first task is to translate this idea into a *generalization* (by using the definition given above). The following might be developed.

Generalization

Complex historical events cannot be explained in terms of a simple, one-to-one cause and effect relationship. A study of the past indicates that "multiple causation" is the dominant pattern.

These statements fit the definition of a generalization because they relate to a higher level of abstraction and appear to be valid and unchangeable. The concepts shown below break down this generalization into units that can be further dissected.

Concepts

1. Causation *is an act or agency that produces an effect.*
2. An historical event *is a significant occurrence in history marking important change from preceding conditions.*

A number of possible subconcepts could be developed from the concepts of *causation* and *historical event.* The most elementary ones might be the following.

Subconcepts

1. *The causes of an historical event are the acts or agencies (personal, institutional, or natural) directly preceding the event in time and without which the event would not have taken place.*
2. *Cause and effect relationships represent a way of comprehending not only historical events but also all events, including those occurring around us every day.*

From these subconcepts, a number of goals could be developed. The following is an example.

Goal

The student should be able to understand the causes and effects of a given historical event.

This goal could be further translated into a series of precise behavioral objectives. Here are a few examples.

Behavioral Objectives

1. *The student will be able to select the simple causes for fifty simple effects from a list of 150 possible causes. The causes and effects will be taken from class discussion of everyday cause and effect relationships. He must do so with 75 percent accuracy within 45 minutes.*
2. *The student will be able to identify all possible causes for each of ten complex effects from a list of fifty possible causes, some of which will be extraneous to all ten complex effects. He must do so with 70 percent accuracy within 30 minutes.*
3. *The student will be able to list in writing the simple causes of ten simple historical events as discussed in class. He must do so with 75 percent accuracy within 30 minutes.*
4. *The student will be able to list in writing the causes of a given historical event as measured on an end-of-term examination. The student must be able to list at least 50 percent of the causes mentioned in class.*

An objective that could follow these might ask the students to list the effects of the given historical event (under the same conditions). Subsequent objectives might ask the student to match given causes and their effects and apply the causes of this historical event to other situations. Later objectives would include analysis and synthesis requirements.

Using the definition of generalizations, concepts, subconcepts, goals, and objectives, let's illustrate with another example. The teacher has decided that teaching the fundamentals of art technique is necessary for achieving artistic expression. The following might be developed.

Generalization

> *The fundamentals and techniques in art provide the means for achieving art expression.*

Concept

> *Elements of Design*

Subconcept

> *Line*

Goal

> *The students will be able to know the differences between types of lines.*

Behavioral Objectives

1. *The student will point out and name from among classroom objects two examples of objects with straight lines, two examples of objects with curved lines, and one example of an object with jagged lines.*
2. *The student will demonstrate his ability to illustrate on the chalkboard one object having straight lines, one object having curved lines, and one object having jagged lines.*
3. *Given a pile of cards with straight, jagged, or curved lines, the student will be able to sort all cards into the three categories.*

Pictorially, let us view how this development of generalizations, concepts, subconcepts, goals, and behavioral objectives might appear. Look at Figure 3, Structure: The Conceptual Organization.

Beginning with the first generalization, a related concept, subconcept, goal, and a number of behavioral objectives are developed. The advantage of this pictorial representation is to show not only the logical relationship between the first generalization and the first set of

FIGURE 3

Structure: The Conceptual Organization. The two conceptual chains derived from Generalization 1 prepare the student for the chain derived from Generalization 2. In each case, the student progresses from simpler to more complex skills; indeed, the chains themselves represent a progression from the simpler to the more complex, with Generalization 4 representing the most complex idea in this structure.

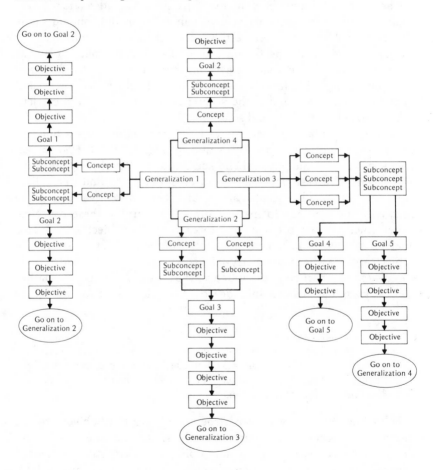

objectives but to show that the first generalization is related to the second and the third and is a prerequisite, like the accompanying concepts and objectives, for all the subsequent concepts and objectives. It is impossible, even in three-dimensional form, to picture all the generalizations and objectives and show their interrelatedness in a subject area. This brief example in Figure 3 gives the reader some idea of the relationship in the organization of knowledge.

Examples 1 and 2 illustrate how the generalization, concepts, subconcepts, and behavioral objectives are charted when a course of instruction is developed. By beginning with the generalization and developing the related concepts, subconcepts, goals, and objectives, the teacher can determine how many objectives will adequately cover what he thinks the students at a certain point in time should know about the generalization. Once this question has been answered, the teacher can begin writing the next generalization and follow a similar procedure. By following such a system, the teacher has the advantage of always being able to determine whether his objectives are related to the generalization and if the second generalization in the curriculum is related to the first, and so on.

For the individual teacher, the task is not as difficult as it first appears. Beginning in the late 1950s and throughout the 1960s, subject area specialists in the physical and social sciences, math, and language arts began to investigate their areas of specialty to find generalizations, concepts, subconcepts, and goals. They also investigated the best ways or methods to instruct others in learning these concepts. (These methods are often unique to each of the subject areas.) This analysis of the methods, generalizations, and other related factors of a subject area has been popularly labeled the study of the *structure of knowledge* of a particular discipline such as history, English, or mathematics. Haas has defined this idea of the structure of knowledge as follows:

> *Structure usually means the theories, concepts, generalizations, data, and "modes of inquiry" used by the practitioners of a particular discipline. The practitioner of a discipline knows the knowledge of the discipline, principles, theories, and the modes of inquiry or methods of collecting and evaluating data within his discipline.*[4]

Following this study of the structure of a given subject area or discipline, teachers, university specialists, subject specialists, and other interested parties began developing and suggesting sequenced generalizations, concepts, and methods for their courses of instruction. Since the middle 1960s, a number of *packaged programs* in biology, mathematics, social studies, and other fields have been developed to

EXAMPLE 1

Partial Social Studies Module

Generalizations	Concepts	Subconcepts	Goal	Behavioral Objective
Rarely can complex historical events be explained in terms of a simple, one-to-one cause and effect relationship. A study of the past indicates that multiple causation is the dominant pattern.	Causation Social change	There is a relationship of cause and effect. Causation attempts to develop a method of thinking as well as a comprehension of causes and effects that surround us. Causes and effects have the characteristic of multiplicity.	The student should be able to understand the causes and effects of a given historical event.	The student will be able to list in writing the causes of a given historical event as measured on an end-of-term examination. The student must be able to list at least 50 percent of the causes mentioned in class.

EXAMPLE 2

Partial Art Module

Generalizations	Concepts	Sub-concepts	Goal	Behavioral Objectives
The fundamentals and techniques in art provide the means for achieving art expression.	Elements of Design	Line	The students will be able to know the differences between types of lines.	The student will point out and name from among classroom objects two examples of objects with straight lines, two examples of objects with curved lines, and one example of an object with jagged lines. The student will demonstrate his ability to illustrate on the chalkboard one object having straight lines, one object having curved lines, and one object having jagged lines. Given a pile of cards with straight, jagged or curved lines, the student will be able to sort all cards into the three categories.

provide the teacher with a ready-made curriculum. These materials involve students in a comprehensive program for their entire school experience. The Biological Science Curriculum Studies materials are one example in which the student is taken through learning that involves a series of sequenced steps and illustrations, always building from the simple to the more complex. The student is asked to form a variety of increasingly sophisticated cognitive and affective operations. Students not only learn facts, but they are also constantly analyzing them and relating them to other facts. The new math and new language-arts reading programs are the result of such efforts.

The development of these programs, however, does not release the teacher from responsibility for planning his curriculum. The teacher must still determine what varieties or alternative programs might be included in a course of study to enhance learning for students who find difficulty using these packages. The advantage of such programs is that they release the teacher from the direct responsibility of developing generalizations and concepts. The teacher must continue to develop objectives and appropriate activities to meet the unique resources and capabilities of the students and the school. This book is directed to the teacher who is in the process of developing his own generalizations and concepts, considering the use of packaged materials, and interested in developing a variety of activities and programs within a consistently sequenced curriculum.

Some years ago, Syracuse University developed a number of concepts and generalizations for the social studies.[5] School districts and teachers have used these concepts as guides for developing their generalizations, goals, objectives, and activities. Educators in other social studies programs, having once developed the concepts and objectives, looked at a variety of programs and asked themselves when each program was most suitably included in the curriculum. Rather than relying completely on the Fenton social studies materials, the Barry Beyer inquiry materials,[6] or the Oliver-Shaver controversial issues approach, they attempted to incorporate elements of these approaches into the curriculum after the teacher has developed a set of objectives. It is in this type of curriculum planning that competency-based instruction is most effective.

A number of school districts have begun to develop a competency-based curriculum. In one instance, a school system established subject matter curriculum committees that scanned the literature and research in each of their fields of study. Using the definition of generalizations, concepts, subconcepts, goals, and behavioral objectives, the curriculum committee began to generate, relate, and sequence these items for the curriculum guides for grades 1 through 8 in each of the subjects taught in the schools. Once the curriculum guides have been completed, the teachers in the individual classrooms will not have to write or develop the generalizations, concepts, or subconcepts. The teachers will, however, develop specific behavioral objectives that are consistent with the goals and concepts contained in the curriculum guides. Teachers will also plan appropriate activities to meet the requirements of the objectives and devise methods and programs unique to the individual classroom.

These competency-based guides will be different from earlier attempts because they provide specific and sequenced direction to teachers. The new guides look at learning from the standpoint of concepts rather than content. The rationale for using concepts is the belief that *students should learn ideas and ways of testing and validating them.* Content is the vehicle to help discuss and analyze ideas. Although not yet accepted throughout the nation, the development of competency-based curriculum guides represents a substantial movement. Coupled with already existing subject area programs, these guides and programs provide a suggested source list of generalizations and concepts that other teachers and schools can use.

Although this chapter requires the student to acquire the technique for writing generalizations and concepts, this task will not ordinarily be within the scope of a teacher's planning. Nevertheless, a minimal comprehension and skill should be attained so that the teacher, if called upon, may work on curriculum committees and evaluate and contribute to the constant revision of guides, units, and lessons.

SELECTING APPROPRIATE LEARNING ACTIVITIES

The second objective of this chapter is concerned with developing appropriate learning activities. Activities are the tasks the student performs as he practices achieving the requirements of a behavioral objective. If the objective required the student to swim 200 yards in 10 minutes using the Australian crawl, the activity would be the student's actual practice of these requirements. If a behavioral objective asks the student to develop inquiry skills by analyzing a series of maps and the objective is to have students draw conclusions about which symbols represent hills, water, swamps, and cities, then the instruction would require the students to practice these activities. This practice would be a preliminary step before the end-of-course evaluation.

The teaching methods refer to the activities the teacher performs in helping the students achieve the skill. The resources might be teacher-developed or a packaged program. In this instance, the teacher might use the Barry Beyer Project Africa materials as a preliminary resource for the students to use in their activity or practice sessions.

Learning activities should be developed directly from the behavioral objectives. These activities must be organized to give the student practice in achieving the necessary skills so that he can accomplish the behavioral requirements stated in the objective.

Activities can be placed in three categories. The first type is a *prerequisite activity.* This refers to the activity and the skills from previous lessons that must have been achieved by the student before he can undertake a more complex objective and accompanying activity. Shorthand skills and practice activities are prerequisite to a behavioral objective that requires students to take shorthand dictation and transcribe the shorthand into a mailable letter.

The second category is *equivalent activities.* This refers to activities that ask the students to perform the *identical* behavior required by the behavioral objective. However, the conditions and criteria may be different. An objective that asks the student to read 500 words without mispronouncing a word within a 5-minute period could have as an equivalent activity the student's reading 500 words in his practice session. During the practice, he might not be asked to complete his reading within the 5-minute period, although he would be expected to keep in mind the requirements of pronunciation and time for the final examination. The teacher might begin by having the student merely read 500 words and gradually include the time limitations and pronunciation requirements in building the student's skill toward the achievement of the objective.

The third category is the *analogous activity.* This activity gives the students practice in developing skills similar to those required in the objective. The analogous activity performs several functions. The skill performed in the analogous activity is so closely allied to the skill required in the behavioral objective that practice on the analogous skill *directly* aids the student in achieving the actual objective. The analogous activity shows the student how various skills and behaviors are related. Another advantage of an analogous activity is that instruction can be varied in order to maintain student interest. A final reason for use of analogous activities is that students may have initial difficulty in performing an equivalent activity, whereas an analogous activity might be more appropriate to their present abilities.

The student, for example, is asked to write an essay answering three questions raised by the teacher in an assignment. During an analogous activity, the student might work in a small group with fellow students discussing group answers to the question. The behavior of the objective is to write, and the condition is an essay. The analogous behavior involves speaking and developing answers in the group instead of individually. Assuming that the student had the necessary skills and practice activities in being able to write, the analogous activity of this illustration would be similar to the requirement in the behavior objective.

A variety of equivalent and analogous activities with different materials and resources can provide for the unique learning capabilities and varied levels of skills of each of the students. The pretest is a valuable and essential tool in determining these differences among students.

Once the teacher has developed his behavioral objectives and has planned the appropriate activities, he should be sure that the resources and methods he uses in the course of instruction allow the student not only to achieve the objective but also to acquire skill in using that method himself. The activities in the course of instruction may be both analogous and equivalent, and there may be a number of methods employed to implement the objective. Nevertheless, at some point in the instruction, students not only have to be assessed for their acquisition of the skill but helped to understand the mode of inquiry (the way that a particular subject area or discipline organizes and focuses upon problem solving).

If an objective, for example, in a biology class concerned dissecting and labeling the various parts of a frog, several equivalent and analogous activities might be performed. The students might dissect a frog, cross-check the specimen with examples shown in lab manuals, discuss with fellow students the recognition of body parts, examine tissues under the microscope, and perform some analysis and formulation of hypotheses regarding the relationship of the frog's body to those of other reptiles. The objectives and activities in this illustration might involve a number of levels in the taxonomic domains, each of which could be evaluated. The use of the microscope, dissecting, referencing, and the design for the formulation of hypotheses would also help the student to comprehend more fully the mode of inquiry used by the biologist.

A mode of inquiry is simply the way in which practitioners of a given subject area develop and use tools to investigate data in their discipline. Hence, the biologist uses a microscope; the historian, historiography; and the English teacher, literary criticism. Within each discipline, there are many modes of inquiry. Sometimes these modes are distinct to that discipline; other times they are shared with other disciplines. The point is, modes of inquiry help teachers and students facilitate learning. Modes of inquiry as tools aid in the activities phase of instruction as vehicles to help the learner reach the intended objective. In the biology module given above, the student has not only fulfilled the objective but he has also been introduced to and had some experience in performing what is called, in popular jargon, "elements of the scientific method" as used by biologists. Teachers in language arts may want to plan activities to provide the students with some basic abilities in critical analysis. Students in a social studies course may be introduced to activities relating to historiography. Similar approaches might be developed by instructors in other subject areas in planning their curriculum.

Figure 4 illustrates how objectives are written from concepts and subconcepts. It shows how appropriate activities and modes of inquiry are developed from a given objective. This mode of inquiry is shown by the teacher during the activities phase of instruction. The mode of inquiry represents the way content and data may be systematically handled in that subject area. The student works through the activities and investigates the data, receives help, and is later assessed on his success in translating the data to subconcepts, concepts, and generalizations. This process is seen in Figure 5, Purpose of Curriculum Development.

Teachers develop precise learning objectives from abstract concepts and generalizations. In turn students should be able to build sets of abstractions by advancing through increasingly complex behavioral objectives and activities. These abstractions provide order and explain the conditions in the world. The teacher's task is to take the abstraction and translate it, through the use of objectives, into precise, teachable experiences. The student, through the process of applying and transferring the knowledge from one situation to another, can begin to form the abstractions, concepts, and generalizations on his own.

The mode of inquiry or method to be used depends on the teacher's knowledge and skills in the subject area. At the simplest level, methods used in promoting activities can be nothing more than grouping students in small clusters to have them discuss a problem. In a more comprehensive situation, the teacher may use a number of programmed and self-instructional materials. Regardless of the modes of inquiry or methods used in developing activities, there is still a simplified way in which all activities can be viewed. Remember that an activity or method that directly teaches the skill contained in the behavioral objective is an equivalent activity and the activity that is similar is analogous. An activity that is not similar or equivalent to the skill required in the objective is *irrelevant*.

FIGURE 4

Development of Activities with Mode of Inquiry

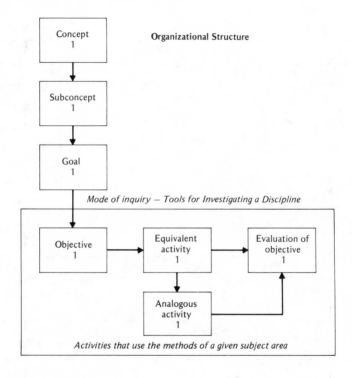

FIGURE 5

Purpose of Curriculum Development: The Learning Process

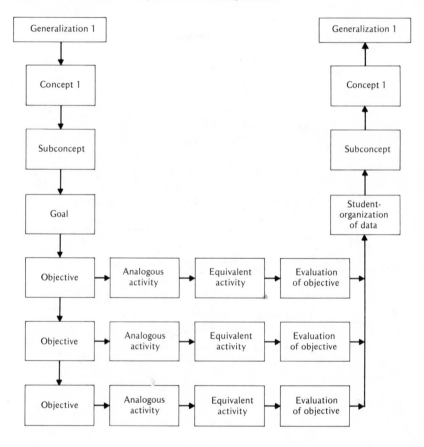

Here is an objective with three activities. Which activity is equivalent? What is analogous? Which is irrelevant?

The student will be able to define orally the terms "concept," "mode of inquiry," "organizational structure," and "behavioral objective."

The activities are these:

1. *The students will discuss in small groups the meaning of the terms "concept," "mode of inquiry," "organizational structure," and "behavioral objective."*
2. *The student will preview a filmstrip that discusses the terms contained in the objective and then write a paper defining the words.*
3. *The student, using the terms of the objective, will find examples of each by examining different cultures and explaining how each of the terms are related.*

The first activity is an equivalent one. The second is an analogous activity with writing skills being emphasized instead of the oral task asked for in the objective. The third activity is irrelevant since it asks for levels of learning not contained in the objective.

Appropriate activities are those based on the student's attainment of prerequisite skills and activities from earlier sessions. Activities are a direct outgrowth of the behavioral objectives and provide both practice in obtaining the objective and help enabling students to visualize how data is investigated within the field of study. Irrelevant activities—those not related to the behavioral objective—may be worthwhile but should be used where they are relevant, perhaps in subsequent planning. The key to developing appropriate activities for the behavioral objectives is first to know the subject matter and the ways to inquire into and investigate it. This means that a teacher should have a knowledge of the available materials and resources. The main point to remember is that *activities are planned after the behavioral objectives have been written.*

DEVELOPING MODULES AND UNITS

The term *module* signifies a competency-based course of instruction. It differs from a traditional teaching unit in that a complete module includes a pretest and posttest and quest or synthesis project for advanced students in addition to the generalizations, concepts, objectives, and activities illustrated in this book. The module also has some kind of formalized system for revision.

Figure 6, Module Evaluation Form, is a checklist that a teacher might use when writing a module. In a more detailed form it consists of all the components necessary for a complete competency-based

FIGURE 6

Module Evaluation Form. This can be used as a checklist during the writing of the module. The text discusses most of the components on the form; those not discussed are self-explanatory.

☐ 1. Rationale
    A. Reason for module
    B. Profile of intended students
    C. Background on methods and curriculum structure to be employed

☐ 2. Title—name of topic or subject area of study

☐ 3. Preassessment device (to determine if student can perform desired behavior without instruction)
    A. Test for skills
    B. Determine if student already has skills planned for instruction during this module
    C. Determine at what objective in module student is to begin instruction

☐ 4. Concepts listed—major

☐ 5. Subconcept and/or skill statements
    A. What the student must *know* to be able to *do* the performance

☐ 6. Objectives expressed in behavioral terms; performance may be observed (enabling objectives followed by terminal objectives)
    A. Who will perform the behavior?
    B. Desired terminal behavior or performance
    C. Conditions of performance
    D. Minimum level of achievement, or criteria
    E. Objectives should be sequenced and matched with taxonomy of learning

☐ 7. Teacher techniques or tasks to be employed (may also refer to motivational approaches to be used). These facilitate the activities.
    A. Materials to be gathered
    B. Books to be read
    C. Learning environments to be designed (space, student deployment)
    D. Media to be used or developed
    E. Experiments to be performed to field test

☐ 8. Learning activities/methods to be employed (activities to be organized into equivalent and analogous learning modes)
    A. Keyed to the objectives
    B. At least one other reading and writing (i.e. tapes, slides, discussions, field trips, simulation exercises, etc., where appropriate)
    C. Reading materials should provide for the varied reading levels of the students
    D. Alternative materials should be listed for students needing remediation

☐ 9. Posttests (evaluation)
    A. Keyed to objectives
    B. Evaluation items or procedures should be stated to include performance conditions and criteria as listed in objectives

☐ 10. Synthesis (quest) opportunities
    A. Individualized learning packages that are behaviorally defined and allow the student either to apply his previously learned skills on the topic in more depth or to relate the skills learned to another topic.

☐ 11. Reassessment of module
    A. Analysis and evaluation of each of the components of module construction and their relationship to the performance of the students. This process is continual.

curriculum. The figure goes into more detail than may be necessary for this introductory book, but it may be helpful to go through all the steps, especially those not covered in subsequent chapters. Several of the steps in writing these modules are really inappropriate for everyday instruction. The Module Evaluation Form must be considered a classical design that should be changed as everyday use requires.

The rationale is the first step that could be eliminated. It is important from a theoretical standpoint. It must justify the type of instruction and tell for whom the instruction is intended. Much of this is obvious to the teacher but not to the principal or supervisor. The title and the following four steps should always be included: the pretest, concepts (which for our purposes encompasses the generalization), subconcepts, and the instructional objectives. Step 7 can be eliminated since what the teacher is to do is implied by the student's learning activities in Step 8. Steps 9 through 11 should be included, although there are times when synthesis (quest) opportunities are not called for. In a continuous-progress curriculum, the student might have the option of moving to the next module instead of doing a quest project. This would require a program that is somewhat self-instructional unless several staff members are available.

Traditional teaching units have a few of the components above. Figure 1, on page 4 illustrates the elements of a module. Neither Figure 1 nor 6 points out one of the significant differences between modules and units: *a well-written module would have several appropriate learning activities for each objective.* These activities, although keyed to the objectives, would fully use resources the teacher had available with the goal of providing as many different ways of learning as possible. This is one way to match activities with the learning needs of individual students. Multiple activities also show the student that the skill he is learning is related to other subject areas and bodies of knowledge. For any given objective, activities might include individual study, small-group work, a field trip, and use of media. All these learning modes help the student see his skill in a more complete light. Using objectives and multiple activities also helps the student who may not pass the objective the first time by allowing him to try one of the other activities. Of course, a teacher need not wait until the posttest to use other activities. Some modules allow students to go through all the activities before the posttest. The focus is upon the student in a module form of instruction because of the constant monitoring and evaluation of the student as he proceeds. This is illustrated in Figure 1.

Let's consider a learning module from an elementary math project.

In this particular module, the teacher has listed for clarity the generalization, concept, subconcept, and goal before giving the behavioral objectives. Accompanying this module is a pretest. There are also a number of other objectives and activities designed to aid the student needing remedial work. The form of this particular example is not the only way to design modules. Another module format could include the topic or subject to be discussed, the specific title of the course of instruction, the prerequisite skills and activities, the behavior objectives for the present course of instruction, the kind of pretest that may be used, the activities for each objective, and the types of posttest or end-of-course evaluation to be used. Regardless of format, modules provide specific instruction to students, teachers, and other interested parties about what will be taking place during the course of instruction and show all the resources and materials required to complete the tasks. Although the authors decided upon a particular modular form, there are others. The differences between these styles are slight. The major difference is the authors' requirement of having the teachers write the generalizations and concepts that they wish to incorporate in their lessons.

It was noted above that learning modules that are part of a competency-based curriculum are under continual reassessment. Modules that are not sequenced probably contain irrelevant objectives or activities that need alteration. If a large number of students do not achieve the objectives, specificity helps the teacher more easily locate the source of difficulty in the instructional program. Such organization helps the teacher overcome the difficulty of not knowing what to change or who to blame when students do not perform satisfactorily.

Let us look at an example of a competency-based curriculum implemented by a school system in all the subjects in the elementary grades. The school district asked each subject area group to develop curriculum guides. Traditionally, curriculum guides are divided by year, or groups of years, for a particular subject. There are guides for second grade math or English guides for grades three through six. The school system organized its guides in somewhat the same manner but included the generalizations, concepts, subconcepts, goals, behavioral objectives, and then *suggested* activities, resources, and techniques that could be used by the teachers.

Example 3 gives an example of such a module for elementary math. The module develops an entire course of instruction from the concept of sets or groups. This particular curriculum guide is divided into a number of sequenced modules. Although these modules might, in their present state, be used by the teacher in actual class instruction, a number of substantial changes are still needed. It may be that in this example the ideas from generalizations through objectives do not need to be rewritten but can be used in the teacher's own lesson modules. The teacher may not want to use all the suggested learning activities or resources that have been listed in the guide. In his own instructional module, he can choose the activities most appropriate for his own class or develop others consistent with the objectives. He may also choose from the suggested resources those that are available and appropriate to his needs or use others more appropriate for his own situation. Although it is unusual for curriculum guides to be organized into modules, it is obviously much easier for teachers developing competency-based curriculum to develop their own instructional modules from such guides. They have less difficulty than teachers who must develop their own generalizations, concepts, subconcepts, goals, and objectives in addition to finding avaiable resources.

Classroom teachers have been using some form of competency-based instruction for a number of years. Although there is merit in the individual teacher's establishing precise instructional objectives and related activities for his particular course, a piecemeal approach to curriculum development is often the end result. Specifically, some teachers build competency-based curriculum while others are content to keep the content approach. This partial curriculum reform within a school or district forces the student to go through a variety of learning situations in which he at times is focusing on the development of concepts and at other times on the mere acquisition of content. More important, schools and districts that have partially implemented a competency-based approach have been faced with the inevitable conclusion that until a districtwide effort is made to base all courses on competency, the subject matter is fragmented and learning is not sequenced. Instead of moving students through increasingly more complex levels of learning, piecemeal programming fails to provide the opportunity for the students to develop consistent, sequential skills.

A School District Becomes Competency-Based

In order to overcome the obvious pitfalls of implementing a competency-based approach in only certain classes and schools, the Catholic Diocese of Toledo made the decision to involve teachers, administrators, and other interested individuals in developing a systemwide competency-based curriculum. They decided to write competency-based curriculum guides for all subject areas, which included language arts-reading, mathematics, science, social studies, art, music, and guidance. Teachers were given in-service instruction in writing

EXAMPLE 3

Elementary Mathematics Module

Generalization	Concept	Sub-concepts	Goal	Behavioral Objectives	Suggested Learning Activities
The idea of number is an outgrowth of the concept of sets or groups.	Sets	Identification of sets	The student will understand the concept of sets and show examples of these from his environment.	The children will identify and make sets of objects that are found in the classroom (erasers, pegs, counters, etc.). The sets of objects will be in groups of five or fewer.	Children will make sets from objects that are available in the classroom: books, pencils, pegs, counters, erasers, pieces of chalk, etc. Children will illustrate sets on the flannel or magnetic board. For objects on the flannel board, children will identify sets by putting a ring of yarn around each set. Children will cut pictures from magazines and newspapers and use these pictures to form sets.

Evaluation	Resources
Children will draw six sets of five or fewer objects with 100 percent accuracy. Given three sets—one set of three objects, one set of four objects, and one set of five objects—the pupil will identify the set of four objects.	**Filmstrips:** McGraw-Hill Films, 330 West 42d Street, New York, New York 10036 Set No. 1, No. 405420, $38.50 "Sets and Numbers" "Numbers and Numerals" "Introduction to Problem Solving" "Learning About Equations" "Learning About Inequalities" "More Numbers and Numerals" **Transparencies:** 3M Company, 3M Center, St. Paul, Minnesota 55101 Lower Elementary Topics, 15-0559-3, $35 "Number and Numerals, 0-9" "Money and Change" "Basic Facts of Addition" "Measurement" **Tapes:** Imperial International Learning, Box 548, Route 54 South, Kankakee, Illinois 60901 Primary Math Skills, PMI 123, Complete Program, $299 PMI 123C, on cassettes, $339 (40 taped lessons, each with 30 pupil booklets, teacher's manual, and pupil placement tests) **Manipulative Materials:** Houghton Mifflin Co., 1900 South Batvia Avenue, Geneva, Illinois 60134 Geoboard and Teaching Learning Kit, No. 1-14482, $3.45 (Contains geoboard, rubber bands, 42 student activity cards, notes for teacher) Kit on Geometric Shapes, No. 1-14440, $1.65 Open-end Abacus Kit, No. 1-14455, $2.10 Kit of Colored Centimeter Rods, No. 1-4423, $1.65 Teaching-Learning Kit, No. 1-14483, $24.45 **Records:** Educational Visual Aids, East 64 Midland Avenue, Paramus, New Jersey "Addition and Subtraction," $1.70 "All About Money," $4.95 "All About Numbers and Counting," $4.95 **Games:** Kenworthy Educational Services, Inc., P.O. Box 3031, 138 Allen Street, Buffalo, New York 14205 "Number Rummy," No. 2023, $1.50 "Addo," No. 2220, $1.65 "Imma Whiz," No. 2218, $1.65

competency-based curriculum, using the approach illustrated in this book. With the help of university personnel, teachers and administrators began a five-year development program.

The curriculum guides are written for levels 1–8. The attempt was made to write units or modules that covered only basic skill areas. Every teacher was required to teach these basic skills. They were also encouraged to plan with their students individualized modules in which students could apply these skills in new and creative ways. There will be continual revision of the guides and a constant reassessment of the objectives, activities, and ways of helping the accelerated and remedial students. The important point in this comprehensive approach is that throughout the district, all students will have the same rights and opportunities whether suburban or inner-city, rich or poor. Learning will be constant—all students are asked to perform certain basic skills, but the time element will be variable. This is in direct contrast to traditional education, in which the opposite is true. By pretesting, allowing students to pace themselves and achieve in their own time, and giving them the continual opportunity to plan their own objectives, the current desire to individualize instruction can be achieved. Involved in developing such comprehensive guides is the task of sequencing modules.

SEQUENCING MODULES

The fourth objective of this chapter is concerned with the skill of sequencing modules. This task is very similar (one might call it an analogous activity) to sequencing objectives.

Modules are sequenced on the basis of the prerequisite skills and activities necessary before beginning the modules. They are also sequenced on the basis of the levels of learning of the behavioral objectives contained in each module. Modules that require the simplest skills are ranked first. More complex modules come later. Modules that require knowledge-level skills would be placed before modules requiring synthesis-level skills. Another way of ranking is also possible: modules that require very simple skills (knowledge through application level) would be placed before modules that require more sophisticated skills (analysis through synthesis level).

It is important to remember when you write objectives and build modules that younger students should be given an opportunity to analyze and evaluate information. This is particularly important at the elementary level. At the secondary level, teachers must remember not to require too many skills too soon. In other words, asking for analysis before comprehension is achieved is not a wise procedure, whereas pretesting and sequencing modules helps the learning process.

Two additional sample modules are seen in Example 4, which shows how the modules are sequenced on the basis of the behavioral objectives. By the conclusion of the second module, the behavioral objective of having the students show a one-to-one correspondence by matching elements is more complex than having students merely identify and make sets from objects found in the classroom. The teacher may put his entire course of study into such sequenced organization. By having the modules sequenced before beginning a course of study, the teacher can visualize the scope of the instruction.

A year's course of study can be planned. By using modules, the teacher can develop objectives that may surpass the normal requirements and develop activities and methods beyond those typically used. In a traditional program organized around some vague learning goals with the textbook as the primary resource, students are expected to complete the requirements and activities in the book by the end of the school year. An Algebra I course following the textbook might be an example. The idea is that it will take 180 school days for the students to achieve the activities contained in the textbook. On the other hand, the teacher writing modules recognizes that some students will achieve the skills earlier and move into more complex operations while others will need special help in obtaining even minimal-level skills. The teacher realizes that both types of students will need far more activities than the textbook contains. Pretesting students allows them to move to the skill areas appropriate to their ability, and this means that students will be working on a number of modules in a given classroom. Modules enable the teacher to know more quickly and precisely where students are working at any given point in time.

Even though the use of modules suggests that students will be doing many different activities at any point in time, this does not mean that the teacher cannot use a competency-based model with learning modules in the traditional, self-contained classroom. It may mean that the teacher will have to use other seating arrangements and view his role in a broader way. When students are working on a variety of tasks, frequent use of a lecture may not be appropriate. On the other hand, teaching techniques that emphasize the teacher as a resource person, explainer, and promoter of open-ended thinking might be more appropriate.

It is true that certain physical arrangements of students and staff can facilitate the use of competency-based models. In the elementary schools, there has been considerable experimentation with developing the *multi-unit* school. The multi-unit school has teaching teams whose members represent different subject matter specialties. These members have designated planning time to develop individually

EXAMPLE 4

Elementary Mathematics Modules

	General-ization	Concept	Sub-concept	Goal	Behavioral Objectives	Suggested Learning Activities
MODULE 1	The idea of number is an outgrowth of the concept of sets or groups.	Sets	Identification of sets	The student will understand the concept of sets and show examples of these from his environment.	The children will identify and make sets of objects that are found in the classroom (erasers, pegs, counters, etc.). The sets of objects will be in groups of five or fewer.	Children will make sets from objects that are available in the classroom: books, pencils, pegs, counters, erasers, pieces of chalk, etc. Children will illustrate sets on the flannel or magnetic board. From objects on the flannel board, children will identify sets by putting a ring of yarn around each set. Children will cut pictures from magazines and newspapers and use these pictures to form sets.
MODULE 2	The idea of number is an outgrowth of the concept of sets or groups.	Sets	One-to-one correspondence	The student will understand the concept of sets and show examples of these from his environment.	Given two familiar sets, the pupils will identify and match the sets having the same number of elements. Given two sets, each having the same number of objects, the child will show a one-to-one correspondence by matching one element of a set with one element in a second set.	The children will make equivalent sets by matching objects in the classroom (chairs with desks, pencils with erasers, etc.). A group of five boys will each pick a girl partner and march around the room. The students will view a filmstrip showing a one-to-one correspondence. The children will illustrate one-to-one correspondence by drawing and matching sets.

Evaluation	Resources	
Children will draw six sets of five or fewer objects with 100 percent accuracy.	Filmstrips:	McGraw-Hill Films, 330 West 42d Street, New York, New York 10036 Set No. 1, No. 405420, $38.50 "Sets and Numbers" "Numbers and Numerals" "Introduction to Problem Solving" "Learning About Equations" "Learning About Inequalities" "More Numbers and Numerals"
Given three sets, one set of three objects and one set of five objects, the pupil will identify the set of four objects.	Transparencies:	3M Company, 3M Center, St. Paul, Minnesota 55101 Lower Elementary Topics, 15-0559-3, $35 "Number and Numerals, 0-9" "Money and Change" "Basic Facts of Addition" "Measurement"

	Tapes:	Imperial International Learning, Box 548, Route 54 South, Kankakee, Illinois 60901
		Primary Math Skills,
		    PMI 123, Complete Program, $299
		    PMI 123C, on cassettes, $339
		(40 taped lessons, each with 30 pupil booklets, teacher's manual, and pupil placement tests)

Shown a transparency of six sets, the children with 100 percent accuracy will identify and match the sets having the same number of members.	Manipulative Materials:	Houghton Mifflin Co., 1900 South Batvia Avenue, Geneva, Illinois 60134 Geoboard and Teaching Learning Kit, No. 1-14482, $3.45 (Contains geoboard, rubber bands, 42 student activity cards, notes for teacher) Kit on Geometric Shapes, No. 1-14440, $1.65 Open-end Abacus Kit, No. 1-14455, $2.10 Kit of Colored Centimeter Rods, No. 1-4423, $1.65 Teaching-Learning Kit, No. 1-14483, $24.45
Given a worksheet of sets, each set having one to five members, the child will match a member of one set with a member of another set with 100 percent accuracy.	Records:	Educational Visual Aids, East 64 Midland Avenue, Paramus, New Jersey "Addition and Subtraction," $1.70 "All About Money," $4.95 "All About Numbers and Counting," $4.95
	Games:	Kenworthy Educational Services, Inc., P.O. Box 3031, 138 Allen Street, Buffalo, New York 14205 "Number Rummy," No. 2023, $1.50 "Addo," No. 2220, $1.65 "Imma Whiz," No. 2218, $1.65

guided instructional programs that are competency-based. As in team teaching at the high school level, such an approach allows some teachers to spend time working with the students who need special attention to obtain minimal skills, allows other teachers to use their time evaluating students and modules, and provides time for still other teachers to work with students at more advanced levels. Such approaches have an added advantage of bringing together teachers who may be skillful in using a variety of methods and approaches and devising a number of activities to implement the objectives. But good instruction and the development of a competency-based curriculum need not wait for the implementation of the new and innovative programs in education. It is unlikely that many schools will soon implement such innovations as team teaching, individually guided instruction programs, continuous progress, or multi-unit schools. In the meantime, teachers can develop competency-based instruction and assess students on the basis of their attainment of the carefully selected behavioral objectives in their own traditional, self-contained classroom.

REVIEW OF BEHAVIORAL OBJECTIVES

Developing Generalizations, Concepts, and Behavioral Objectives

Now that each of the behavioral objectives of this chapter have been examined and discussed, here is an opportunity to practice implementing them. To begin, let us review the first objective:

1. *The student will write appropriate generalizations, concepts, and objectives from a subject matter area of his choice. The objectives must directly relate to the concepts and generalizations. The objectives must be measurable and organized so that they can be used in planning subsequent appropriate activities.*

Before beginning this exercise, it may be helpful to refer to the part of this chapter in which the terms *generalization, concept, subconcept, goal,* and *objective* are defined. Once the definitions are clear, consider the following problem.

Remember that there are a number of possible generalizations, concepts, subconcepts, and so on that might be developed. There is probably no one right answer. But a correct response for each term will contain all the components listed in the definition. The generalizations, concepts, subconcepts, goals, and behavioral objectives must be related to each other and be sequenced.

This section provides an opportunity for writing competency-based curriculum that includes the skills for writing generalizations through objectives and the skills for writing objectives from goals. Writing objectives from goals is a simpler task and more typical of the kind of situation most teachers will face. The initial concern of these activities is not so much gaining sophistication in writing generalizations and concepts as it is understanding the logical sequence of curriculum development and achieving skill in putting ideas into some kind of order.

The first problem concerns a high school social studies teacher.

The teacher is presented with the task of discussing economics and showing how there are certain principles or concepts that help economists (and those individuals possessing knowledge of these principles) to predict and understand how economics may affect a given society. The task is to build on this example a generalization from which a number of concepts, subconcepts, goals, and objectives could be written.

The key to translating this idea into a generalization is to refer to the definition of a generalization, which states that we must take the idea to its highest form of abstraction. This means that we want to make the generalization statement broad and general enough so that it is as nearly universal as possible. The generalization should not be written entirely from one's own opinion or experiences but should be logically applicable to all places and all times (or all places within a stated period of time).

The most important words in the problem above are "principles," "predict," and "understand." These words imply that there is some kind of *regularity* and order in economics that can explain and *predict* the influences of economics on society.

The two key ideas, "regularity" and "predict," should be included in the generalization. The task is to write a statement that includes both these terms and suggests that they are true in every economic system, at least to some extent. The creativity of each individual writer may produce slightly different statements, but the following appears to be consistent with the definition and incorporates the key terms.

Generalization

Every economic system possesses regularities that make certain forms of prediction possible.

This generalization can now provide a working base from which a large number of concepts can be developed.

Recall that a concept is defined as a representation of the generalization and is the way of delineating some of the ideas contained in the generalization. Because economic systems have regularity, the concept could be formulated that economic systems are the outgrowth or are one manifestation of a political system. As such, economic systems are controlled, at least in theory, by the political system. This concept can be written in two ways. It could be written in the lengthy manner just given, or it could include a sentence that economic regularity is the result of its relationship to, and control and reinforcement by a political system. Or the whole statement might be reduced to the concept of "social control".

Concept

   Social control

As will be demonstrated below, the elements of political authority controlling and reinforcing the concept could be written later. Using the same system of logic, a number of concepts could be developed that would be concerned with comparative advantage, power, social change, and the modified market economy. All these concepts come from the ideas contained in the generalization. There may be more concepts, but these seem to be the most obvious.

The next task is to write some appropriate subconcepts from the concepts. Here is where the elements of authority and relationship may be included. The subconcept is a closer examination of the main concept. One of the first appropriate subconcepts that could be written would be this:

Subconcepts

1. There are many types of economic systems but all have underlying principles that regulate them.
2. Economic systems are related and largely controlled by a political system.

Some learning goals for the first subconcept might be the following:

Goals

1. The students will learn the main principles of economics and be able to recognize how they function in society.
2. The student will be able to comprehend and discuss how an economic system operates in a given society and helps regulate and is in turn regulated by other forces in that society.

There are many more goals that could be developed for each of these subconcepts.

Some behavioral objectives developed from the first goal might be:

Behavioral Objectives

1. *The student will be able to define at the end of the course of study the economic principles discussed in class as measured on an end-of-term examination in which the minimum level of acceptability is the complete definition as given in class.*
2. *At the completion of the course of study, each student will be able to identify given principles of economics and match them with given economic systems as measured on a final examination. The student must be able to correctly identify and match all the problems given.*

It becomes clear that this generalization of economics can be used as the basis for a rather long course of study involving a great number of objectives. In fact, the teacher may deal with only one or two generalizations during an entire semester. It depends on how much depth and how comprehensive the course of study is intended to be.

Let us see how the generalizations, concepts, subconcepts, goals, and objectives might look when placed together as in Example 5.

The second example in this section concerns an elementary school teacher who wants to develop a course of study that considers key elements in the English language. The first concern is to look at words and then instruct the students about how the words are divided into groups. From this task the module illustrated in Example 6 was developed.

The teacher is writing the generalizations and concepts in their simplest forms. Instead of making a concept statement regarding nouns, the teacher has simply stated the term "noun" as the concept. The subconcept has been written as a definition of nouns, which is correct in that it explains and begins to operationalize the concept.

By examining the goal, it becomes more obvious that the course of instruction will center around the identification of nouns. The behavioral objectives are concerned with nouns in their singular and plural forms and with the types of nouns that designate persons, animals, places, things, or ideas.

In this case, the teacher has written behavioral objectives that have the student immediately begin working on nouns in singular and plural forms. It may have been necessary for the students to begin by naming the various kinds of nouns and distinguishing them from verbs and other parts of speech. This skill is a *prerequisite* to having students work with singular and plural endings of nouns. The objectives given are appropriate for the second subconcept and represent a very adequate operationalization of part of the original generalization.

EXAMPLE 5

Partial Economics Module

Generalization	Concept	Subconcepts	Goals	Behavioral Objectives
Every economic system possesses regularities that make certain forms of prediction possible.	Social control	There are many types of economic systems but all have underlying principles that regulate them.	The students will learn the main principles of economics and be able to recognize how they function in society.	The student will be able to define at the end of the course of study the economic principles discussed in class as measured on an end-of-term examination in which the minimum level of acceptability is the complete definition as given in class.
		Economic systems are related and largely controlled by a political system.	The student will be able to comprehend and discuss how an economic system operates in a given society and helps regulate and is in turn regulated by other forces in that society.	At the completion of the course of study, each student will be able to identify given principles of economics and match them with given economic systems as measured on a final examination. The student must be able to correctly identify and match all the problems given.

EXAMPLE 6

Partial English Module

General-ization	Concept	Sub-concepts	Goal	Behavioral Objectives
There are four main classifications of words in the English language.	Nouns	A noun is a word that names a person, animal, place, thing, or idea. Nouns have forms that give the meaning of "one" or "more than one."	The students will understand the term "noun" and identify the various kinds.	The student will explain orally and in writing the term "singular" as meaning "one" and the term "plural" as meaning "more than one" and give at least three examples of each. Given a list of twenty nouns, the student will form the plural by adding s with at least 90 percent accuracy. Given a newspaper article, the student will be able to list the nouns that are in the singular form and rewrite them in plural form. By looking up the plural forms of designated words in the dictionary, the student will discover and write the principle that nouns ending in s, ss, x, z, ch, and sh add es to form the plural. The student will make a chart explaining that nouns ending in s, ss, x, z, ch, and sh add es to form the plural.

Writing Appropriate Activities for Behavioral Objectives

The second objective for this chapter reads as follows:

2. *The student will write appropriate analogous and equivalent activities for a set of behavioral objectives that he is given.*

Earlier in the chapter three kinds of useful activities were mentioned. The prerequisite activity referred to the skills the student must have experienced or possesses *prior* to undertaking the present course of study. The equivalent activity provides practice of the *same* skill required in the objective. The analogous activity involves skills that are *similar* to those required by the objective.

It may be useful to reexamine the discussion about activities before beginning this section. The example used to illustrate the development of generalizations, concepts, subconcepts, and so on, considered curriculum planning for an English course that operationalized the concept "nouns." Let us use this example to develop some activities that would operationalize the behavioral objectives. These behavioral objectives were as follows:

1. *The student will explain orally and in writing the term "singular" as meaning "one" and the term "plural" as meaning "more than one" and give at least three examples of each.*
2. *Given a list of twenty nouns, the student will form the plural by adding s with at least 90 percent accuracy.*
3. *Given a newspaper article, the student will be able to list the nouns that are in singular form and rewrite them in plural form.*
4. *By looking up the plural forms of designated words in the dictionary, the student will discover and write the principle that nouns ending in s, ss, x, z, ch, and sh add es to form the plural.*
5. *The student will make a chart explaining that nouns ending in s, ss, x, z, ch, and sh add es to form the plural.*

From these five objectives, let us examine some activities that would be appropriate.

Learning Activities for Objective 1

The student will classify pictures of objects as "singular" and "plural."

Under the captions singular *and* plural *on the blackboard, the student will list singular and plural nouns.*

The student will play the game "tucho" by touching singular and plural objects according to the directions of the leader.

Learning Activities for Objectives 2, 3

Given a list of words, the student will form the plural by adding s.

From a paragraph in the book, the student will list the nouns that form the plural by adding s.

Working in teams of two, one student will flash a card showing the singular form of a noun and his partner will spell or write the plural form.

The student will compile a simple dictionary of common nouns, supplying singular and plural forms.

The student will write shopping lists of plural nouns according to specific categories such as groceries, toys, clothing, and so on, using nouns that form the plural by adding s.

Learning Activities for Objectives 4, 5

The student will make a poster explaining that nouns ending in s, ss, x, z, ch and sh form the plural by adding es.

The first activity for the first objective in which the student is asked to classify pictures is an *analogous* activity. The first objective asks the student to explain and write singular and plural nouns and give examples of each.

The second activity, in which the student is listing on the blackboard, appears to be an equivalent activity. Listing assumes writing, and this activity implements part of the first objective.

The last activity involved in the first behavioral objective has the student play the game "tucho." This is an *equivalent* activity, because the student is asked to provide examples of singular and plural nouns.

The next group of activities relate to the second and third behavioral objectives. Which of these activities are equivalent to the objective? Which are analogous? The first two activities in this set appear to be equivalent. The third is analogous. The fourth is equivalent, and the final activity is analogous.

At lower levels of the taxonomy concerned with basic knowledge, comprehension, and application skills, the teacher should provide equivalent and analogous activities. He should remember that on the final examination, the student should be evaluated for his skill in achieving the equivalent activity. If the objective is to have the student write, it is often functional, in the activity section of the course, to have the student speak and write; but on the final examination, the student's evaluation should rest solely on his writing. At higher levels, when students are asked to analyze and evaluate, the activities center around attaining skills that in turn can be applied to problem solving.

It would be acceptable, for example, in a history class to have an objective that asks the students to analyze several aspects of the Civil War and have them practice this in an activity section followed by an end-of-course examination that asks them specifically to analyze the Civil War. A more appropriate way of devising equivalent and analogous activities at higher levels of learning would be to use objectives requiring the students to learn precise skills, such as the use of historiography and content analysis as they relate to Civil War problems. During the activities section, the students might practice a number of exercises, both equivalent and analogous. The final examination might ask the students to use these skills to solve a specific but new problem that requires their analysis and evaluation. Merely to have the student reproduce specifically on a final examination what he has learned in practice sessions is not analysis but recall and application of information. The teacher who lectures on the Civil War, analyzing both sides of a given question, and then provides the same question for student debate and ultimate consideration on a final examination is not having students perform the analysis he desires. It is more appropriate to instruct the students in a number of analytical tools and give them problems to solve using these skills. As long as the activities are consistent with the objectives, the teacher will be able to get an accurate measurement of student achievement. In the evaluation chapter, ways of measuring and assessing performance will be developed; but a few comments should be made about evaluation.

Evaluation of Competency-Based Instruction

There are two kinds of evaluation in competency-based instruction. The first is *product evaluation;* the second is *process evaluation.*

Product evaluation refers to measuring the student's performance at the completion of the module. The product is the student's change in behavior and his acquiring a new skill after completing the module. There are a number of concerns in product evaluation, and the first one is philosophical. What are *worthwhile* skills, behaviors, and experiences? What do we want students to become? One of the initial criticisms of competency-based instruction was that many teachers were writing taxonomically low-level objectives that merely restated typical end-of-chapter questions. Developing objectives from concepts helps to overcome that criticism, but the question of what constitutes appropriate skills and learning is still open to debate. With competency-based instruction, a system exists for determining whether the skills given the student are relevant to his needs. Relevancy is certainly one way of determining the worth of instruction.

Another concern in product evaluation is how to determine student success. What constitutes adequate proficiency? How much of a given set of problems must an individual do in order to master the topic? Setting criteria is a difficult task. It is a problem that frequently is left unanswered in traditional curricula. How many misses can a student make when adding two-digit numbers and still be considered competent in two-digit addition? Answers are still being formulated, but at least competency-based education allows us to look at the problem and attempt some approximations. Several books now on the market deal with the topic of mastery learning.[7]

The final concern in product evaluation is designing the appropriate test instruments to measure the learning. In a given objective, the criteria and condition statement specifies what the student is to know at the completion of the module. Still, the task is to package a number of those criteria and condition statements into a test format. The chapter on evaluation attempts an elementary consideration of this topic. It also discusses the changing of a criteria-referenced system to a norm-referenced system and what both those terms mean to teachers in today's schools. *Criteria referencing* is the form of evaluation used in competency-based instruction. The student meeting the criteria of an objective should be given merely a pass with the opportunity of immediately moving to the next module. This ideal, continuous-progress curriculum, is only a reality in a few classes. The likelihood is that the teacher will have to set a number of performance levels in an objective and convert those levels to a *norm-referenced* letter grade.

Ethically, product evaluation is the instructor's completion of the contract he has entered into with the student. The teacher has given an objective to the student, and the student has performed the necessary activities. He now has the right to be tested to see whether he has acquired the necessary terminal behaviors. Although this book focuses upon more objective evaluation, there is no intent to belittle other more subjective forms such as observation or self-evaluation. In the elementary school, the most functional type of evaluation may be something other than an objective, paper-pencil test. The question of test construction in order to make a product evaluation is always answered by the form of testing that will prove to be most accurate. The authors suggest that the choice depends entirely on the objective and its intent.

Process evaluation refers to the evaluation by the teacher of each component of the module. In this evaluation, the teacher acts as a monitoring device to decide what revisions, if any, are required at each step of the module. Figure 1 shows the teacher's task in process evaluation. The reassessment block with the arrows pointing to each of the instructional components illustrates the need to isolate each part of the module and evaluate it for possible change. The arrows from the reassessment box going to and coming from all the other boxes represent the teacher's constant assessment of each segment of the module. Data from student performance, student perception, and teacher perception are ways of judging the appropriateness of the module components.

There are a number of indicators that may be used to help the instructor determine whether a change is necessary in a module. Perhaps the most important indicator is the degree of student success after completion of the module. If fewer than 70 percent are successfully completing the module, it is obvious something is wrong. A task analysis may determine that the objectives were too difficult or that the activities did not match the objectives. The analysis may show that the posttest was poorly designed and not really indicative of student learning. Another indicator is the student's perception. The student's evaluation of both the module and the instruction can be a worthwhile aid in helping a teacher improve. The teacher's subjective feelings are also extremely important. There are a number of other indicators, such as affective attitudes of students, time-cost factors, the loss or addition of resources to implement the module, and decisions that new objectives or requirements be added. The important point is that process evaluation is a never-ending task. Modules do not lend themselves to yellowed file card folders used yearly on a given date with little change. Process evaluation keeps both the teacher and the curriculum current. It helps overcome some of the problems generalized in such books as *Compulsory Mis-Education* and *How Children Fail.*[8]

Developing Modules and Explaining a Competency-Based Curriculum

The third chapter objective reads:

3. *The student will write a learning module that includes objectives, appropriate activities, evaluation items, and other components illustrated in the chapter. The student will be able to define and defend his use of competency-based skills in curriculum planning.*

Several learning modules have been illustrated in this chapter. A learning module is defined as a self-contained course of study somewhat similar to a lesson plan but with behavioral objectives developed from generalizations, concepts, subconcepts, and goals plus a variety of activities that may include diverse methodologies. The activities and methodologies operationalize the objectives. The evaluation items for assessing a student's development are the direct translation of the criteria and conditions in the behavioral objective into some type of test form. Remedial or recycling work is available if some students need extra time to achieve the objective. These are the basic elements of a module.

In the following example, let us develop a module in art in its most comprehensive form, listing generalizations through resources.

Generalization

The fundamentals and techniques in art provide the means for achieving art expression.

Using the definitions and methods discussed in this chapter, develop an appropriate concept, subconcept, behavioral objectives, activities, and evaluation items. Also list some necessary resources.

The module shown in Example 7 is one that was developed from the generalization. Do all the elements meet the criteria discussed in this chapter? Are the objectives, activities, and evaluation items appropriate? The development of the concept, subconcept, and behavioral objectives seem entirely appropriate. The objectives are very elementary, knowledge-level requirements. Therefore, the module was probably written as one of the first in a course of instruction. However, no goal was stated. Nor has there been any indication that a pretest is available. A pretest should always be included, because some students may already possess the skills asked for in the objectives.

The learning activities are entirely appropriate. Both activities are analogous because they do not specifically ask for the skill stated in the objective of "drawing primary colors using crayons and paper." The first activity asks the student to name objects while the second asks the student to present color cards requested by the group leader. A defense for not using equivalent activities might be based on the premise that if the student can recognize the color both by pointing to the objects and giving colored objects to the instructor, it would be a very simple task to select the appropriate crayon and color the object.

In this instance, it may be hard to challenge that argument except that in the evaluation the student is asked not only to color but also to color correctly the set of five items. The skill of coloring items correctly is somewhat more sophisticated than merely making the correct color splotches on a paper when requested. The evaluation should measure the objective specifically—no more and no less. It is easy to imagine the confusion and difficulties in evaluation at later stages of complex learning when assessment tests are developed that far exceed the requirements stated in the objectives.

In the module developed by the reader, it might be helpful to review it using the same arguments as above. It may be necessary to refer to the definitions and example forms discussed earlier in the chapter.

The second part of the third chapter objective requires an explanation of the term *competency-based curriculum* and *module develop-*

EXAMPLE 7

Art Module

Generalization	Concept	Sub-concept	Goal	Behavioral Objectives
The fundamentals and techniques in art provide the means for achieving art expression.	Elements of design	Color		The student will be able to identify the primary colors red, yellow, and blue by reproducing them with crayon on drawing paper. Given an assortment of colored cards and the specific labels of red, yellow, and blue, the student will match the cards with the proper labels.

Learning Activities	Evaluation	Resources
Name objects found in the room that are of the same color as the color flashed by the teacher. Given one card of red, yellow, or blue, the student, on hearing his color name, will present the card to the leader of the group.	The student will draw and color correctly the five items listed: 1. A yellow bird 2. A red ball 3. A blue boat 4. A blue top 5. A red kite	Color cards, crayons, colored objects found in the classroom, and drawing paper.

ment, and the reader is asked to defend their use in curriculum planning. Consider this problem:

> *As an instructor, you have been requested to develop a rationale and system preliminary to developing a year's course of instruction to implement some of the new methods and resources available to your subject area. Also, the principal, representing the school district, recognizes that each student's learning capabilities are different. Your course of instruction must allow for these differences. You must be able to identify slow learners and students with special learning difficulties from those who have been popularly labeled gifted. This must be done so that the school will have a basis on which to make decisions about whether special instruction is needed for pupils outside the class.*

How can this assignment be fulfilled?

Stripped to its essentials, a competency-based curriculum is nothing more than a map containing the necessary directions, activities, and resources for reaching goals. It is a systematic way of looking at learning. In building courses of instruction, it allows a teacher to have specific objectives, variety in methodologies and resources, and accountability in that student performance may be measured against the requirements listed in the objectives. This accountability provides the teacher with necessary information so that he can isolate student learning problems at the particular level and see where further help is needed. Gifted students are also aided because they are allowed to advance to learning opportunities at their higher skill level.

In defining and defending a competency-based curriculum and module development, one can discuss the components, which include continuous progress, constant assessment, pretesting, and posttesting. A competency-based curriculum, since it is a skeletal framework for outlining curriculum development, allows any type of new method or resource to be included if it directly implements the objectives. This clarity and precision in curriculum planning allows a more accurate assessment of the kind of physical resources and organization of students than is frequently the case. Rather than adopting team teaching or the multi-unit school merely for the sake of innovation, there is now a solid basis for change and regrouping of students and teachers. These basic points (and several others discussed earlier) can be elaborated in developing any rationale that both explains and defends the use of a competency-based curriculum and module development in curriculum planning.

Sequencing Modules

The behavioral objective for this section is this:

4. *Given a set of modules, the student will sequence them from the simple to the complex. This is to be done by referring to the behaviors con-*

tained in the objectives of each module. The student will supply his rationale for ranking the modules.

The key to sequencing modules is to examine the *level of complexity* of a given set of modules. Modules requiring simple behavioral skills should be placed first. Modules requiring more complex skills should be placed last.

The two modules in Example 8 are in the correct order. The objectives of the first module merely ask the students to recognize and define a noun, as well as understand nouns in their singular and plural forms. The second module represents a course of instruction in which students are assumed already to have considerable knowledge of nouns—knowledge that may have been learned from a number of previous modules. The second module is relatively complex; its behavioral objectives ask the students to identify common and proper nouns.

SELF-EVALUATION ACTIVITIES

This section of the chapter is a posttest. The problems relate directly to the chapter objectives. To check the correctness of your answers, it may be necessary to refer to the sections of the chapter dealing with the discussion of the topic.

1. *Examine and respond to the following problems. They require analogous and equivalent skills. The first objective is concerned with writing appropriate generalizations, concepts, subconcepts, goals, and behavioral objectives from the subject matter of the reader's choice. These problems involve an equivalent skill and ask for the following:*

    a. Assume in this problem that you are to develop a course of instruction for the subject matter of your choice. In order to write some appropriate and related objectives, you will first develop an idea and subsequently translate it into a generalization, concept, subconcepts, goals and objectives—as many of each as you choose. The objectives must be measurable and organized so that they implement the generalizations and can in turn be used in planning subsequent appropriate activities.

    b. Assume that in your school a new foreign student has enrolled in an exchange program. After an initial acceptance, it has been brought to the attention of the staff that the foreign student has been excluded from school activities and is extremely unhappy. It has been decided in the faculty meeting that a week's course of instruction should be given to help the student body appreciate and in some manner accept the new foreign student in the school.

Taking this general idea, develop a generalization, a concept, subconcept, goal, and some behavioral objectives to implement this assignment. The

EXAMPLE 8

English Modules

	Generalization	Concept	Subconcepts	Goal	Behavioral Objectives	Learning Activities
MODULE 1	There are four main classifications of words in the English language.	Nouns	A noun is a word that names a person, animal, place, thing, or idea. Nouns have forms that give the meaning of "one" or "more than one."	The students will understand the term "noun" and identify the various kinds.	The student will explain orally and in writing the term "singular" as meaning "one" and the term "plural" as meaning "more than one" and give at least three examples of each. Given a list of twenty nouns, the student will form the plural by adding s with at least 90 percent accuracy.	The student will classify pictures as singular and plural. Under the captions singular and plural on the blackboard, the student will list singular and plural nouns. The student will play the game "tucho" by touching singular and plural objects according to the directions of the leader. Given a list of words, the student will form the plural by adding s. From a paragraph in the reader, the student will list the nouns that form the plural by adding s.
MODULE 2			Common and proper nouns	The students will understand and know what is meant by common and proper nouns.	Given a list of ten or more sentences containing both common and proper nouns, the student will identify at least 90 percent of the common nouns by circling them. Given a paragraph of not less than fifty words, including both common and proper nouns, the student will identify at least 90 percent of the proper nouns by underlining them.	The students make a collage of common nouns using pictures cut from magazines. The students make a collage of proper nouns using pictures cut from magazines. Divided into two teams of equal number, the players on Team A will name a common noun and players from Team B will name a corresponding proper noun.

Evaluation	*Resources*
The student will explain orally and in writing the meaning of the term "singular" and give three examples.	Paper, pencil, chalk, magazines, scissors
The student will explain orally and in writing the meaning of the term "plural" and give three examples.	
The student will write with 100 percent accuracy the plural form of the following nouns: arrow, number, author, kitchen, brother, school, problem, crow, wing, father, teacher, pattern, driver, topic, cousin, stream, river, and canal.	
Given a list of ten sentences containing both common and proper nouns, the student will identify at least 90 percent of the common nouns and circle them.	
Given a paragraph of not less than fifty words, including common and proper nouns, the student will identify them with 90 percent accuracy.	

EXAMPLE 9

Mathematics Modules

	General-ization	Concept	Sub-concept	Goals	Behavioral Objectives	Suggested Learning Activities
MODULE 1	The idea of number is an outgrowth of the concept of groups or sets.	Sets	Equivalent and non-equivalent sets	The students will understand equivalent and nonequivalent sets.	Given two sets of numbers, the student will be able to identify those sets which are equivalent and those which are nonequivalent. Eighty-five percent accuracy on a post-test is necessary for successful pass.	As the teacher displays a set, the pupil will make an equivalent set or a nonequivalent set on his pegboard. Given several sets on the flannel board, the pupils will show by matching which sets are equivalent and which are non-equivalent. The children will take turns making sets on the magnetic board. Children at their desks will form equivalent sets on their peg boards. Children will make sets with pegs on their desks. They will form corresponding equivalent sets with their counters.
MODULE 2			Comparing sets	The students will understand and recognize the difference between sets.	Given two nonequivalent sets, the pupil will match the members one to one and discover which set has more or less.	A set of four books is placed on a front desk. Have three children take a book. The teacher will then ask, "Are there more books or children? Which set has more members? Which set has fewer members?" Children of Group I draw three sets on the board, each set having a different number of objects. Children in Group II will also draw three sets. The class will then compare Set 1 of Group I with Set 1 of Group II, indicating which set has more members, which set has fewer or that sets have the same number of objects.

Evaluation	Resources
Using a peg board, the student will form equivalent or nonequivalent sets as the teacher displays a given set.	Filmstrips: McGraw-Hill Films, 330 West 42d St., New York, New York 10036
	Set No. I, No. 405420, $38.50: "Sets and Numbers" "Numbers and Numerals" "Introduction to Problem Solving" "Learning about Equations" "Learning about Inequalities" "More Numbers and Numerals"
Given two set cards, the pupils with 100 percent accuracy, will compare the sets, stating which set has more and which set has fewer. Given a test sheet with ten illustrated sets (five groups of partners), the pupils, with 100 percent accuracy, will draw a red line between the equivalent sets. With a black crayon, they will mark an X through each set that has more members than its partner.	

generalizations through objectives do not have to represent the initial modular lesson plan. The objectives might be those presented on the third, fourth, or final day of instruction. The object of this problem is merely to go through the exercise of developing curriculum writing skills. Be sure to include all the elements involved in writing generalizations, concepts, subconcepts, goals, and objectives.

2. *Develop some appropriate analogous and equivalent activities for the following behavioral objectives. This problem relates to the second behavioral objective of this chapter.*

   a. Develop one analogous and one equivalent activity for the following behavioral objective.

   The student will demonstrate his knowledge of the school's fire regulations by listing in writing the correct procedures to be followed during the first drill exercise as measured on a test developed by the teacher in which the student will be able to list correctly all the steps in sequential order. The student will also be able to demonstrate all the proper procedures to be followed during an actual fire drill.

   The activities you write should conform to the definitions of analogous and equivalent activities discussed earlier in the chapter. The objective is typical in any classroom situation and allows the teacher an opportunity to develop a range of activities. (The activity above is equivalent to the chapter objective.)

   b. Take a behavioral objective of your choice and write a set of equivalent and analogous activities.

3. *The first part of the third chapter objective involves the skill of writing a learning module. This requires the development of generalizations, concepts, subconcepts, goals, and behavioral objectives with corresponding activities, evaluation items, and resources.*

   a. Choose a generalization (perhaps from your subject area) and develop the generalization through resources for this idea. In other words, write a learning module. Be sure that the module's objectives and activities are sequenced and that they operationalize the generalization.

   In planning activities, it is important not only to consider the use of equivalent and analogous activities but also what unique and useful teaching methods, materials, and resources in your subject area could be used. Be sure the evaluation (how you assess the student's achievement of the objective) relates directly to the behavioral objective. In other words, if the objective asks the student to write, be sure your evaluation item asks the student to write.

   b. The second part of the third chapter objective requires the ability to explain and defend the terms *competency-based curriculum* and *module development* in curriculum planning. You may respond to the following problem in a number of ways. You can list items in the rationale for each of these terms and discuss their advantages in curriculum planning or you may write an essay that develops a rationale for planning new curriculum in the school that has decided to use a competency-based, modularized program.

4. *Place the modules in Example 9 in proper sequential order. Remember that the key is to look at the behavior and skill required of the student as outlined in the* behavioral objective. *(As an added learning opportunity, you may want to take two modules that you develop and put them in sequential order.) Defend your rationale for placing the modules in the order you have chosen.*

NOTES AND REFERENCES

1. Fred T. Wilhelms, "Curriculum Sources," in *What are the Sources of the Curriculum: A Symposium* (Washington, D.C.: ASCD, 1962).
2. *Ibid.*
3. Benjamin Bloom, *Cognitive Domain*, pp. 25–39; and Robert Travers, "On Transmission of Information to Human Receivers," in *Theories of Instruction*, J. McDonald and R. Leeper, eds. (Washington, D.C.: ASCD, 1964), p. 29.
4. John D. Haas, "The Structure of Knowledge and the Act of Inquiry" (unpublished position paper, University of Colorado, 1969), p. 14.
5. Roy Price, Warren Hickman, and Gerald Smith, *Major Concepts for Social Studies* (Syracuse, N.Y.: Social Studies Curriculum Center, Syracuse University, 1965).
6. The inquiry materials by Barry Beyer are to be released by Thomas Crowell Publishing Co., New York.
7. James H. Block, *Mastery Learning* (Englewood Cliffs, N.J.: Prentice-Hall, 1971).
8. Paul Goodman, *Compulsory Mis-Education* (New York: Random House, 1964); John Holt, *How Children Fail* (New York: Dell Publishing Company, 1964).

SUGGESTED READINGS

Blount, N. S., and J. H. Klausmeier. *Teaching in the Secondary School,* 3d ed. New York: Harper & Row, 1968.
   This is a standard methodology text. Klausmeier's abilities in system-analysis model construction and statistical design complement the areas discussed in the present text.

Cooper, J. M., W. A. Weber, and C. E. Johnson. *A Systems Approach to Program Design.* Berkeley, Cal.: McCutchan Publishing, 1972.
   The book presents a good philosophical and theoretical framework for competency-based teacher education.

Dickson, George E., and R. Saxe. *Partnership for Renewal: Competency-Based Teacher Education and the Multi-Unit School.* Berkeley, Cal.: McCutchan Publishing, 1973.

The book descriptively illustrates the relationship between competency-based teacher education and the multi-unit staffing of teachers.

Houston, W. R., and R. B. Howsam. *Competency-Based Teacher Education.* Chicago: Science Research Associates, 1972.
More than a status report, the work delves into the theoretical framework of competency-based teacher education.

Olsen, A. V., and J. A. Richardson. *Accountability: Curricular Applications.* Scranton, Penn.: Intext Educational Publishers, 1972.

Popham, W. James, and Eva L. Baker. *Planning an Instructional Sequence.* Englewood Cliffs, N.J.: Prentice-Hall, Inc., 1970.
The complete audiovisual filmstrip and tapes accompanying this book are prerequisite to reading the present text. Mastery of the Popham materials makes investigation of modes of inquiry, synthesis, and so on, very logical next steps.

Rosner, Benjamin. *The Power of Competency-Based Teacher Education: A Report.* Boston: Allyn and Bacon, Inc., 1972.
What the future of education might be within a competency-based teacher education framework is within the discussion of the many facets and implications of CBTE to present educational institutions.

Schwab, Joseph, and Paul F. Brandwein. *The Teaching of Science.* Cambridge: Harvard University Press, 1962.
This illustrates Schwab's conception of structure in the framework of a science curriculum.

Senesh, Lawrence. "Organizing a Curriculum Around Social Science Concepts," in Irving Morrissett (ed.), *Concepts and Structure in the New Social Science Curricula.* West Lafayette, Ind.: SSEC, 1966.
The book of readings provides a series of examples of modes of inquiry plus a variety of opinions about each one.

Short, Edmond, and George Marconnit. *Contemporary Thought on Public School Curriculum.* Dubuque, Iowa: William C. Brown Co. Publishers, 1969.
As a basic reader, this compendium is both functional and complete. Curriculum is considered from every perspective.

Soltis, Jonas F. *An Introduction to the Analysis of Educational Concepts.* Reading, Mass.: Addison Wesley Publishing Company, 1968.
This work offers an excellent rationale for considering the use of a series of goals for instruction.

Taba, Hilda. *Curriculum Development, Theory and Practice.* New York: Harcourt Brace and World, 1962.
Hilda Taba provides a thorough treatise on developing the perimeters of a cognitively ordered curriculum.

Vargas, Linda. *Writing Worthwhile Behavioral Objectives.* New York: Harper & Row, 1972.

Verduin, John R. (ed.). *Conceptual Models in Teacher Education.* Washington, D.C.: Association of American Council for Teacher Education, 1967.

This is a highly recommended collection of readings providing short articles on curriculum by such authors as B. O. Smith, Hilda Taba, J. Richard Suchman, and Asahel Woodruff.

Weigand, Makes E. (ed.). *Developing Teacher Competencies.* Englewood Cliffs, N.J.: Prentice-Hall, Inc., 1971.

This book is similar in outline to the present text and provides a number of good examples in a self-instructional package that illustrates each of the domains in curriculum building.

Evaluation

Note to teachers: These sample questions cover all of the objectives included in the chapter on evaluation. The teacher may wish to use a shorter pretest for a variety of reasons (for example, to test only the less complex objectives in the chapter, to exclude some because of personal preference, or simply to make a shorter test). Some of the questions may be seen as more appropriate for a take-home exercise rather than a classroom evaluation. Sample answers to equivalent questions can be found in the following chapter.

1. *Pick four of the following six test items and (a) identify the faulty aspect(s); (b) rewrite the item in an improved form.*

   a. (Second grade; verbal) Name the two animals that are opposite one another in the picture.
   b. (Fifth grade) If three boys each had $6 in their pockets and wanted to buy a game costing $3.75, would they have enough money left to buy a $5 book?
   c. (Sixth grade) The most famous of the explorers of the New World was (1) Cabot, (2) Erikson, (3) Columbus, (4) Cortez.
   d. (Eighth grade; true-false) If heat is added to salt water at normal room temperature (at sea level), the water must eventually boil out the sodium and chloride, leaving only some residual nitrogen and any impurities the water might have.
   e. (Ninth grade) List the four causes of the Great Depression of 1929–1933.
   f. (Eleventh grade) Compare and contrast the Mexican and Spanish-American Wars.

2. *From the following three behavioral objectives, select two and write two appropriate evaluation items for each.*

a. (Sixth grade) The student will demonstrate the application of percentages by correctly answering ten of the fifteen word problems requiring percentage use.

b. (Seventh grade) The student will demonstrate his knowledge of the locations, length, and use of American rivers by correctly answering at least thirty-five of fifty multiple-choice questions, each question containing four choices.

c. Given five statements, three of which are sentence fragments and two of which are complete sentences, the student will (1) correctly identify the three incomplete sentences, and (2) rewrite them with correct English usage.

3. *Examine the following affective educational goals and identify and defend two behavioral indices for each that would translate them into behavioral objectives.*

a. To develop increased support for the school's drama program.

b. To promote improvement in the social life of the school's students.

c. To improve the attitude of C-tract students toward school.

4. *At the beginning of a geography unit, Mrs. Jones gives her sixth grade class a sixty-item multiple-choice test to evaluate her students' knowledge and understanding of the facts and concepts she wishes to teach. Each item has four choices. The pretest results show the following distribution of scores:*

Number of Correct Answers	Number of Students	Number of Correct Answers	Number of Students
1–10	3	31–35	2
11–15	6	36–40	2
16–20	5	41–45	4
21–25	2	46–49	4
26–30	1	50–60	1

a. To what extent do these results indicate a knowledge of the material? State an explanation of your interpretation.

b. What implications does this interpretation hold for future teacher behavior?

INTRODUCTION

Thus far in our development of the competency-based curriculum, we have considered problems of evaluation only minimally, noting that it comprises the necessary beginning and concluding steps in the development of behavioral objectives. Since evaluation is the moment of truth for the competency-based curriculum, it is both necessary and functional that we now broaden and intensify our focus. The term *evaluation* itself often presents problems; it is frequently perceived by students as just another guise for the overtly evil term of testing. In the scope of this chapter, we shall include consideration of testing and its implications for an educational program. A competency-based curriculum, however, must do more than test. If the only goal of testing is to rate students, then we are restricting both the student and the teacher to a narrow path of learning. Tests should not, and need not, be viewed with distaste by all concerned. Indeed, as Jerome Bruner pointed out, examinations "can also be allies in the battle of curricula and teaching."[1]

Since we wish to use evaluation as an ally, our primary focus in this chapter will be on the diagnostic functions of evaluation. Specifically, this chapter will zero in on skills in the recognition and writing of test items, the writing of questions from cognitive objectives, developing objectives in the affective domain, and interpreting test results for their implications for students and teachers.

Implicit in this kind of focus is our belief that the teacher must build evaluation instruments from his educational objectives and then look at the student's performance to see whether or not that performance meets the predetermined objectives. If it has not met these objectives, the teacher must look at a variety of factors (such as the pretest, objectives, activities, final evaluation) to determine where the learning sequence may have broken down. Diagnosis of evaluation necessitates looking at both student and teacher behaviors for possible necessary changes. The teacher can no longer say "the students loused up the test" and throw it back into the file for use again next year.

EXAMINING SOME FREQUENTLY HEARD CRITICISMS

Before delving into concepts relating to the objectives, we will address ourselves to some of the criticisms that have permeated much of the educational literature in recent decades. Evaluation generally, and testing specifically, have undergone widespread and prolonged criticism in recent years. Jacques Barzun, John Holt, Martin Mayer, and others have zeroed in on testing with varying critical themes, seeing testing as making an essentially negative contribution to their conceptions of education.[2] Numerous themes emerging from these and other authors mandate some consideration. We shall examine the most predominant of these and comment on what we perceive to be their validity and implications for learning.

The first of these criticisms is that tests discourage what Holt calls a search for honest understanding by promoting a right-answer mentality. There is little doubt in the authors' minds that many tests do just this. When the student is asked to list *the* seven causes of the Civil War (which the teacher has previously written on the board) or recite the multiplication tables from one to twenty, he is forced to engage in behaviors that fail to promote any understanding of the concepts involved. Must tests necessarily dwell in the domain of simple recall, repetition, or memorization? Questions above the knowledge level are both feasible and desirable, as demonstrated by Bloom's *Handbook I* of the *Taxonomy of Educational Objectives*[3] in the cognitive domain or Norris Sanders' *Classroom Questions*.[4] Such questions are not written without effort and thought; when written, they can *require* the student to demonstrate skills of understanding and analysis (the higher levels of the taxonomy). The teacher should be wary of using evaluation items that artificially test such higher-level cognitive skills. Because teachers are anxious to produce results to demonstrate that they have indeed "taught," they often prime students with practice items that are virtually identical to the test items. As Holt indicates, these children are conditioned like the laboratory animal and respond to the proper stimulus when it is placed in front of them. Such behavior does not demonstrate learning in the sense we have talked about but is a change of behavior involving only superficial skills. Although teachers might see the questions as on the application level of the taxonomy, *the more important behavior of the student* is that he is giving a meaningless rote response. Building and giving tests in such contexts precludes the possibility of their functioning as a diagnostic tool and thus avoids one of their major purposes. There is another unfortunate by-product of tests oriented to right answers; they tend to produce answers that are not understood rather than producing processes that are. Our efforts in later parts of this chapter will be more directly and extensively related to this question.

A second criticism is that tests tend to produce a climate of anxiety that permeates the educational climate of the school and impedes the child's learning. If, however, we are to regard learning as a change in behavior (or, for example, the demonstration of intellectual skills), how can such changes be determined if we do not test or evaluate in some form? The authors would argue that a term paper or verbal demonstration involves tests that are as anxiety-laden as a formal test. The use of a single testing device for the make-or-break evaluation of a student (thus inducing anxiety) is an improper use of testing. It not only creates an impending emotional climate for the test, but it also fails to recognize that multiple evaluation instruments will furnish a more valid and reliable indication of a student's ability than will one long final test.[5] In a competency-based program, evaluation procedures should be made available to the student in smaller, multiple doses, and as soon as possible after the student has completed a module. This mode of operation will help to minimize student anxiety.

A corollary of this anxiety theme is the use of grades by teachers, either consciously or unconsciously, as a means to intimidate the child's behavior. Its most common overt form is the threat of "If you don't stop causing trouble in this classroom, I'm going to flunk you." Such an approach is not only morally indefensible, but is also dysfunctional from a learning standpoint; it equates learning with the student's conformity of behavior rather than with his demonstration of skills. In its covert or unconscious form, the grade as a weapon is more difficult to identify. How can the teacher objectively determine whether or not John's troublemaking has influenced his evaluation of John? This is certainly no easy task. We would argue that such a possibility is minimized by the use of behavioral objectives. In this method, the teacher's attention is more clearly focused on the attainment or nonattainment of those behavioral objectives and will tend to exclude factors extraneous to the teacher's legitimate evaluation.

A third critical theme frequently heard is that objective tests (such as true-false or multiple-choice tests) are not objective, nor can they measure anything but the most trivial kind of knowledge. Again, this claim can be seen as valid if we examine sloppily constructed tests, the failure of teachers to look at the results produced by tests, and tests constructed without intellectual effort. An examination of Bloom and Sanders will show the student numerous examples of higher level "objective" items. Efforts will be made later in the chapter to confront these problems more directly.

Lastly, tests have been criticized in a general sense as labeling the child, often in such a way as to penalize the child from a lower class or from a minority group. Such criticisms are generally associated with IQ tests and standardized achievement tests. Henry Dyer has very effectively responded to this criticism.[6] Such tests are not represented (and should never be) as infallible instruments that precisely evaluate a student's capabilities. *Any* test is only *one* attempt to assess a student's capabilities. The absurdity of assuming that John is smarter than Mary because his IQ score is 5 points higher can be shown by giving them the test again; their scores may well be reversed. A child's IQ score, for example, will probably vary about 5 points when he retakes the same test or an equivalent form of it. A second point Dyer stresses is that it is not the *test* which is penalizing the child, but rather the inequities in the child's educational opportunities. The latter is what we are seeking to change. Thirdly, such test results are meant to be used as diagnostic tools, not as ready-made labels. They should be used as aids to decisions and are not to represent decisions in themselves. IQ tests and achievement tests must be seen, then, in the light of the purpose for which they are designed and *not* in the way in which they are most easily used.

A last critical point surfaces here and is directed to those who would do away with all tests. If not tests, what tools, devices, and so on, do we use to evaluate in the educational process? The presumption here is that it is neither feasible nor functional for everybody, by his own choice alone, to become a doctor, lawyer, nurse or electrician. Some readily used tools come to mind. Interviews, written recommendations, and self-evaluation are three that are often mentioned. If we examine all the evidence, however, we find that such measures present so many problems in reliability and validity that their objectivity is continually questionable.[7] Rather than rely on such weak crutches, we find testing (in the broadest interpretation of the term) to be a *fairer and more efficient* way to evaluate whether or not the teacher has achieved his objectives. The social consequences of not testing, as Ebel has indicated, leave educational decisions to prejudice and caprice.[8]

SUGGESTED BEHAVIORAL OBJECTIVES

Having focused on some of the frequently voiced criticisms of testing, we shall now identify the skills we are seeking to promote in this chapter.

1. *For four of six given examples of faulty test items, the student will (1) identify the faulty aspects of the questions, and (2) rewrite the questions with improved clarity and precision.*
2. *Given examples of three behavioral objectives in the cognitive domain, the student will choose two and write two appropriate evaluation items for each.*
3. *Given three goals in the affective domain, the student will identify and defend two behavioral indices for each that would translate them into behavioral objectives.*
4. *Given the specific characteristics of an evaluation problem, the student will (1) supply an interpretation and defense as to whether student learning has been demonstrated, and (2) diagnose the results for their implications for subsequent teacher behavior.*

MEANS OF EVALUATING COGNITIVE SKILLS

Although it is not our purpose to develop a *comprehensive* statement about the great variety of cognitive testing techniques, we would like to explore some of the more salient characteristics of the most commonly used (and misused) methods. For more extended consideration of these evaluation techniques (and their specific application to different levels and subjects), the student is directed to the Suggested Readings at the end of this chapter.

Modes of cognitive testing are frequently broken into two categories: objective tests and essay tests. The objective label denotes a consistency in the scoring process characteristic of most objective tests, as contrasted with essay tests, which frequently show inconsistent evaluation when judged by different readers. We will briefly consider some of the particular characteristics of five kinds of objective tests—true-false, multiple choice, completion, matching, and word problems—and of essay tests generally. When writing the evaluation criteria for his objectives, the teacher should bear in mind the strengths and weaknesses of these various modes of evaluation. Examples of each type of item will be demonstrated in the later section dealing with the behavioral objective.

True-False

Although this test is generally easy to build and easy to score and can cover a great amount of content, the teacher should be extremely wary of several unavoidable weaknesses. Because each question must be either true or false, the student has a one in two chance of choosing the correct answer whether or not he knows anything about the content of the question. This naturally will mask much student guessing, a point we will explore later. Second, true-false tests are best suited to low-level, recall kinds of content. Attempting to get around this by lengthening questions to include more context or concepts merely results in lessening validity and reliability. Adding frills to true-false formats, such as asking the student to defend his choice, can help to lessen the effects of these limitations. Overall, the effectiveness of the true-false item should be seen as limited.

Multiple Choice

This type of test is more difficult to construct than the true-false test, but it is easily scored and can cover much in the way of content. Because there are multiple choices, the chance of guessing the right answer is reduced. Examination of test responses yields a more specific diagnosis of student errors than it does with a true-false test. Morever, the nature of the multiple-choice item more readily lends itself to questions at higher cognitive levels and to a wider variety of formats (such as analogies, graph interpretation, and reading comprehension).

Completion or Fill-In

Again we have a format that is generally easy to construct, easily scored, and potentially comprehensive. It suffers from one of the same limitations as does the true-false question in that it must restrict its use to simple recall or low-level cognitive items. Moreover, it suffers from a sort of schizophrenia in that it is open-ended ("fill in the blank with your choice") but seeks only one desired response. Because of sloppily written items and the natural ambiguity of language, these items are frequently low in validity and reliability. For example, how many legitimate responses can you think of for the question, "Before becoming President, Woodrow Wilson was ———."?

Matching

This type of question takes more effort to construct and will likely cover less ground than the previous three formats, but it does have the advantage of simple scoring. Its potential for complex questions is similar to that of the multiple-choice test. Matching can involve a variety of factors (for example, names, places, concepts, theories). It can be used with one list of choices (which are matched with a number of questions) or as two lists matched with each other. To minimize the effects of guessing (in this instance arriving at the answer by elimination), the number of choices should be several more than the number of items in the original list.

Word Problems

Of all the objective modes, these questions are usually the most time-consuming to construct. Although they are easily scored, their usual length limits the amount of ground they can cover. Their basic strengths, however, should not be minimized. They virtually eliminate the guessing problem and can require the student to demonstrate many high-level cognitive skills. They are particularly applicable to the areas of math and science. Since they involve the need for the student to comprehend a more complex verbal statement, they demand reading comprehension skills beyond those of other items. For these reasons, the validity and reliability of these kinds of questions are lower than the validity and reliability of other objective methods.

These five techniques by no means begin to exhaust the number of objective test techniques. Each level of school and subject area may lend itself to a different mode of evaluation. For example, chronologies are particularly applicable to history, map location to geography, music listening to music, and slide viewing to the visual arts.

Essay Questions

This relatively subjective means of evaluation is surrounded by a sea of misunderstandings of which teachers should be aware. First, properly designed essay tests are *not* easily constructed. An essay test that is put together in a few minutes very likely measures little but recall skills and is probably difficult to understand. Nor is it easily scored. The teacher who designs a challenging test and then skims the answers is *increasing* the problems of low validity and reliability that are built into all essay tests. A further contrast with objective questions can be noted in the potentially limited coverage. Since an essay test likely includes only a few questions, it will tend to cover less in the way of content. Because it samples more in depth, it can deal with more complex cognitive skills in a broad variety of formats (such as comparison and contrast of two views, analysis of given quotations, creative writing). These factors tend to make them generally more suitable to a secondary school classroom.

Because essay tests do lean heavily on verbal expression skills, the teacher must be wary of several potentially risky implications of this dependence. First, the student with high verbal skills and creative imagery—regardless of his knowledge and understanding of the content—will tend to be evaluated more highly than the person without those skills. Second, the already noted subjectivity of evaluation must be considered. The longer the verbal content of an answer, the less reliable will be the evaluation of that response. A third limitation is related to this factor. Most of the student responses will be written in hand, and this has been shown to be an influential variable. The person with neat handwriting will tend to be evaluated more highly than the student with poor handwriting. In addition, "nice" girls and boys tend to get better evaluations than boys and girls not seen as "nice" by the teacher. Combating these problems is difficult but not impossible.

A first general aid to limit these effects is to be aware of these often unconscious influences. This is particularly true of poor handwriting. Minimizing the effects of helping the nice student (versus the troublemaker) can be achieved by having the students put their names at the *end* of the test only (rather than on the front page). If the teacher sets out the points, skills, and/or processes he would like to see in an essay response, he can minimize the problem of reliable evaluation. Screening out the effects of verbal skills (if they are not part of the evaluation) is the most difficult to accomplish. Following the suggestions given in this paragraph will help, along with a generally careful reading by the person doing the evaluation.

ADDITIONAL PROBLEMS OF COGNITIVE EVALUATION

In addition to the points we have made about specific techniques of evaluation, we would like to focus on some broader problems of cognitive evaluation that are applicable to a wide variety of formats.

The first of these is the goal of attaining clarity of communication in the test instrument itself. Certainly, several rereadings for clarity and grammatical correctness are necessary. Beyond these obvious steps, however, a more reliable means exists to identify specific problems. Giving your instrument to a teacher peer is a good way to attain this goal. His editing eye is far more observant than yours, which by the time of the fourth reading is likely to be less than critical. When potential problems of vocabulary exist, giving the language in question to an individual student whose verbal abilities are equivalent to those of your students can reveal whether you are communicating. These simple steps can do much to assure that you have a valid measurement instrument; that is, that you are measuring what you want to measure.

A second concern centers around the reinforcing effects of tests. Testing is viewed by most students as important. (Many would legitimately argue that its positive or negative *value* is dependent upon how tests are used.) Tests are, therefore, a critical reinforcing factor in the classroom. The type of correct response required on the test is positively rewarded; being reinforced, that behavior is more likely to increase. Are we willing to examine our test items critically in light of the question, "Is this the kind of student response we are trying to perpetuate?" For example, the behavioral objective "The student will be able to list the fifty states" is explicit and very easily evaluated; at the same time it rewards lower-level behaviors (memorization, recall) and encourages dysfunctional learning tricks.

Another problem we have already mentioned: that of the teacher's use of artificial questions at the higher levels of the cognitive taxonomy that are actually answered at the knowledge level, in which the student uses only recall and/or memorization responses. Some classroom examples will perhaps clarify the point. Mr. Green spends considerable time in his government class comparing and contrasting the different causes of the American and French Revolutions. On the subsequent exam, he gives the item, "Analyze the similarities and dissimilarities between the causes of the American and French Revolutions." In this case, only the student who reviewed and criticized Mr. Green's own analysis or who missed the discussion would be responding at the analysis level. The student who merely fed back Mr. Green's discussion by recalling his own notes would be responding at the *knowledge* level. This pitfall is a common one that can be illustrated in other academic areas. Mr. Brown takes one of his chemistry problems from the "good" problem used on page 86 of the chemistry workbook. To "change" the problem, he substitutes new numbers in front of the symbols. Such a problem is identified by Mr. Brown to be at the concept level but is really working at the recall level. Likewise, the child who solves the fourth grade math application problem by *recalling* the multiplication tables is working at the knowledge level. Again, the essential point in this discussion is that the sole determinant of the taxonomy level of a question is the level of activity *on the part of the student*. The teacher may minimize this dilemma and avoid self-deception by building and using test items that require *original* thinking by students. The teacher's review of materials covered by students will help assure that test items do require original thinking by students.

A fourth focal point in our concern about building test instruments is the selection of items for a test. Because behavioral objectives in the curriculum reflect a broad variety of behaviors, test items must then consistently sample a broad variety of those desired student behaviors. In doing this, the test instrument can furnish a more complete diagnostic picture of the student's capabilities. The most common error in this area is for teachers to make all questions "tough" or concentrate on the most difficult behavioral objective. The common rationale is that "nothing should be too easy for the student." Since most classrooms represent a broad variety and range of abilities, this approach often produces results that identify two groups: one small group that solves those difficult problems and one large group that cannot. Since most or all of the test problems have been in one domain, we cannot distinguish among the variety of individual problems in the "poor" group. For example, if students are given only analysis-level problems (which they cannot solve), we do not know whether they are capable of handling problems at the knowledge, understanding, or application levels.

In relation to this problem, tests should be sequenced much like behavioral objectives, with the easiest skills first, working up to the most difficult. In this way, the student is not bogged down early in the test with a perplexing math problem. For example, if we were constructing a test on subtraction, we might use the following kinds of problems in sequence. First, start with simple one-digit subtraction. Next proceed to problems with two digits without carrying or borrowing. Third in the sequence might be two digits with carrying or borrowing. Next might be word problems involving the need to subtract one-digit numbers. Last in sequence might be word problems with more complex subtraction. In terms of our language system, this mode of approach means starting with the simplest knowledge items and working up through the cognitive taxonomy to comprehension, application and higher levels. Sequencing test items serves both to make possible better diagnosis of student learning (about which more will be said later) and also to increase the likelihood of the student's completing the test.

RELATING TEST ITEMS TO BEHAVIORAL OBJECTIVES

In any performance-based approach, test items must be written from the given behavioral objectives. The format of the evaluation should be made evident in the behavioral objective itself, and sample questions should be provided, both for the sake of furnishing activities to build the skill and to clarify the kind of problems to be used in the evaluation. The chapter on building a curriculum clarifies the function of utilizing such equivalent and analogous activities to develop skills.

The need to clarify the kinds of problems used in evaluating the objective is important for both the student and the teacher. Writing sample items from behavioral objectives is functional for the student because it will illustrate specifically what kind of problem he will face on a test and thereby reduce the "fear of the unknown" anxiety that accompanies all examinations. The student at any level, when confronted with the behavioral objective or a descriptive statement of the evaluation procedure, may not always understand specifically what that test will require in the way of skills and in what context he will be asked to demonstrate them.[9] In addition, sample evaluation items can serve as effective practice items to help the student build the required skill.

When the teacher writes examples of test items at the same time he writes his behavioral objectives, he effectively tests the soundness of the objective itself. If he finds that the objective cannot be meaningfully evaluated, he must rewrite the objective in such a way that it is explicit about the behavior to be evaluated. Even if the objective is behaviorally explicit in this respect, the simultaneous writing of evaluation items tests whether the teacher himself is capable of writing items for the objective in question. If the diagnosis shows that he cannot, it is important that he know at a time when he can remedy the deficiency with outside help, rather than waiting until the night before the examination.

Several positive examples of the kind of evaluation procedures that clarify and correlate with objectives will help to demonstrate these points.

> *The student will demonstrate his knowledge and comprehension of the Constitution by correctly responding to a minimum of seventy-five out of one hundred multiple-choice questions.*

In the case of this objective, the teacher must examine the content and concepts involved in the unit to determine their suitability to this kind of evaluation. If the answer to this question is positive, he should attempt to write *both knowledge- and comprehension-level* multiple-choice items on the unit materials. With the objective, the student should be given examples of these items to clarify his expectations about the skills to be demonstrated. Supplementing the problems should be information about the evaluation setting (such as the amount of time available). A second illustrative objective deals with arithmetic skills.

> *Given ten word problems involving addition, subtraction, and multiplication, the student will demonstrate his ability to apply these skills by correctly answering a minimum of seven.*

The importance of supplying illustrative examples is more important as the objective becomes more complex. Since the objective on word problems is more complex than the one on the Constitution, we may legitimately assume that the teacher will have more difficulty writing problems and that the student will have more difficulty understanding what the objective means. In building problems for this objective, the teacher should be sure to make the problems require *application* of the stated addition, subtraction, and multiplication skills, rather than problems requiring only that the student add all three numbers mentioned in the problem to get the correct answer. Such examples demonstrate the greater complexity of these problems to the student and also demonstrate other important features, such as their length and the verbal comprehension skills required.

The teacher's writing of items relating to the objectives also serves another important function in a competency-based approach. Since we are interested in assessing the skills of students before they start a learning experience, we need to pretest them, both to determine whether they possess the necessary entering skills and to determine which of the terminal skills the students may already possess. Thus some items evaluating the skills to be learned *must* be written before the learning experience starts, since they must be a part of the pretest.

A third objective involves even more complexity.

Given ten quotations from the works of ten twentieth-century novelists, the student will pick eight and (1) identify a possible author of the passage; (2) defend his choice of that author.

Because students would not likely *know* these passages from recall, this task becomes one of analysis. The selection of the potential author is far less important than the rationale used to defend that choice. The teacher's task is one of selecting items that are *representative but not obvious* passages written by the authors studied. The student's task is not to memorize passages, but to read widely both the author's works and about his writing. In this way, he will be better able to demonstrate his understanding of the author by use of the application and analysis skills required in the task. The teacher *must* supply sample problems and *adequate responses* to such problems. Because the task is a higher-order one, and because there is no one right answer or a specified quantity of success, sample responses must serve to furnish the student with some insights as to the *process* involved and the skill level he must demonstrate.

EVALUATING THE AFFECTIVE DOMAIN

The most difficult task of all is to measure effectively in the affective domain. Even those trained in measurement techniques find it difficult to accurately and reliably measure such traits. How, then, can the teacher in the classroom be expected to do what experts in the area find difficult? He can if he (1) limits in complexity the affective traits he is attempting to measure, (2) specifies which behaviors he is equating with those traits, and (3) follows up to determine whether in fact those behaviors are actually demonstrated.

On examination of a curriculum guide or text, one frequently finds some vaguely stated goals relating to some desired change of attitudes or behavior on the part of the students. Here is a typical one: "To demonstrate an increased appreciation of poetry." A noble goal, but how do we evaluate it or translate it into a measurable behavioral objective? This depends on how we choose to define the word "appreciate." A few attempts in this direction will help us to focus more clearly on the problem. Might we not define "appreciation" as showing an increase when the student *says* he appreciates poetry more? This obvious means of evaluation has several overriding drawbacks. First, quantifying the concept of "appreciation" in a measure of attitudes is difficult to do. If the student says he likes it a lot, how does this achieve any comparative meaning? Even if the concept of appreciation is quantified on an attitude scale, how do we know what it means when the student circles the choice "a great deal"? Does the student mean a great deal more than Mary or a great deal more than he used to? There is a second and even more severe limitation in trying to ask the student about his appreciation. Almost always he will see some explicit or implicit relationship between his response and the evaluation he was given for the work in question. Even if the teacher assures him that his response will in no way affect his grade, the student (or the teacher!) is never fully sure of this. Assuming that this ideal condition should prevail, there is still the strong wish on the part of the student to be perceived favorably by the teacher. In an analogous sense, we are very unlikely to tell Aunt Bertha that we never have liked her rhubarb pie simply because we don't like to face the consequences of making such a statement. This confrontation factor is too much to face, whether it be Aunt Bertha or our teacher that we are confronting.

A second means by which we might attempt to assess a gain in "appreciation" would be by equating this with a gain in the student's knowledge, understanding, or ability to write poetry. Would not an increase in the skill level of the student be fairly correlated with an increase in the same person's appreciation of poetry? Perhaps in some cases, but by no means in all. The rewards accompanying such a skill demonstration, whether they are in the form of grades, gold stars, or merely gaining a teacher's satisfaction, might motivate a person to perform any number of skills; at the same time that person's appreciation of the intellectual content of those skills might remain constant or even diminish. Where poetry is concerned, we have all confronted persons whose negative attitudes toward poetry were greater *after* the unit than before; yet some of these persons demonstrated a high competence level in spite of their negative values. As we noted in the chapter on taxonomy, we are in a better position to infer gains in the affective domain (such as appreciation) when the student has performed at a higher cognitive level rather than at a lower cognitive level.

A third approach to evaluating appreciation might attempt to define certain specific behaviors related to such an increased appreciation and note any changes in these behaviors after the unit or lesson had been taught. For example, if we had the goal, "The students will increase their appreciation of poetry," what behaviors on their part might we reasonably expect to change after the unit had been taught? Several come to mind. First, does the use of library books in the poetry section increase? Were these books checked out by students in your class? Do students continue to ask questions or make comments related to poetry after the poetry unit has been completed? Do a greater number of students elect to read a poetry book when a reading choice is offered to them? These techniques are but a few of many that attempt to look at the change of students' behavior that follows a unit and that *demonstrates* an overt behavioral commitment rather than the shallow and often empty phrase "I like poetry."

Such a preference for behavioral indices should not be taken to imply that there are no means by which attitude questionnaires can assess reliably. Many simple and straightforward questions can be asked of students with confidence that their responses represent a valid answer. If we were to ask students to rank novels, short stories, and poetry in their order of preferred reading, we could fairly expect to get their actual preference. Where we must be suspect of such responses are those areas in which the student's evaluation by the teacher is most directly related. Attempts to relate a course grade to a student's response to "how much I gained from this course" merely force most students to consciously or unconsciously deceive themselves. Overt behaviors tend to be more reliable responses than do responses to attitude questionnaires.

Several questions about affective evaluation still remain. First, how can we best assess the growth factor over the time span of a learning experience? In order best to assess a change of behavior, we should have entered measures on the behavioral and attitudinal traits of concern to identify where the student started. Success can be assessed more explicitly if we can see the degree of gain (or loss) on the part of students over the time span of the learning experience. Such data also is valuable in reassessment, both in terms of evaluating learning activities and the original objectives.

In addition, how do we know whether such changes are a result of the unit taught or rather the result of some other influence that might have occurred at the same time? The answer to this is that we are never fully sure that the prime cause of the change is *the unit* taught by Miss Smith. This issue is not, however, the primary concern; the primary concern is whether the students did change on these dimensions of behavior, regardless of what factors are responsible. The teacher must not be so shallow as to assume that all good flows from his influence.

Nor does the primary focus of such affective evalaution focus on the individual student. This kind of evaluation should primarily be directed back to the teacher, to tell him whether or not some of his goals are in fact being achieved. The evidence should not be brought to bear as to whether Johnny Jones appreciates poetry, but whether or not a greater number of students in his class are now reading poetry books on their own. It cannot be expected that a horde of students will immediately start to read poetry at the conclusion of the unit; at the same time, if no students at all exhibit behaviors showing an increased appreciation of poetry, then the teacher should critically review his teaching procedures. The functionality of translating goals into specifics is best illustrated by example. Our original learning goal of "To demonstrate an increased appreciation of poetry" might be translated into the following specific objective:

> The students will show an increased appreciation of poetry as indicated by (a) increased selection of poetry books from the leisure reading list, (b) increased voting for poetry selections to be included in the student publication Literary Choices, and (c) increased choices for poetry to be read in the oral reading period.

FOCUSING ON DIAGNOSTIC EVALUATION

When the teacher is confronted with a set of test results, he is usually under several pressures. Students are anxious to learn whether they passed or failed (and thus whether they get to take the car on Saturday night). The office is anxious for the teacher to get the tests evaluated so that they may get student grades on time. Because of these pressures, the function of evaluation or testing is frequently limited to the grading function alone, rather than focusing on what we consider to be more important factors—diagnosis of learning and teaching. Such a limited approach further intensifies the make-or-break, anxiety-laden atmosphere that surrounds tests. ("Aren't grades the only reason teachers give tests?" a student will ask.)

If a behavioral system with behavioral goals is to be meaningfully implemented, then the diagnostic function of testing must be taken seriously. Necessarily built within the system is a process of recycling and reevaluation, one that continually asks itself the question, "Did we succeed in producing the skills, behaviors, and so on, that we were seeking to produce?" Examination of test results with such a critical attitude is indispensible for the use of behavioral goals.

What specifically do we mean by *the diagnostic use* of a test? Let us first examine this question as it relates to the issue of student learning. When a significant number of students fail satisfactorily to perform the behavioral objectives, it means that the teacher, rather than attributing it to such factors as "dumb troublemaking students" or "this stuff just can't be taught," must ask himself a more profound set of questions. Four questions of concern confront us at this point.

First, *does the total previous performance record of the students indicate that they are likely to be capable of such skills?* This question relates to the issue of the relevant and realistic curriculum, an issue that is too broad and complex for meaningful consideration here. Yet a very important judgment must be made by the teacher; namely, that of whether such efforts to master skills are undercut by the need for remedial work preceding the effort of mastery. This question is crucial because it is frequently incorrectly assumed that fourth grade students know how to add because they are fourth grade students. This concern furnishes additional rationale for the use of pretests.

Second, *did the students perform the accompanying learning activities designed to promote the development of the skills?* The answer to this question tells the teacher whether or not he needs to reexamine his curricular organization with an eye to a complete restructuring, or whether he merely needs to verify that students are doing the learning activities they are supposed to be doing. If they have been doing them and have failed, then a critical question needs to be asked concerning these learning activities; that is, in what way do they promote the development of the skills necessary to perform the desired behavioral goals?

Third, *is the mastery of such skills necessary to master subsequent skills in the sequence attempted?* This issue, seemingly obvious, is often ignored. It would seem logical that we should not ask children to perform skills for which they are ill prepared, but pressures frequently dictate otherwise. Teachers are under considerable pressure (both internal and external) to cover the material. Teachers in all areas and at all levels (and the authors acknowledge having been guilty of the charge) feel uneasy if they don't get to the last lesson by the end of the academic year or cover all the wars and peace treaties in a history course. There is a feeling of sympathy for the child who has missed a part of the course, for he must certainly have an empty space in his intellectual life or a blank spot in his mind! Such arguments parallel the *exposure theory* of teaching (that is, that exposing the child to great ideas, concepts, and so on, is in itself valuable to the child whether or not he demonstrates any meaningful learning. Beyond all this internal pressure, there is the sometimes real pressure of the principal or curriculum evaluator who insists that all the material be covered. Regardless of the source of the pressure, of course, asking the child to go on when he has not mastered the necessary skills makes about as much sense as asking the child to run before he has learned to walk.[10]

And fourthly, *given the answers to the previous questions, what teacher actions become necessary to produce the desired student skills?* The answer to this question is to a large degree answered in the previous statements. Several teacher actions have already been suggested. A central point, however, perhaps needs restating: if the bulk of the students have not performed the skills necessary for the mastery of future skills, then the children should be involved in a reexamination and possibly a restructured curriculum designed to produce the desired behaviors. Even if such skills are not deemed necessary for the mastery of subsequent skills, the diagnosis of results should result in some reexamination of the curriculum related to subsequent teaching. In either case, such a restructuring is not an easy task; it involves both considerable additional work and a psychological loss for the teacher. Its educational defensibility is based on the simple assumption that the skills children do or do not develop is *the* focal question of the educational enterprise.

THE PROBLEM OF GRADING

The issue of relating grading to evaluation cannot be ignored. Our plea is that the reporting of student progress to parents can be made more of a diagnostic communication. Indeed, many school districts, instead of using the simplified five-category rating systems, have moved to student reports that explicitly focus on the degree to which specific desired behaviors have been mastered. A sample of such a report system in social studies is shown on the next page. Note that this diagnostic reporting system covers low-level through high-level cognitive skills. Unlike the traditional report card, it communicates more specifically in what skills Johnny is having difficulty or success; thus the parent is in a better position to know in what specific area his child could use additional work. The entry in the first blank would show the frequency with which the student has performed the skill in question. The entry under Growth would simply indicate any change since the last reporting period. Even if As, Bs, and so on, were used in a reporting system, relating those grades to different skill areas would serve a helpful diagnostic function.

A related issue should perhaps be considered at this point. Because of the grouping process present in almost all American school systems, achievement comparison across groups (for example, between A and C groups) introduces both confusion and complexity. "Why," the student in the A section asks, "Should I get a lower grade for a better performance than a student in a C section?" This dilemma has been dealt with by numerous techniques; the central focus of most of these has been to designate the level of the group as well as the progress and grade received. More functional for diagnosis from our standpoint would be the identification of the student's achievements, at least once during the school year, with regard to three continuums: (1) how the student's performance compares with that of other students in the same class; (2) how the student's performance compares with that of other students in the school; (3) how the student's performance compares with his capabilities, as identified by his performance on achievement and IQ tests. Thus even when using a criterion-referenced report system (such as that illustrated in Figure 7), the school is not absolved from reporting to parents about how their child is performing with regard to local and national norms. In terms of priorities within a performance-based curriculum, however, the latter information must be seen as *secondary* in importance to that provided by a more diagnostic reporting system.

THE FUNCTION OF PRIOR INFORMATION

Much attention has been focused recently on the effects of the teacher's having background information on the child prior to the child's entering the class. Rosenthal and Jacobson's study found significant IQ changes among first and second graders who were randomly identified to their teachers as late bloomers when these students were compared with students in the same classes not so identified.[11] Thus the teacher's expectation may influence the child's intellectual growth (although it should be noted that the extent of such influence is a topic of continuing debate).

FIGURE 7

Sample Grade Report Form

Subject Social Studies	Always or almost always	Usually	Some of the time	Seldom or never		Significant growth	Some progress	Performing at same level	Performing at lower level
Has knowledge of facts					Growth				
Has knowledge of procedures					Growth				
Has knowledge of generalizations					Growth				
Understands what he/she has read					Growth				
Shows ability to interpret written materials					Growth				
Can correctly read maps					Growth				
Shows ability to apply knowledge and understanding to new problems					Growth				
Shows ability to identify and analyze the different parts of a communication					Growth				
Shows ability to identify the relationships between the different components of a given problem					Growth				
Shows ability to plan, organize, and communicate the solution to a large-scale problem.					Growth				

COMMENTS: _____

_____

_____

_____

_____

A critical question emerges: should the teacher be given background information (such as achievement results, IQ scores) on the children entering his class? Our first response to this question is another question: for what purpose will the information be used? If the teacher has the skills to interpret the behavioral meaning of test scores and will use the test scores and following diagnosis to develop a strategy to cope with the child's problem(s), then we would argue that such information is wisely given to teachers. By contrast, if such information is given to teachers who, at best, can make only the broadest of interpretations and who will label the students rather than develop meaningful strategies for behavioral change, then it is inappropriately given.

A specific case can perhaps further clarify this distinction.

Six-year-old Mary has had frequent difficulties with her tasks in the first grade. While her reading level is only slightly less than satisfactory, her skill development in writing letters and other hand-manipulation skills is markedly retarded. This problem has had a contagious effect on her other classwork and has several times drawn the ridicule of other students. Her personal student file reveals that a physical examination shows no physiological handicap. She was referred for an individual intelligence test and scored 93. Her verbal score was 108 and her performance score was 78.

How might such a case be properly and improperly diagnosed? An improper diagnosis might be made by a teacher in the following way. The teacher would see the child as just another problem to handle. The test results might well indicate to this teacher that the child is dumb and clumsy. He might seek out the child's kindergarten teacher to reinforce these beliefs. His classroom strategy would be to avoid the issue; that is, place the child in situations that would isolate her from the class.

A proper diagnosis by the teacher does not come as easily nor does it arrive at such simplistic answers. He would seek information from a counselor, student file and the parents as to the possible causes. The differential performance by the child on the two sections of the intelligence test would be a clue that the child might have specific hand-manipulation problems related to her previous experiences (rather than merely being dumb). In this instance, a conference with the mother revealed that the child had no pencils or crayons in the house to play with, nor had she had any since she was three. They were taken away from the child at that age when a younger sister continually chewed on her pencils and crayons and had serious digestive problems. Thus the child's normal progress toward the development of these skills had been impeded. Given this evidence, the teacher then developed a strategy to speed up the development of these skills. The mother was fully sympathetic to the idea of furnishing the child with crayons, pencils, and games to foster these skills. In her domain, the teacher provided special kinds of hand-manipulation exercises for this child, designed to start at her current skill level and then progress as the child's skill progressed.

In this case an individualized program was provided to attempt to change the undesired behavior. The available information on the child was the source of a strategy for dealing with the child's problems. Without such information, the formation of an effective strategy would be much less likely. Before determining the merit of giving the teacher the child's background information, then, we must be assured that this information will be used in these appropriate ways (and follow up to see that it is).

INTERPRETING TEST RESULTS

How in fact do we know whether a child has demonstrated a particular skill that we are interested in developing? At the knowledge level this question is easily handled, since a simple comparison of answer sheet to answer suffices to evaluate clearly. As we progress above the knowledge level, however, this determination becomes more difficult. As noted before, behavioral objectives need to have some statement about the specific performance criteria required. This creates a problem in the use of higher-level items. If the criteria are made *totally* explicit in the objective, the student can memorize the facts specified for the test. For example, rather than listing the explicit analytical steps the student is to take in fulfilling the behavioral objective, examples should be furnished to illustrate the *process* of analysis. Translating behavioral objectives into test items should not result in tasks that require students to "lockstep" their way to *the* answer; they should be translated in such a way to allow for the creative process; that is, for students to demonstrate the same analytical process by different means.

The preceding remarks pertain largely to essay types of examinations. Short-answer objective tests present different kinds of problems for interpretation. Of particular concern are the most frequently used types: the true-false and multiple-choice tests. As we have already noted, interpreting these tests presents a different kind of problem, that of the probability factor. Students frequently see the two examinations (true-false and multiple-choice) as of the same breed, referring to multiple-choice tests as "multiple-guess" tests. This is not a valid evaluation, as we will show in our examination.

When forced-choice tests of any kind are used, the probability factor *must* be considered if the tests are to be meaningfully evaluated (that is, in terms of learning demonstrated by students). For example, if Miss Black gives a true-false test to her seventh grade class, she may have problems interpreting the results. If Mary gets twenty-five of the fifty items correct, what does Miss Black know about what learning the student has demonstrated? Does Mary know half the material? Does the student know only the easy items? Does the student "know" anything?

The answer to these questions is that we do not know what Mary knows or does not know. Assuming we have a fair test, the results do not demonstrate that she has learned anything. Why do we make these statements? Because if Mary had stayed at home and, without seeing the test, had written true-false opposite numbers one to fifty on a sheet of paper and sent it to school, she would likely have done as well as she did by coming to school. Since on a true-false question, she has a half-chance by guessing (she must be either right or wrong), we can legitimately multiply this likelihood by the total number of items (in this case fifty) and determine the score she would likely get by chance alone. The score by chance alone is obviously twenty-five. If the other members of the class did not "know" any more than did Mary, most of their scores would be about the same. It is probable that most students would do slightly better or worse, depending on how the "dice" fell for them, but the scores (in a class of thirty) would probably range from about 15 to 35.

On a four-choice multiple-choice test, a chance score would be one-fourth of the total number of items; thus on a fifty-item multiple-choice test, the chance score would be between twelve and thirteen, with a possible range of eight to sixteen. (The range in this case is reduced because of the same probabilities that reduce the chance-level score below that of the true-false test.) Thus we can see that the use of a four-choice multiple-choice test has an advantage over a true-false test: it furnishes results that more clearly indicate whether learning has been demonstrated by the students. In the previous case, on the true-false test, a student who scores thirty-three is almost impossible to diagnose with regard to demonstrated learning. We know that one student could score that by guessing alone. If two or three score thirty-three, however, we could legitimately presume that at least one student was guessing; the problem, however, is that *we would have no means of knowing which one(s)*. Using a four-choice test gives us more room for analysis; the narrowed range of scores clearly indicates whether learning has been demonstrated. Any student who scores above twenty has clearly demonstrated learning; on the true-false test, a student would have to score above thirty-five before we could assume with any degree of certainty that he had demonstrated learning.[12]

An additional advantage of the multiple-choice test is that it enables the teacher to test at higher levels of the taxonomy more effectively than with a true-false format. Let us examine an item to further demonstrate this.

World War I was to Lenin as the Treaty of Versailles was to:

    a. Clemenceau
    b. Harding
    c. Mussolini
    d. Hitler (the desired answer)

Unless the student is very widely read in history and has seen the question, to make the correct choice he must be able to contrast and interrelate the events and persons involved in this question. (He must come to the conclusion, utilizing his understanding of the period, that the reaction to World War I in Russia promoted events that brought Lenin to power as the reaction to the Treaty of Versailles in Germany promoted events that brought Hitler to power.) Again, in this format, he has only a one-in-four chance of guessing the answer. What happens if we put the same question in a true-false form?

True or false: World War I was to Lenin as the Treaty of Versailles was to Hitler.

First of all, the student is forced to much less analytical activity, looking at only one comparison instead of four. He then falls into the mentality of "it looks true (or false)," rather than a process of critical thinking. Moreover, the student has a one-in-two chance of getting the item correct by guessing alone.

Several procedures can help to minimize the problems of interpretation that surround true-false tests. The first is to use enough items (for example, fifty) so that the results can more clearly indicate whether overall learning has been demonstrated on the test. This procedure does help much in identifying the specific areas in which the student has had difficulty. A second remedial step is to penalize the guessing student by counting all wrong answers double. (The student's score would be the number of answers right minus the number wrong.) Whether this procedure evaluates a student's cognitive knowledge or his willingness to gamble is still open to question. In sum, true-false items fall prey to a number of weaknesses that, in our judgment, outweigh their potential merits. We shall examine true-false and multiple-choice items again when considering the complexities of the probability factor in our review of the behavioral objectives.

An additional use of the probability factor relates to the setting of proficiency levels in the behavioral objectives. Teachers should be sure that minimal proficiency levels are set significantly above a chance score level. For example, if a true-false format were used, the student should be asked to demonstrate at least 75 percent correct responses. (If the test involves fewer than twenty-five items, the percentage would have to be higher.) Setting proficiency levels involves other factors, as noted in previous chapters. If the skill in question is a mastery skill, such as learning the alphabet, the mastery criteria would take precedence over the probability factor involved.

REVIEW OF BEHAVIORAL OBJECTIVES

Revising Faulty Test Items

Another look at the suggested behavioral objectives in this chapter is now in order. Let's look at the first one.

1. *For four of six given examples of faulty test items, the student will (1) identify the faulty aspects of the questions, and (2) rewrite the questions with improved clarity and precision.*

The following test items all have faults making them ripe for revision.

   a. (Third grade level) John Kennedy was born in —————.

Accepting the limitation that this is a simple recall item, we can see that it is further limited by the imprecise cues. The student could legitimately respond with "Massachusetts," "1917," "a hospital," "in the presence of his mother." The teacher might respond with the statement, "That's not what I meant," but the *meaning* of the question is in the beholder's eye, not in his. In this instance, it is a simple task to rewrite the item:

   a. John F. Kennedy was born in the state of —————.

Such a change minimizes the chances of misinterpretation.

Next to consider is a confusing matching question.

   b. *(Fifth grade level) Match the rivers in the first column with the European countries given on the right.*

1. Rhine	( )	*a.*	*Switzerland*
2. Thames	( )	*b.*	*France*
3. Loire	( )	*c.*	*Germany*
4. Volga	( )	*d.*	*Italy*
5. Maas	( )	*e.*	*Poland*
6. Rhone	( )	*f.*	*Netherlands*
7. Po	( )	*g.*	*Great Britain*
8. Vistula	( )	*h.*	*Russia*

Several faults built into this question make it invalid. Because there are the same number of countries as rivers, the student is in a better position to guess or get the correct answer by elimination. A first revision would be to add several countries to the number of countries given on the right. This does not serve to rectify the question, however, as additional confusion will be caused by the fact that the Rhine runs through three countries (Switzerland, Germany, and the Netherlands) and that the Rhone River runs through both France and Switzerland. The student will easily become confused about whether or not he is to use a country more than once since both the Loire and Rhone are in France. Assuming that we are only concerned in this case with the student's ability to match the country and the river, we could clarify the question with the following revision.

b. *Match the rivers in the first column with the European countries through which they pass the greatest distance. Use each country only once.*

1. *Rhine*	*a. Switzerland*
2. *Thames*	*b. France*
3. *Loire*	*c. Ireland*
4. *Volga*	*d. Italy*
5. *Maas*	*e. Austria*
6. *Shannon*	*f. Poland*
7. *Po*	*g. Netherlands*
8. *Vistula*	*h. Spain*
	i. Great Britain
	j. Germany
	k. Russia

The question has been clarified by the additions to the stem (for example, using each country only once). The chance factor has been lessened by adding three countries to the right-hand column. Replacing the Rhone River with the Shannon has served to eliminate the ambiguity about the former. Although we still have only a knowledge-level item, it is now clarified enough to be understood by the student.

Consider this third faulty question:

c. (Seventh grade level) T-F Many people opposed our entry into World War I.

We should, of course, immediately note that the true-false format leaves *much* to be desired. Nevertheless, there are distinctions between true-false items. In this case, the imprecise language impairs a clear meaning. Does the word "many" in this question mean 10? or 10 million? We do not know. The word "opposed" does not clarify what constituted opposition. Thus it might include silent protesters and/or those who refused to fight. How might this question be clarified?

> c. True or false: More than ten U.S. senators voted against our going to war with Germany in World War I.

The fourth faulty question is in a multiple-choice format.

> d. (Eighth grade level) The biggest health problem confronting the people in American cities today is (1) poor diet, (2) lack of medical care, (3) substandard housing, (4) communicable diseases.

The ambiguity inherent in this item is readily apparent. All the options can be seen as potentially the biggest problem, depending on how one sees the problem and chooses to define the different terms in the question. The correct choice, then, is a matter of opinion, and this should be made clear in a revised form of the question. Assuming that the implications of the choices had been made clear, the question might read: "In the view of Dr. Smith, the biggest health problem confronting the people in American cities today is. . . ." By this means, the ambiguous source problem is clarified.

A fifth question is a poorly stated word problem.

> e. (Tenth grade geometry) Mr. Smith wants to fly his plane from Maryville to Springfield, a distance of 400 miles. If the plane averages 200 miles an hour and he stops for two hours in Raytown (50 miles north of Springfield), how much total time will the trip take?

In this case the student's efforts to solve the problem would be frustrated by his not knowing the directional relationship of Springfield and Maryville. The solution to the problem would be different if Springfield were east, west, north, south, or another direction in relation to Maryville. We can clarify the question and convert it to a right-triangle problem by adding the phrase "directly east" after the phrase "400 miles." This will give the student the two sides of the right triangle, and he can then solve for the hypotenuse, which will give him all the necessary components to solve the rest of the problem. Note in this question that the ambiguity is cleared up with the addition of only two words that the teacher might easily leave out if he did not reread his test before its administration.

A last faulty question is of the essay type. Let's look at one in the domain of English.

> f. (Twelfth grade English) Discuss John Steinbeck's *The Grapes of Wrath* as a novel and as a social commentary.

The teacher's stated goal in this case would probably be to find out "how much the students know about it and whether they can think."

Unfortunately, what the student ends up writing will depend largely on how he interprets a vague question. Since the clues in the question itself are minimal, the student will probably go in the "wrong" direction, or will take his clues from the other behaviors of the teacher. The student will write what is rewarded in an answer, such as a long answer, clever remarks, neat organization, in his attempt to "psych out" the teacher. These behaviors are often extraneous to the skills the teacher is trying to produce, but he ends up rewarding such extraneous skills because his evaluation system is unreliable owing to unclear goals. Assuming certain liberties about what took place in this teacher's unit, we will try to rewrite the question.

> *A critic has written: "John Steinbeck's* Grapes of Wrath *is a study of artistic compromise. Rather than developing the character in depth, he chooses to paint a picture of the character's economic sacrifice; rather than developing the plot, he chooses to paint a picture of society's political and social upheaval. These choices result in his book being a great period piece rather than a great novel."*

f. Discuss the validity of this position in light of:

1. The *Essence of Character Development* by John Miller
2. The *Elements of the Plot* (as developed and discussed in class)
3. Your own criteria (develop at least two) of what makes a "great novel"

The question now gives the student a clear sense of direction *without* putting him in a straitjacket; he must demonstrate high-level cognitive skills that require some creativity on his part. Beyond this, the teacher has established some explicit guidelines for his own evaluation; rather than "lousy" and "good" reactions, he can evaluate more precisely the reasons why the student did or did not demonstrate skills required by the question.

Writing Items from Behavioral Objectives

Our second suggested objective requires that we write cognitive test items from given objectives.

2. Given examples of three behavioral objectives in the cognitive domain, the student will choose two and write two appropriate evaluation items for each.

Here is a first objective in the area of ecology, intended for a potential audience of seventh graders.

> *The student will demonstrate his knowledge and comprehension of recycling and ecological balance by correctly answering at least thirty of forty multiple-choice items (each item with five choices) based on Chapters 5 and 6 of* Science for Today.

The format of multiple choice is clear, as is the fact that these questions should reflect knowledge and comprehension skills. The following items reflect only two of many evaluation items that would meet the specifications of the objective.

1. *Which of the following bodies of water reflects the best effort by man to preserve its natural ecological condition? (a) Lake Michigan, (b) Hudson River, (c) Lake Ontario, (d) Lake Tahoe, (e) Lake Okeechobee.*
2. *Which of the following processes would be least likely to produce a condition of ecological imbalance (as defined in class)? (a) The building of a new power plant on a river, (b) eliminating deer hunting, (c) doubling the fish catch in an ocean fishing area, (d) spraying fruit trees with a pesticide, (e) cultivating deserts by irrigation.*

In the first item, the student must merely *know* that the greatest preservation efforts have been made with Lake Tahoe. This would necessitate only his recalling of a fact given at some point in the unit. In the second question, the student must not only know the given definition of ecological balance, but he also must be able to translate that definition in identifying which of the five choices best fits it. Beyond knowledge, then, he must show comprehension.

The second objective relating to the skill of question writing relates to arithmetic and might be used for fifth graders. We used it in another context earlier in the chapter.

Given ten word problems involving addition, subtraction, and multiplication, the student will demonstrate his ability to apply these skills by correctly answering a minimum of seven.

Again, a variety of problems would serve to achieve this objective. Here are two.

a. *A farmer has 30 acres of land on one farm and 10 on another. Of his total acreage, 2 acres are occupied by buildings and another 23 are covered with trees and already planted crops. If the farmer wanted to plant 69% of the remaining land with alfalfa and 40% with wheat, how many acres of wheat should he plant?*
b. *John and Harry both have $4.25 and want to take Bill, Don, and Jim to a baseball game. The tickets are $1.35 each. If they pool their money to buy tickets for everybody, how much money would each boy have left?*

In each of these problems, the student must not only know the skills of addition, subtraction, and multiplication, but he must also comprehend those skills as they are related to the problems and be able to apply them to reach a solution. Note that the factors given in the problem are clearly identified, and that the verbal comprehension of the student is not impaired by a long, drawn-out statement.

The third potential objective for this question is directed toward a senior high school class in American problems.

Given eight short statements involving faulty cause-effect relationships, the student will pick six and furnish a rationale why each stated cause-effect relationship is faulty.

The following two statements would test such an objective.

    a. Whenever teacher salaries go up, there is a corresponding increase in alcoholic consumption. Therefore, it is obvious that when teachers get paid more, they will spend more on alcohol.

    b. High-speed driving has frequently been found *not* to be a decisive factor in highway fatalities. Because of this, the highway speed limit could be raised by 10 miles an hour without any significant increase in highway fatalities.

Although these statements contain several obvious flaws, the skills required here are those of analysis; as such, they do not lend themselves to one right answer. The skill of identifying and explaining fallacious assumptions and non sequiturs must be one developed by the teacher in learning activities. To do this, he must furnish the student with similar (but not identical) examples of such faulty statements for practice work. Only in this way can the student have clear expectations of the skills required and can the teacher know that he is testing what he set out to test.

Assessing Affective Outcomes

As we have already pointed out, measurement of affective goals is the trickiest of the evaluation problems. We will try our hand at it after reexamining the third suggested behavioral objective.

3. *Given three goals in the affective domain, the student will identify and defend two behavioral indices for each that would translate them into behavioral objectives.*

Goals in the affective domain are often written in such broad and ambiguous terminology that they seem to defy measurement. If we are to take them seriously, we *must*, however, identify specific indices for their measurement. This may involve the teacher's creating his own index for measurement in order to understand and communicate what is happening in the classroom.

The first of these affective goals might be directed toward a kindergarten class:

To improve skills in getting along with peers.

We can translate this goal into a behavioral objective by starting with

the phrase "students will demonstrate improvement in peer relationships by" and then listing the indices chosen to measure the goal.
What indices might the teacher use to assess this noble and yet vague
goal? He cannot retreat to a statement like "all the kids got along
just swell," because this has no clear meaning. There are behaviors,
however, that the teacher *can* assess and that *do* have meaning. For
example, because we are interested in the improvement of the children
over a period of time, we could look at the frequency of equipment
sharing during a week of class, first in September and then in May.
If this is too difficult to observe, we could look at the frequency with
which *failure* to share occurs among student work groups in September and May. A second index of this goal might be the number of
acts of physical and/or verbal aggression between peers (again, over
a specified period in September and May). These are only two ways
of many in which the objective might be assessed; note that in each,
however, we must see an increase of positive behaviors and a decrease in negative behaviors before we can say that the students'
skills in "getting along with their peers" have improved.

A second affective goal falls in the area of music education, directed toward a seventh grade class.

> *At the conclusion of the unit, the student will show an increase in his
> appreciation of folk music.*

Can "appreciation" be evaluated? The answer to this is an unqualified
"yes," *if* we define the term to show what students *do* to demonstrate
their appreciation. Given the context of a seventh grade setting, there
are many indices that could translate this goal into an objective. We
will suggest five.[13] The students would show an increase in their
appreciation of folk music by increases in:

1. *Number of folk music records checked out in the library by your
   students (compared with a time period previous to the unit).*
2. *Number of students talking to you about folk music after the unit
   (compared with periods after studying other kinds of music).*
3. *Number of requests to play folk music records.*
4. *Number of students attending voluntary folk music programs after
   school (compared with the session previous to the unit).*
5. *Number of students who say they like folk music better than they did
   before the unit.*

In each of these indices, we have a quantitative measure of what students *do* to demonstrate their appreciation or the lack of it. We should
again emphasize that if there is not an increase in these measures, the
teacher can in no way legitimately infer that the students have shown
an increase in their appreciation of folk music. By contrast, if the

teacher has evidence to show such a gain, he is in a position to state his case with authority rather than falling back on a meaningless cliché.

The third affective goal might be one found in a "brotherhood" program.

The students will demonstrate increased racial harmony.

This is a noble and yet pathetic goal, if only for the single reason that people make no attempt to see whether or not there are any changes in the behaviors of students. This fault can be remedied, however, by looking at some specific occurrences in the school that might indeed indicate better racial harmony. The students will demonstrate increased racial harmony by:

1. *Increases in the number of students sitting at integrated lunch tables in the cafeteria (compared with a time period previous to the program).*
2. *Increases in the number of minority group members in school clubs and activities (compared with the year previous to the program).*
3. *Increases in the number of students volunteering for "Brotherhood Week" programs.*
4. *Decreases in the number of fights related to racial factors occurring in the school.*

If we have an increase in indices one, two, and three and a reduction in index four, we can meaningfully say that the program to achieve better racial harmony has had some tangible positive effects. If the evidence is to the contrary, we have more than just data for suggesting the program has failed; we have a solid rationale for revising the program for next year.

Interpreting and Diagnosing from Evaluation Problems

Our last critical objective in this chapter relates to the important skill of interpreting test results and determining the implications of those results for future teacher behavior.

4. *Given the specific characteristics of an evaluation problem, the student will (1) supply an interpretation and defense as to whether pupil learning has been demonstrated, and (2) diagnose the results for their implications for subsequent teacher behavior.*

Bearing in mind the foregoing behavioral objective, consider the following evaluation problem:

You are a fifth grade teacher who has just taught a set of concepts in math. At the conclusion of the unit you give the students a test based on the concepts. The ten questions are problem-solving; that is, the students must work through several steps to obtain the answer. The results show a wide disparity. Three children score 100 and five others score between

70 and 90. Twenty score less than 50, with fifteen of these under 30.
(Partial credit is given on questions.) After several days of indecision on
your part, the students ask you what grades they received on the test.

In this case we may reasonably diagnose that at least half the class
failed to demonstrate any significant ability in applying the concepts.
Could we not legitimately "fail" the twenty students who failed to
score at least 50 (that is, get at least half the questions correct)?
Before failing a majority of the class, however, we would argue that
it is mandatory to consider several of the questions posed earlier in
the chapter. Does the previous performance record of these students
indicate that they are capable of the skills required by the test? If
there is doubt about this, some preliminary skill-building is in order.
Did the students perform the accompanying learning activities designed to develop the skills measured by the test? Although this question *should* have been asked during the learning period, it can
partially be determined at this point by reexamining records of student work during the learning period. (This work, while not being a
complete evaluation, should have been the type that required the
student to demonstrate his *own* understanding of the concept.)
Evidence showing that there was minimal student demonstration of
these skills during the learning period would indicate to the teacher
that these concepts need to be attacked again; if such concepts were
essential to the mastery of subsequent materials, then such a reexamination is mandatory.

The last point relates to the second specification of the behavioral
objective; namely, that of future teacher behavior. Future teacher
actions would necessarily take a different course if the total evidence
indicated that the students *had* demonstrated individual mastery of
the concepts during the learning period. The first action would be a
reexamination of the accompanying learning activities with regard to
the following question: do they require the student to demonstrate
the same or analogous skills as those required by the behavioral objective? The inverse question needs to be asked with relevance to the
validity of the test: were the skills required on the test consistent with
those of the learning activities? Given the inverted curve of the test
results (few middle scores), we should ask another question about the
test: did the teacher sample evenly from all areas in the unit or did
he concentrate on one or two of the more difficult concepts? If the
latter were the case, the future use of a test instrument with a broader
range of skills (from the easier to the more difficult) would furnish
results giving a more precise diagnostic picture.

A second problem relating to this objective requires that the student
deal with probability factors.

After teaching a unit on poetry, Miss Jones devised a test to determine what kind of learning had taken place in her eighth grade English class. Miss Jones's last test was evidently too easy and almost all of her students earned perfect or near-perfect scores. As a result, she made a concerted effort to make this one harder. The results indicated to Miss Jones that she had indeed given a hard test, but she was confused by the results. The test was composed of (1) twenty fill-in items and (2) thirty multiple-choice questions (each having three choices). The possible points were 50. Two students did score 35 (each correctly answering about fifteen fill-in and twenty multiple-choice questions). Not counting these two, however, the rest of the class fared this way: the mean score was 15, with scores ranging from 7 to 22. The mean score of the multiple-choice section was 10, with almost all students within 2 or 3 points of this. On the fill-in section some students had none correct, and none had more than eight correct. The mean on this section was 4.

Has knowledge, understanding, and so on, been demonstrated by the students? The chance score on the multiple-choice section of the test would be ten (one-third of thirty); because almost all students were within two or three points of this, we can assume that no learning was demonstrated by the majority of the students. The students' responses on the fill-in items cannot be precisely evaluated with regard to probability factors; yet we can note that the mean was four, meaning that of the twenty responses elicited, only one-fifth were answered correctly. Chance factor *would* play a part here, but we do not know how much. In sum, the fill-in results supply no evidence of significant learning; added to the multiple-choice results, they indicate (with the exception of the two students who scored 35) that no knowledge, skills, and so on, were demonstrated on the test.

We are then placed in the position of reexamining the status of the learning program in the class. Thus we must consider some of the critical questions already noted (for example, can we proceed to the next skill area, knowing the students' degree of inability?). The evidence suggests that some review work is needed for the students, very likely with a different approach from that attempted the first time. Individual contract programs might be worked out for the two students who *did* demonstrate learning.

A Last Critical Point

There is no substitute in test construction for a great deal of effort, with respect to both higher cognitive skills and time expended. The test should have a logical construct and represent the whole variety of skills being fostered. Beyond these factors, however, we must not forget that the ultimate test of an evaluation instrument is whether it

measures what it intends to measure (that is, has validity). To vali-
date our test, we must evaluate our test results. Individual responses
should be examined to determine how students with the best scores
did when compared with students with the lowest scores. (The
method presumes an *overall* validity of the test, which, in turn, assumes some significant efforts in the initial test construction.)

Numerous patterns can emerge in such validation technique. If we
find on one item that only three of ten high scorers get it correct, as
opposed to six of ten low scorers, we would seriously consider remov-
ing or rewriting the item. If the pattern of scores were reversed (with
a greater number of high scorers getting it correct), we would have a
validated item. When almost all students (high and low) get an item
correct, then we need to examine the question to see whether it is
measuring anything of significance. If almost no students get an item
correct, we then need to look at it for its possible faulty construction
or its relationship to the skills being learned.[14]

While it is not feasible to include the foregoing test skill within the
scope of this book, we stress that it relates to an important theme
here; namely, that a test needs both to evaluate meaningfully and be
evaluated meaningfully. Pulling old tests out of the file to administer
them is indefensible if done merely to avoid work; only when old
tests are reevaluated and refurbished can they serve as valid evaluation instruments. Whether the teacher elects to design new tests or
refurbish old ones, however, there is no easy way out.

SELF-EVALUATION ACTIVITIES

Here are some more evaluation problems relating to the chapter objectives.

1. *Try your hand with the following poorly written questions, following
the guidelines stated in the first suggested objective for this chapter.*

   a. (First grade) Which is bigger, an elephant or a giraffe?
   b. (Second grade) Who is the character we meet earliest in the story?
   c. (Third grade) Why is Texas bigger than Montana?
   d. (Fourth grade) If we go to the store with $1 and buy eight oranges
      at 5¢ each, we should have left: (1) $1, (2) 60¢, (3) 10¢, (4)
      nothing.
   e. (Fifth grade) If two boys each had $5 in their pockets and wanted
      to buy a book costing $3.75, paying 4% tax, how much money
      would they have left?
   f. (Sixth grade) The most popular President of the United States was
      (1) John F. Kennedy, (2) Thomas Jefferson, (3) Abraham Lincoln,
      (4) Franklin Roosevelt.

g. (Seventh grade) The greatest composer of piano concertos was
_____.

h. (Eighth grade) True or false: The biggest carnivorous amphibious mammal we studied living on the North American continent today is the grizzly bear.

i. (Ninth grade) Consider the following characteristics:
(1) Heavily industrialized
(2) Dense population
(3) Large unpopulated spaces
(4) High in agricultural production
(5) Marked seasonal weather changes

Match these characteristics with the following states:

(a) California
(b) Texas
(c) New York
(d) Montana
(e) Ohio

j. (Tenth grade) The Renaissance began in the year _____.

k. (Eleventh grade) The most important cause of overweight is (1) overeating, (2) lack of exercise, (3) unbalanced diet, (4) all of these, (5) both 1 and 2.

l. (Twelfth grade) Discuss the merits of Charlotte Bronte's novels.

In each of these, have you been able to identify the faulty aspects of the original question? Has your rewriting served to clarify and improve the original?

2. *The second objective in this chapter requires the student to write examples to meet the specifications of given objectives. Can you write at least two items for each of the following?*

a. (Sixth grade) Given a paragraph description of each of the nine planets, the student will be able to correctly identify at least seven of the planets described.

b. (Eleventh grade) Given a list of ten historical events relating to the American Revolution, the student will rank them in the correct chronological sequence.

c. (Fourth grade) The student will demonstrate his ability to apply the concept of addition by correctly answering four of five word problems requiring addition.

d. (High school physics) Given the specifications of wind strength and direction, field size, and kite string length, the student will correctly solve for the direction and length of string release that he must use to fly a kite at its maximum extension.

e. (High school typing) Given the specifications of a business format, the student will, without error, type a 500-word letter in correct business style within a 20-minute time span.

Do your questions meet the specifications of the objectives? Are they consistent with the taxonomy level suggested by the objective?

3. *In light of the third chapter objective, examine the following goals and devise two indices for each to translate them into measurable behavioral objectives. Briefly defend your choice of indices.*

    a. (Second grade) To promote growth of good citizenship.

    b. (Fifth grade) The students will demonstrate improvement in their mental health.

    c. (Seventh grade) The students will show evidence of improvement in their boy-girl relationships.

    d. (Eighth grade) To improve dental health practices.

    e. (Eleventh grade) The students will grow in their respect for American institutions.

    f. (Twelfth grade) The students will show an increase in their appreciation of Shakespeare.

Has each of these general goals been translated into a specific objective? Can all of your proposed indices be effectively measured?

4. *The following problems are suggested for use in evaluating the fourth behavioral objective.*

    a. After a unit on multiplication, Mr. McDonald gives a ten-problem test to his students. There are no easy problems, because he doesn't want to "give any points away." All problems require the students to demonstrate application-level skills. The test results show a wide disparity. Six students get seven or more problems correct, but the remaining twenty-four students score three or fewer correct. No partial credit is given, as Mr. McDonald believes that "you only get paid for right answers in life."

(1) What inferences can be made about student learning in this problem?
(2) What implications does this hold for future teacher behavior?

    b. While giving your seventh grade class a test in geography, you discover a widespread "cheating ring." Coming back from a trip to the office, you find many students copying from others. Further investigation reveals that several students have made and used "ponies" with all the names of the state capitals on them. You have talked briefly about cheating in the class, saying that all students are expected to do their own work.

(1) Interpret this event with regard to its implications for student learning.
(2) Diagnose this event as to its implications for future teacher behavior.

    c. After giving your eighth grade science class two 40-item tests, one a multiple-choice test (each item with *four* choices) and the second a true-false test, you find the following distribution of scores (number correct):

Multiple-Choice Test		True-False Test	
Score	*No. of Students*	*Score*	*No. of Students*
36–40	3	36–40	1
31–35	2	31–35	2
26–30	7	26–30	4
21–25	12	21–25	12
16–20	3	16–20	7
11–15	1	11–15	3
6–10	2	6–10	1
0–5	0	0–5	0

(1) What inferences could you draw about student learning from the results of these tests?

(2) What future teacher strategies would you advise in each case in light of this evidence?

  d. You are a new first grade teacher and have been asked by the reading teacher which of your thirty-five students you would recommend for the special reading preparation sessions. These sessions can involve any number of students and are designed to help those who have demonstrated a lack of aptitude on the reading readiness Test. This test has been shown to identify effectively children in need of prereading help. Although no one on the staff knows specifically how to interpret the results of this test, you do have a copy of the test and the scores your students made on it. The test consists of thirty items, in which the student is given a word, sign, symbol, or letter that he must correctly match with *one of three* following words, signs, symbols, or letters in the same row. The scores on the test, which show the following distribution, are the only information on which you can base your decision.

Score	*No. of Students*	*Score*	*No. of Students*
1	0	16	0
2	0	17	0
3	0	18	0
4	0	19	0
5	0	20	1
6	1	21	0
7	2	22	1
8	1	23	2
9	4	24	1
10	5	25	1
11	3	26	0
12	3	27	2
13	4	28	0
14	3	29	0
15	1	30	0

(1) How can these results be interpreted with regard to the students' reading preparation skills? Explain your answer.

(2) *How can these results be diagnosed with regard to the teacher's need for curriculum planning?*

(3) *What suggestions would you make for future reading diagnosis of students?*

NOTES AND REFERENCES

1. Jerome Bruner, *The Process of Education* (New York: Cambridge: Harvard University Press, 1960).
2. Jacques Barzun, *The House of Intellect* (New York: Harper and Brothers, 1959); John Holt, *How Children Fail* (New York: Dell Publishing Co., 1964); Martin Mayer, *The Schools* (New York: Harper and Brothers, 1961).
3. Benjamin S. Bloom *et al.*, *Taxonomy of Educational Objectives, Handbook I: Cognitive Domain* (New York: David McKay Company, 1956).
4. Norris M. Sanders, *Classroom Questions: What Kinds?* (New York: Harper & Row, 1966).
5. *Valid* and *reliable* are used here in their general measurement meaning. A test is valid if it measures what it intends to measure; it is reliable if it produces relatively consistent scores with repeated measures of this or equivalent tests.
6. Henry S. Dyer, "Is Testing a Menace to Education?" *New York State Education* 44 (October 1961), pp. 16–19.
7. Fred N. Kerlinger, *Foundations of Behavioral Research* (New York: Holt, Rinehart and Winston, 1965).
8. Robert L. Ebel, "The Social Consequences of Educational Testing," *School and Society*, November 14, 1963, pp. 331–334.
9. Furnishing behavioral objectives to students at elementary grade levels would not be educationally functional; in many elementary and secondary classrooms, the use of sample exercises relating to the objectives would be the simplest and most direct means of clarifying student expectations.
10. See Benjamin Bloom's "Learning for Mastery," in *Formative and Summative Evaluation of Student Learning* (New York: McGraw-Hill, Inc., 1971), for some insights into mastery learning potential.
11. R. Rosenthal and L. Jacobson, *Pygmalion in the Classroom* (New York: Holt, Rinehart and Winston, 1968).
12. Determining whether a student has demonstrated learning is a more complex probability problem. For example, the probability that a student would score six on a ten-item four-choice test by chance factors alone is less than .02. Thus it is very unlikely that this score was attained by guessing. We arrive at this probability by the formula:

$$P = \frac{N!}{R!(N-R)!} \, (p)^R \, (q)^{N-R}$$

where N = number of questions, R = the number of right answers, p = the probability of a right answer by chance, and q = the probability of a wrong answer by chance. Six factorial (6!) = 6 × 5 × 4 × 3 × 2 × 1.

In this case, $P = \dfrac{10!}{6!(10-6)!} \left(\dfrac{1}{4}\right)^6 \left(\dfrac{3}{4}\right)^4 = .016$

13. See Robert Mager's *Developing Attitudes Toward Learning* (Palo Alto, Cal.: Fearon Publishers, 1968) for some excellent examples of how affective traits can be measured.
14. See *Making the Classroom Test: A Guide for Teachers* (Princeton, N.J.: Educational Testing Service, 1961), for a more extended explanation of this process.

SUGGESTED READINGS

Bloom, Benjamin S., *et al. Handbook on Formative and Summative Evaluation of Student Learning.* New York: McGraw-Hill, Inc., 1971.
A long-needed reference work for teachers that includes a section on basic evaluation concepts and individual chapters applying those concepts to specific academic levels and areas.

Collins, Harold W., *et al. Educational Measurement and Evaluation.* Glenview, Ill.: Scott, Foresman and Company, 1969.
Here is a handy workbook that requires the student to study and then demonstrate a broad variety of evaluation skills.

Dyer, Henry S. "Is Testing a Menace to Education?" *New York State Education* 44 (October 1961), pp. 16–19.
Dyer critically examines eight misconceptions about testing, noting how these misconceptions impair the effectiveness of evaluation.

Ebel, Robert L. "The Social Consequences of Educational Testing." *School and Society*, November 14, 1963, pp. 331–334.
The author points out ways in which testing can be made to have more beneficial social consequences. Also noted are the social consequences of not testing.

Ebel, Robert L. *Essentials of Educational Measurement.* Englewood Cliffs, N.J.: Prentice-Hall, 1972.
This book furnishes an excellent overall survey of the uses and meanings of classroom and standardized tests.

Mager, Robert F. *Developing Attitudes Toward Learning.* Palo Alto, Cal.: Fearon Publishers, 1968.
This excellent manual develops skills of measurement in the affective domain.

Making the Classroom Test: A Guide for Teachers. Princeton, N.J.: Educational Testing Service, 1961.
This short handbook clearly explains the basic skills of testing.

Sanders, Norris M. *Classroom Questions: What Kinds?* New York: Harper & Row, 1966.
Sanders has developed many examples of the varieties of questions that can be asked at the different levels of the cognitive taxonomy.

A Curriculum
Synthesis

INTRODUCTION

It has been the authors' intent to suggest that classroom planning requires a thorough and comprehensive analysis of a number of factors. The book has
looked at real and artificial learning, student self-
discipline and motivation, a behavioral-objectives
approach to curriculum planning, and ways of
evaluating students on the basis of performance.
It has been assumed that minimum skills in each
of these areas are necessary for effective planning
and instruction. The objectives contained in this
book provide a teacher with at least the beginning
skills needed to plan a comprehensive course of
instruction.

The point to be made in this closing chapter is
that a *competency-based curriculum is a model for
planning* this course of instruction. From a curriculum standpoint, it is a structure on which a
teacher can build whatever he chooses. Competency basing is not a teaching method because it
does not tell us *what* a teacher should do or *how*
he should do it. It merely provides a format for
the teacher's own creativity or synthesis.

A logical synthesis in curriculum planning would
operationalize the objectives of this book. Although
these objectives represent only an introduction to
curriculum planning and classroom management,
by blending this information with the teacher's
skills, methodologies, and subject matter, a curriculum can be achieved that is true synthesis.

Some authors use the term *synthesis* for creativity. This is true to the extent that synthesis, like
creativity, consists of putting parts together in
order to form a new whole. A form of creativity

is present when the teacher builds a curriculum module and the student uses previously learned skills to solve problems and see the relationship between a number of elements.

In developing a synthesis curriculum, the teacher must make special preparations in order to make the curriculum a potential source of creativity to the learner. This goes far beyond establishing sequenced learning, providing an acceptable learning climate, or modifying unacceptable student behavior.

SUGGESTED BEHAVIORAL OBJECTIVE

In order to produce a synthesis curriculum, one that has creative potential for the learner, consider the following chapter objectives.

1. *The student will demonstrate his ability to synthesize competency-based theory in the development of a cluster of modules.*
   a. *The student will first state the subject area for which his curriculum is to be developed.*
   b. *In developing a synthesis of competency-based theory in curriculum development, the student will incorporate in his behavioral objectives, activities, and evaluation the conditions discussed in this chapter that promote pupil learning. The student will list and defend those elements in his planning that promote this learning.*
   c. *The student will field-test the modules in an educational setting and then .make the necessary revisions in the modules based on his analysis of the students' performance, school resources, and time allotted for instruction.*

A SYNTHESIS OF COMPETENCY-BASED THEORY

The best way to discuss the use of competency-based theory in curriculum development is to provide an illustration. In the curriculum and taxonomy chapters, there have been numerous illustrations of curriculum modules. These modules can be grouped together in a cluster. The style of these modules may be used as models for building your own synthesis curriculum.

An approach similar to these models could be developed for a course of instruction for college seniors as a terminal class before graduation. Five modules might be written to include learning, taxonomy, curriculum, self-management, and evaluation. These modules could contain the skills that students should acquire during their previous undergraduate courses in education. The first part of the course would include a pretest on these skills. Based on the student's performance on the pretest, he would be assigned all, none, or only some of the modules to be studied during the first half of the course. The emphasis would be to reacquaint or provide the student with the necessary minimal skills all teachers should possess.

All five modules could be in operation at once. A self-instructional center with materials could be provided so that students could proceed at their own speed through the course. Ideally the student should be able to test himself on these modules whenever he feels he has acquired the necessary skills and completed all the activities. However, the structure of the physical plant and the requirements of the school may necessitate a midterm examination when the student would be tested on all the modules for which he is responsible. A number of class sessions should be devoted to each module and should consist of discussions with equivalent and analogous activities. The student who successfully completes the modules for which he is responsible, as measured on the midterm examination, could proceed to a synthesis project. His project might be to develop a field problem representing some combination of the skills learned in the modules. Students who still do not meet the minimal requirements on the midterm could receive intensive, one-to-one help until they achieve the necessary skills. Then these students would also proceed to a synthesis project.

This process is shown on the curriculum map in Figure 8. The student enters the course, is pretested, and begins working on one or more modules. A number of students could demonstrate on the pretest that they already possessed the minimal skills required in each of the modules, and these students could be allowed to begin work on the synthesis project immediately. A number of the projects might represent the students' creation and evaluation of a competency-based curriculum. Others might investigate social or psychological problems existing in the community.

When starting his project, the student should write a brief outline including the methods, resources, and subject matter that the project will encompass. Then a meeting with the teacher should be held to finalize the contract. The teacher's role is to serve as a resource in selecting possible avenues for finding data or suggesting alternative ways of handling information. Just as this particular curriculum outline developed by the teacher would represent a synthesis of the objectives contained in this book, the project developed by the student would also be a synthesis of the skills outlined in his course of instruction. Figure 9 is a chart called 'Synthesis Project Evaluation Form' and would be an appropriate device for evaluating a student's synthesis project.

Faced with the task of evaluating synthesis, two options appear possible. Judgments could be made on the basis of process (technique)

FIGURE 8

Curriculum Map

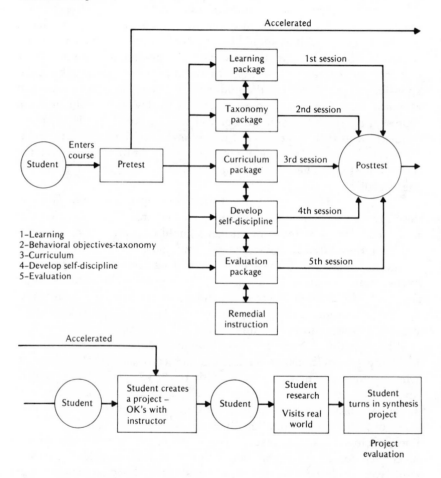

1-Learning
2-Behavioral objectives-taxonomy
3-Curriculum
4-Develop self-discipline
5-Evaluation

FIGURE 9

Synthesis Project Evaluation Form

The classifications listed below categorize the elements that are contained in your papers.
The letter with each category signifies according to our evaluation E—excellent; A—adequate; or L—lacking.
More discreet evaluation may be found in reading the individual comments on the projects.

I. Knowledge

   The statement of the project in an accurate, clear and precise manner ☐

II. Comprehension

   The statement of the project in such a way that the student effectively communicates his understanding of the problem undertaken ☐

III. Application

   The effective utilization of abstractions and concepts in the problem undertaken ☐

IV. Analysis

   Breakdown of the communication into its constituent elements such that the relative hierarchy of ideas is made clear and/or the relations between ideas expressed are made explicit. ☐

   Facts distinguished from opinions and unstated assumptions recognized. ☐

   Systematic, logical, and persuasive structural organization developed for the project. ☐

V. Synthesis

   Project developed in such a way that elements are put skillfully and effectively together to form a whole ☐

   Set of conclusions developed and structured to either explain or classify data, with a set of generalizations produced from the data ☐

or skill (qualitative expertise and product). In determining process, the quest is to ascertain the rationale, justification for the rationale, assessment of the methodology, degree and type of analysis, and the consistency of conclusions drawn from the earlier procedures. In viewing the final product, the skills employed (verbal, concrete, symbolic, logical sequences, persuasiveness, and the sophistication of generalizations) are all measures of achievement. At some point, the evaluation moves from "hard," classifiable categories for judgment to "soft," rather personal decisions. Nevertheless, the building of evaluative category systems is a step toward standardizing or at least clarifying criteria.

Projects that are not completed may not result in failing grades but in an "incomplete" mark until such time as the skill is achieved. The synthesis projects, like the class itself, attempt to implement learning research under a given set of conditions. The projects should be developed as much as possible from experiences in an actual classroom and should represent some combination and use of skills from previous courses of instruction.

Synthesis is a way of tying together a variety of learned skills by providing the student with the opportunity to illustrate the relationship of these skills in solving a problem. Some form of synthesis should be attempted at all levels of instruction after the completion of a few modules. The elementary student who has acquired three or four basic skills needs the opportunity to bring them together by creating some kind of synthesis. This not only positively reinforces the skills learned but makes it very clear that the skills are relevant to situations in the real world. This is particularly true with the synthesis projects discussed above for the college seniors. The students will often translate educational theory into the development, analysis, and evaluation of a particular curriculum. These projects should be field-tested in an educational setting and the data gathered from actual classrooms. This allows the student to alter his curriculum to better fit the requirements of the individual students in the class.

The course of instruction outlined above is just one possible way of adapting competency-based theory to a given educational situation. The most obvious way of implementing a competency-based approach would be for the classroom teacher to take the model outlined above and begin to assess and restructure his courses of instruction as necessary. During this process, a number of skills and experiences could be classified as basic and necessary for all students to possess. In this segment of the course, the teacher would provide learning opportunities to all students. Coupled with this would be some form of remedial or tutorial work in which the teacher could devote part of certain class periods to working with the students having difficulty obtaining the basic skills. A team-teaching approach is advantageous at this point; however, it is possible in a self-contained classroom to give the students learning activities that free the teacher from his traditionally conceived role as lecturer to one of resource person and helper. Following a posttest on these basic skills, the teacher might provide or plan with the students a number of individualized learning programs. This individualized instruction segment of the course would require the teacher and/or the student to state as clearly as possible the skills and experiences necessary for each individualized program. This is particularly crucial when the student has a cooperative role in planning curriculum. When the student can state his own goals, he can decide just how much he wants to attempt in his program and what kinds of activities he must perform to achieve the desired results. By using a competency-based model with explicit objectives, the student can assess his own productivity and success in meeting the goals he has helped set.

Figure 1, on page 4 illustrates what we have been discussing. Basic skills are determined for the course of instruction, and these skills are outlined in the form of concepts, goals, and objectives. Then there is a pretest of the skills (the objectives). This test is followed by the instructional program. As in all competency-based programs, there are a number of treatments representing the capabilities, interests, and needs of the students. At the completion of the learning activities, all the students are given a comprehensive posttest. This can be followed by teacher, student, or teacher-and-student development of individualized learning programs. As the figure suggests, these programs should require at least application-level skills. Hopefully skills and experiences from other courses and life interests will be developed during this phase of the program. The focus on individualized learning is always twofold. The first goal of individualized instruction is to allow for application of previously learned skills. It should also provide the student with an opportunity to integrate the skills and experiences he is presently learning with the other skills previously learned. The second focus of the individualized learning program relates to the discussion in the curriculum chapter. Students need to build and relate skills so that they may form concepts and generalizations. These concepts and generalizations are the abstractions that provide order and explain the conditions in the world.

In a competency-based curriculum, even an individualized learning program has specific focus, precise objectives, and some type of evaluation device. The outline in Figure 1 shows a possible synthesis evaluation activity. This synthesis segment of the course might take a number of directions. This could include tests, small group discussions, or projects. In this instance, the outline suggests that all the individuals in the course would be brought together to share and evaluate the basic skills and their application to the individualized learning programs. The program should have continual assessment during each phase.

The two examples discussed above represent only two possible ways of organizing a competency-based curriculum. All curricula using a competency-based model would have in common these integral parts: objectives, appropriate learning activities, and evaluation measures, which determine the attainment of the skills contained in the objectives.

In the previous example of a college-level course and in the last example, the desire has not been to limit the experiences, thought processes, or any other possible benefits that might be involved in any course of instruction. In writing objectives and specifying at least minimal skills and experiences, the teacher is not closing the door to student curiosity or value formation. *Objectives only specify the items on which the student will be assessed.* Any other benefits the student realizes are important and worthwhile; if these experiences need to be assessed by the teacher, subsequent instruction may plan for their evaluation.

A competency-based curriculum does not limit any more than the traditional curriculum does what students will internalize or what they will do with the information given to them. The differences between competency-based and traditional curricula is that a competency-based curriculum more accurately measures some of the specific skills or conclusions the student has acquired from the information or experiences provided.[1]

PROGRAMMING ACTIVITIES TO PROMOTE PUPIL LEARNING

Early in the chapter on curriculum, it was suggested that planning multiple activities for a given objective was one way of providing a better match between pupil learning and resources. There are a number of ways to arrange activities within a given objective or module. The creative teacher can use these two guidelines as a starting point:

1. *Write the concept curriculum within or across subject matter areas.*
2. *Program the activities in a linear (sequential) or vertical (simultaneous) format.*

Figure 10 shows linear and vertical programming.

For ease of instruction, this book has focused on writing modules

FIGURE 10

Programming Instruction

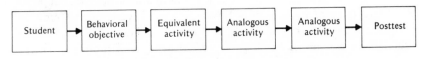

Linear (sequential)

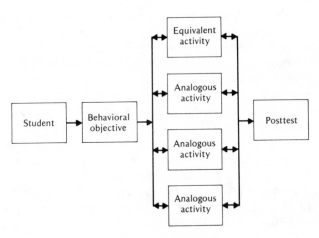

Vertical (simultaneous)

within a given subject area. At the elementary school level, it is entirely possible and often desirable to write modules on general topics that cut across subject areas. In a cross-discipline approach, activities written for a given objective can illustrate the skills of several disciplines. In a module on pollution, for example, some activities might require math skills as well as scientific data gathering, social studies analysis of the effect of the particular pollution on local culture, and the entire exercise might be put in written form, using the skills of language arts. At least in theory, the multi-unit school developed at the University of Wisconsin's Research and Development Center attempts to develop curricula in this manner. The multi-unit school, which uses a team of teachers representing specializations in each of the elementary teaching areas, has the goal of developing cross-discipline modules through its individually guided instructional programming.

Whether the curriculum is cross-disciplined or not, the task still facing the teacher is how the activities will be presented. The most traditional form is *linear programming*. This might involve the presentation of an equivalent activity followed by several analogous activities and concluded by the posttest. The students may or may not be excused from all or part of the instructional activities depending on their pretest skills. This design is sequential in that it may imply that one must possess the skills in the first activity before moving to the next activity. From a time standpoint, this instruction is sequential.

Vertical programing makes entirely different assumptions about the activities. There may be simultaneous activities that a student can engage in with the belief that he has the necessary skills to enter in any or all that he chooses or is assigned. Modules displaying the vertical presentation of activities show students working at a variety of learning stations using a number of different media. The option is to have a number of equivalent activities or one equivalent and a number of closely related analogous activities. Vertical programming is more difficult in a self-contained classroom. It requires the teacher to move and act as a resource agent. It also calls for learning to be more self-instructional. Linear programming is more teacher-directed, while vertical programming sees the teacher as a diagnostician and resource person. There is an advantage to vertical programming: where a cross-discipline approach has been used, students can be placed in a learning situation that forces them to practice skills in which they may be deficient. A student with weak language-arts skills may have the task of writing the final report for a group-assigned project on pollution. He not only learns about pollution but gets necessary practice and writing skills.

Multiple activities are not required in module construction, but their advantage is hard to disclaim. When students have the opportunity of seeing their objectives in a variety of activity settings, the student can see that knowledge is not compartmentalized but goes across a number of subject areas and modes of inquiry. When students can choose activities, it enhances their interest and may provide enough motivation to see them successfully through the module. The likelihood of a student's failing an objective is lessened when he has had a variety of activities for practice before the post-test. In fact, multiple activities may lessen the need for remedial work or at least the number of students recycling.

Each module presents different opportunities in the programming of activities. This is perhaps the greatest area for teacher creativity. A sound decision will be based on a teacher's comprehensive assessment of the time and resources available, objectives of the module, and a thorough understanding of the personalities and learning characteristics of his pupils.

PROMOTING CREATIVITY IN THE COMPETENCY-BASED CLASSROOM

In its most elementary form, *creativity* is any new or unique product developed by an individual. The product builds upon previously learned skills and knowledge. The product may, in its final form, represent a new way (or synthesis) of looking at data. More typically, synthesis provides an extension and development of an already established way of doing something.

Let us illustrate by considering the creation of a musical symphony. In composing his own unique works, Beethoven used the previous knowledge, skills, forms, and techniques of his predecessors. However, he created out of the old forms and techniques an entirely new form never written before. One of Beethoven's contemporaries, Schubert, used some of Beethoven's forms and style in his own composing. Even to the untrained ear, it is obvious that much of Schubert sounds very similar to Beethoven and is in large measure an *extension* of Beethoven's form. Both of these men *created*. Schubert developed a unique composition. The elements were borrowed and the product is an extension of an already existing form, but the act of developing a unique composition of individuality allows the music to be placed in the same category of creativity as Beethoven's works.

While one particular Frenchman may have developed Impressionistic painting, no one would claim that Degas, Monet, Manet, or

Renoir (who worked in the same frame of reference) were less creative than any others. It is not within the scope of this book to become involved in establishing the criteria of "most creative" or "least creative." The aim is to suggest that *each student has creative potential. To develop it, the teacher must provide careful and considerate planning.*

When students are only gaining knowledge and comprehension skills, there is little opportunity for creativity. The student is asked merely to recall material for which there is a right or wrong answer. As instruction moves into the higher levels of the taxonomy, there is less emphasis on right and wrong answers. More stress is placed upon the *procedures* or *mode of inquiry* that the student uses to solve the problem. There is little creativity in naming the battles and generals of the Civil War. More creativity is allowed in considering the causes, conditions, and possible alternatives of the war. *Students working at this level are evaluated on the method used and its correct application in developing answers.* Another means of enhancing creative potential is to allow alternative solutions to a problem, using as the criteria for evaluation the student's application of a methodology and his ability to defend his solution.

These are a few conditions that promote creativity. E. Paul Torrance, in his book *Encouraging Creativity in the Classroom,* discusses in more detail some specific means for building creativity into class instruction. This is a valuable resource book for incorporating creative techniques into a competency-based curriculum.

The conditions for creativity must be planned for and not left to chance. Although the final product itself may go beyond any particular course of instruction, the creative act is always built on precise skills that have been previously learned. Beethoven's creation of a symphony with its unique form and style went beyond any previous forms and structure. Yet to achieve this new wholeness required a thorough application and analysis of previously learned techniques and forms. It is the teacher's responsibility to teach the necessary techniques and forms of his subject area and provide behavioral situations in which the student can attempt to create.

IMPLEMENTING A COMPETENCY-BASED CURRICULUM

A number of school districts have begun to implement competency-based curricula. Earlier illustrations in this book have been built around school districts that have developed competency-based curriculum guides. The teachers in a school system, working cooperatively with students, community, and university resource persons, began to generate objectives and incorporate a number of teaching methods and programs in an attempt to give their students the most complete and comprehensive learning opportunities.

This brings us to a final approach that might be used in developing a competency-based curriculum. Using the skills contained in this book and other resource references written on the topics of behavioral objectives, classroom management, and criteria-referenced evaluation, experienced teachers might use the competency-based model for re-structuring curriculum in their classroom; they might cooperatively rewrite the curricula of their school systems. This would be feasible if teachers attended a workshop and acquired the necessary skills. Admittedly, such a thorough and comprehensive approach to instruc-tion is time-consuming and can appear to be a Herculean task to the teacher. Developing modules over a year's course of study, planning individualized instructional programs *with students*, and providing a number of different methods and activities to reach as many students in the class as possible requires the teacher to use a number of intel-lectual skills. Some writers have suggested that such a rigorous under-taking is beyond the creative capability of many teachers.[2] It is true that using a competency-based model helps the teacher use his skills in developing a creative enterprise. Hopefully those writers are wrong who claim that teachers lack the necessary creative or intellectual potential to undertake this task. If they are right, the result will be either the continuation of rather poorly developed instruction or pre-packaged programs that require the teacher to perform in only a technician's role. A competency-based curriculum is time-consuming to develop, but the most compelling reason for attempting a thorough approach to instructional planning is that such an approach provides *the student* with a comprehensive design for learning. After all, the primary reason teaching takes place is to provide students with the opportunity to learn, and a competency-based curriculum attempts to provide the best possible learning opportunities.

REVIEW OF BEHAVIORAL OBJECTIVE

Recall the behavioral objective of this chapter:

1. *The student will demonstrate his ability to synthesize competency-based theory in the development of a cluster of modules.*
   a. *The student will first state the subject area for which his curriculum is to be developed.*
   b. *In developing a synthesis of competency-based theory in curriculum development, the student will incorporate in his behavioral objectives, activities, and evaluation the conditions discussed in this chapter that*

promote pupil learning. The student will list and defend those elements in his planning that promote this learning.

c. *The student will field-test the modules in an educational setting and then make the necessary revisions in the modules based on his analysis of the students' performances, school resources, and time allotted for instruction.*

Before attempting the development of a curriculum that represents a synthesis and application of competency-based principles, consider the following module that represents an adaptation of some of the behavioral skills required in this book. This module, although somewhat vague, is still more expertly constructed than modules teachers would typically be confronted with when developing competency-based curriculum. As an analogous exercise before developing your own curriculum, look at this unit. Analyze and evaluate its synthesis of competency-based elements. Do the activities correspond to the objectives? Are the assessment items precise? Can students receive remedial help and advance at their own pace? Are creative conditions provided in the course of instruction? The reader should form his own conclusions based on the objectives in this book as to how well the unit meets the criteria for a competency-based model of instruction. It is not necessary for the reader to be a social studies teacher to determine whether the behavioral objectives move through both taxonomic domains and to see whether the activities, methods, and evaluation complement the behaviors contained in the objectives.

How Should People Treat People in the Supermarket?
Grade Two Social Studies
Sample Unit

OVERVIEW

As an outcome of this unit, children should develop a sense of responsibility for the effective operation of their neighbourhood. Pupils should be aware of honesty and dishonesty in the interaction of community members—specifically the interaction which occurs at the supermarket or local grocery store. Thus, the value objectives of this unit relate to **responsibility, empathy** and **honesty.**

Since most second-year students are familiar with many visible aspects of the supermarket or store, **this unit is designed to explore the less obvious problems.** The unit should be more a sociological study than an economic one. The major concept to be learned through this unit is **goals.** Skills to be emphasized include classifying (analysis) and hypothesizing (synthesizing).

This unit will concentrate on four aspects of a supermarket and afford opportunities for pupils to organize information, pose problems, suggest possible solutions for them and, in some cases, test their solutions. The four aspects are:

1. *Employer-employee relations.*
2. *Customer relations.*
3. *Advertising.*
4. *Packaging*

Teachers should not feel that they are committed to study an urban supermarket if this is not pertinent to the needs of their pupils. The objectives of the unit can be realized by a study of a corner store, a village store, a country store or even the mail-order catalog.

Again it must be emphasized that it is not the aim of this unit to merely increase the child's knowledge or skills but, above everything else, to provide opportunities for building his value system.

The authors wish to thank the Department of Education, Province of Alberta, Canada, for permission to use this unit. The Department of Education gratefully acknowledges the work of the following teachers who developed the Social Studies Unit on the Supermarket: Mrs. Thelma Pendergast, Red Deer County Elementary Consultant (Chairman); Mrs. Diane Averill, Grandview School, Bowden; Mrs. Gwen Clark, River Glen School, Red Deer; Mrs. Marie Mann, John Wilson Elementary School, Innisfail; Mrs. Helen Marshall, Grandview School, Bowden; Mrs. Christine Murphy, Spruce View School, Spruce View; Mrs. Agnes Riley, River Glen School, Red Deer; Miss Lexie Stevens, John Wilson Elementary School, Innisfail; Mrs. Edna Whittemore, River Glen School, Red Deer.

OBJECTIVES

A. Value Objectives

Students will make value judgements concerning the advantages and disadvantages of:

1. Respecting the rights, feelings and ideas of others (Empathy).
2. Recognizing the worth of other people's contributions to the neighbourhood (Empathy).
3. Accepting responsibility in job activities (Responsibility).
4. Treating others justly, fairly and honestly (Honesty).

B. Skill Objectives

1. Students will *locate* and *classify* information on the supermarket in picture and chart form.
2. Students will *hypothesize* and *solve problems* related to the interaction of people in satisfying their basic need for food.
3. Students, by *conducting a survey*, will give evidence of the ability to *tabulate and interpret information* by means of a bar graph.
4. Students will develop speaking and listening skills, such as *speaking clearly and telling the facts in order.*

C. Knowledge Objectives

1. Understanding of such terms as advertising, wants and needs, services, division of labour, employer, employee, customer, cashier will be indicated in student oral or written examples and explanations (System).
2. Students will be able to recognize and explain when presented with picture examples of interdependence, how people of a neighbourhood are dependent upon each other (Interdependence).
3. Students will be able to identify from listed examples those which require people to cooperate to get a lot accomplished (Cooperation).
4. Pupils should gain an understanding of the following generalizations, all of which relate to the major concept of goals:
   a. The members of society have different wants and needs. (e.g. The supermarket owner needs people to shop there. The customer needs food to satisfy his basic need of hunger.) Certain institutions (such as the supermarket) have available a variety of goods to meet the demands made by the members of society.
   b. A variety of personnel provide the services that the members of society require.
   c. All individuals have a responsibility to do their jobs well and thus provide a worthwhile contribution to society.
   d. How an individual performs his job or role affects all others involved.
   e. All well-done jobs make a worthwhile and necessary contribution to society.
   f. All individuals make choices to meet their needs.

LEARNING EXPERIENCES

Generalizations or Values to be Stressed	Questions	Activities (See Bibliography for sources)
A. Opener The supermarket is a major part of the neighbourhood.	1. What is happening? 2. Where is it happening? 3. What is a grand opening? 4. Why is it happening?	Bulletin board display with captions, pictures, balloons, flags, "Grand Opening." Each child writes one reason for the grand opening. These are read, discussed and tabulated on the board. Later, one member of class makes a chart.
Neighbourliness	5. Where do you shop? 6. Whom do you meet there?	Children start title page on grand opening for a booklet on the supermarket. (Pupils' own creative work—not ditto worksheets.) Read *Communities at Work*—"Food for the City."
Differing needs and wants	7. Why do your parents shop at the supermarket?	Make a combined checklist from pupil responses. Have parents check their reasons. Tabulate the responses by using objects which could be stacked. One object for each response. Convert these to a stencil bar graph for their booklets.
B. Development 1. Employer-employee Relations Institutions provide a variety of goods and services to meet the society's needs and wants.	1. What things are bought at the supermarket? 2. Where do you find these goods? 3. What departments are there at the supermarket?	Bring grocery lists from home or make their own. Classify the groceries (Meat, Produce, Grocery, Miscellaneous). Game: Shopping at the Supermarket Purpose: To strengthen auditory discrimination of beginning sounds. Players: Four Materials: Twenty word-cards each of which indicates something that can be bought at the supermarket; a shopping bag; a master word-list for the leader, representing the beginning sounds on the word-cards.

Generalizations or Values to be Stressed	Questions	Activities (See Bibliography for sources)
		Directions: The leader gives five cards, randomly selected, to each player and says, for example, "Who has bought something that begins like banana?" The players listen intently and those whose words answer the question give their cards to the leader who puts them in the shopping bag if they have been correctly selected. (Examples in this case are beans and biscuits.) If a winner is desired, he will be the one who first disposes of all his cards. (It should be noted that this is a game in which skill and luck may combine to determine the winner, thus the slower child has a chance to win.)
		Adaptations:
		a. Blends could be used as well as medial sounds.
		b. The game could be made more difficult by using more cards.
		c. This game could be adapted to the vocabularies of arithmetic, science and social studies.
A variety of personnel provide the services that society requires.	4. What workers are needed because of the variety of departments?	Read "Let's Go to the Supermarket" from *Your World.* Reclassify if necessary and include along with pictures in the booklet. Pupils list employees for booklets as a result of their research.
	5. What are the duties of each employee?	
Interdependence-responsibility	6. What happens if each worker does not fulfil his job?	Small groups prepare oral or written reports. May make stencils of reports for booklets. These can be put in riddle form.
Cooperation		
Equality		
How an individual performs his role affects others (empathy).		

Role Play:

Contrasting a job well done to one poorly done.

1. How would the other workers feel?

   What would happen if?

   a. Peter was late returning for work. Bill was waiting to go home for supper.

   b. Mary forgot to order the plastic bags needed to wrap the meat.

   c. Harry does not come to work and does not let the manager know in time to get someone to take his place.

   d. Groceries well packed as opposed to those poorly packed.

   e. Bob does not want to go to work today. He would rather accompany his friends to the lake for a swim. Someone suggests he phone his manager and say he is sick.

2. How would the customers feel?

   What would happen if?

   a. Housewife finds the eggs broken or bread squashed.

   b. Housewife sees the meat packer or baker with dirty hands and dirty apron.

Picture discussion of one or more workers.

Making Decisions When Hiring Employees

1. Which of these would be good employees? Why? Some could be acted out.

   a. Jim Brown was hired by Mr. Fox, manager of the local grocery. Jim's job was to pack groceries and take them to the cars. Jim put heavy tins at the bottom of the bags and then put the bread on top of the tins. Was he the kind of worker Mr. Fox wanted?

7. If you were the manager, what would you look for when hiring employees?

Honesty

Responsibility

Loyalty

Courtesy

Personal appearance

Empathy

Generalizations or
Values to be Stressed

Questions

Activities (See Bibliography for sources)

b. Bob did not like to carry the bags out to the customers' cars. He often packed the bags so that eggs, bread or doughnuts were squashed by heavy cans of juice or boxes of soap. Was he the kind of worker Mr. Fox would want?

c. Harry always seemed happy and cheerful. Everyone liked to talk with Harry. He always thanked them for shopping and hoped that they would return. "See you again soon" he'd say.

d. Dick Farley was also a bagger at the local grocery. He was always neatly dressed, had his hair combed and changed his apron daily.

e. Betty was glad when coffee time arrived. She met a friend for coffee and was so interested in talking that she took fifteen minutes longer than she should.

f. Sue was asked to mark the cans of soup as 2 for 19¢. She was not paying attention and marked the soup 23¢ a tin.

2. Which of these would be good employees? Why:

a. Today the grocery store was having a sale on cranberry sauce and turkey. Sam was to keep the shelves full. Mrs. Long wanted a turkey and cranberry sauce but there was no cranberry sauce on the shelf.

b. Tom was asked to move a display of pop from the back storeroom to a counter in front of the store. In a short time he had made a very attractive display.

c. Miss Hill, when ringing up Mrs. Long's groceries, rang up three tins of canned ham instead of two. This was not the only time she had done this.

d. Mr. Cork, the popman, is putting pop on the shelf. Mr. Fox had ordered ten cases but no one is around just now and Mr. Cork would like some pop for himself. So he takes some.

e. Jack did not like many of the people he worked with. He thought he knew all about groceries and he would argue with the others, point out what he thought were mistakes and generally make trouble.

Define customer for booklet. Illustrate with a picture or drawing.

Discuss example stories of customer behaviour.

Students make decisions and give reasons for them.

2. Customer Behavior

A variety of personnel provide the services that the members of society require.

1. Why are employees needed in the supermarket?
2. What do you call the people who shop at the supermarket?
3. What do you call the people who work at the supermarket?
4. What is a customer?
5. Where do they come from?
6. What responsibilities do customers have?

Honesty
Empathy
Courtesy

Customer Behaviour

1. What would you do? Why? How would the employees and customers feel?

a. At the end of an aisle is a display of cans of peaches. Mrs. Clay takes a can from the center of the display since she can reach it without much trouble. The cans fall over.

Generalizations or
Values to be Stressed

Questions

Activities (See Bibliography for sources)

b. Mrs. Snatcher walks up and down the aisles of the grocery store picking up her groceries. She decides she doesn't want the bottle of soap she has picked up. She is some distance from the soap counter and is quite tired. She leaves the soap on the bread counter.

c. Mrs. Stopper is taking her groceries through the check-out. She decides she forgot the ice cream. There is a line of people behind her but she goes to get it anyway.

d. Mr. Black has some spoiled meat to return.

e. Sue and Jill happen to meet each other in one of the aisles of the grocery store. They decide to visit since they haven't seen each other for such a long time. Other shoppers find it difficult to go by them.

f. Mrs. Hall has two bags in her grocery cart. Her husband could not pick her up and take her home. She could either carry her groceries home or take them in the cart.

g. There are some chocolate bars and gum on the shelf. Jim could help himself to some candy and he does. He puts the candy in his pocket and leaves the store.

h. Fred saw a bag of chips on the shelf. He broke open the bag and ate some. What do you think of that?

i. Mrs. White knocked a bag of flour on the floor. The bag broke.

j. Kathy went shopping with her mother. She bought a bag of popcorn with her quarter. The cashier gave Kathy her popcorn and a dime and her quarter back.

Class summary for booklets—
"A good customer is _____"
"A good customer will _____"
"I am a good customer because _____"

Group work. Students gather ads. Discuss why people buy the goods.

For booklets, pupils take two ads—one item they would buy and one they would not buy—and tell why.

Set up situations where the child has a limited amount of money, e.g., what would you buy if you had twenty-five cents and could buy chocolate bars, gum, apples, candy, pop? Tell why they choose as they do.

Read "Wishes, Wishes, Wishes," page 59, *Families at Work*, and *Camera Patterns*.

Read decision stories from *Basic Social Studies Series - Living Together in the Neighborhood*.

Decision Stories To Finish
1. Marie had twenty-five cents to spend in the neighbourhood store. She saw a doll for fifteen cents

3. Advertising

Refer to bulletin board display or teacher-gathered ads.
1. What do you call these signs?
2. Why are ads used? (to get people to buy)
3. Why are famous people used in ads?
4. Since people's money is limited, how do they decide what to buy?
5. Can you think of a situation in which you might have chosen differently?

Generalizations or Values to be Stressed	Questions	Activities (See Bibliography for sources)
		and one for twenty-five cents. She liked the fifteen cent doll but the twenty-five cent doll was bigger and had a pink dress. Marie bought the twenty-five cent doll. On her way home, Marie saw her friends running to meet the ice cream wagon. She . . . . .
		2. Tom had a dime. He was going to the store to buy candy. On the way he met Harry and Peter, who went with him. Inside the store, Tom looked at the candy. He saw the kind of candy bar he liked. He could buy it for a dime. There were jelly beans too. He could get a lot of those for a dime. Tom . . . . .
4. Packaging Respect for others' needs Honesty Justice Choosing	1. How are goods packaged? 2. Why are goods packaged?—convenience, weight, cleanliness, what ingredients, advertising, customer protection (Canadian Food Rules), safety (plastic, glass), some people use the package. 3. Can packaging be misleading?	Students bring sample packages (ahead of time). Discuss the actual package. Booklets. Find pictures of a variety of packages. Items are packaged because . . . . . Use examples to show—sometimes unable to see the whole product, sometimes misrepresentation on package, e.g., will your cake look as good as the one on the package?

C. Conclusion

The culmination would first be approached as a class project in the areas of decision making, planning and supply. It would then be divided into group projects, each group or person being responsible for his or her job. This type of culmination would give the teacher an excellent chance to perform a subjective evaluation of the entire unit by observing the children and watching for the manifestation of internalized values.

The Supermarket—The class plan to set up a miniature supermarket in their room. Decisions would have to be made with regard to—which day, what time, how long, what items to bring, number of departments (e.g., popcorn, candy, cookies, toys, etc.), what classroom pupils in the school will be the customers.

After these decisions have been reached a letter and check-list could be sent to the parents to confirm the kind and amount of "merchandise" available. When this list is returned, the children would classify the items and list on a chart, thus arriving at a definite number of departments their store would consist of. The next step would be to divide the class into groups and assign each to a particular facet of running the store. You would require: advertising people, packaging people, cashier, people to set up counters, cleanup personnel, people to keep counters stocked, clerks, one or two people to act as manager throughout the operation. Make ads to advertise products that they are bringing to sell. Post ads in halls in advance.

Once divided, the children would have a group discussion and possibly list what their particular jobs entail. They are then responsible for carrying them out in the best possible way. The teacher could rotate among the groups, offering guidance if requested. The sale is held and afterwards the children gather in their groups to discuss with the class how things went, what was a particularly good feature and why. The money from the sale would be listed and totalled. The operating expenses are listed, totalled and subtracted from the proceeds. Any remaining money is profit. Throughout the various stages of the conclusion the teacher would guide the various groups to review what they had covered throughout the unit, particularly in relation to their own jobs. As a final project the children could perhaps write in their booklets their ideas of their venture into the supermarket business and what particular things they learned from it.

D. Evaluation

	Often	Some-times	Very Rarely	Never

Teachers' Checklist:

1. Pupil shares ideas and materials willingly.
2. Pupil shows consideration for others by waiting his turn.
3. Pupil displays responsibility by collecting materials and bringing them to school.
4. Pupil shows understanding or respect for others' feelings in role playing.
5. Pupil shows ability to reach decisions on the basis of materials presented.

Pupil Self-Evaluation

1. Group Work
   a. How well did we share our materials today?
   b. Did I do my job as well as I could?
   c. Did I give any worthwhile ideas?
   d. Did I put away all the materials I used?
   e. How could we improve next time?
   f. Did I keep the group from working by interrupting, too much talking about other things or pushing and bothering the others in my group?
   g. Was I polite?

2. Listening
   a. Did I get ready to listen?
   b. Did I look at the speaker?
   c. Did I keep very quiet?
   d. Did I have a question in mind as I listened?
   e. Did I get an answer to my question?
   f. Did I act as if the speaker had something important to tell me?
   g. Did I listen so well that I can retell what I heard?

3. Oral Reporting
   a. Did I have something worthwhile to say?
   b. Were my ideas in order?
   c. Did I look at my listener?
   d. Did I talk to them in a conversational tone, neither too loud nor too soft?
   e. Did I pronounce my words correctly so the listeners could tell what I was saying?
   f. Have I done a good job of reporting?

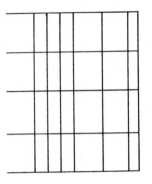

4. Booklets
a. Is my booklet the best I could make it?
b. Did I find good pictures to illustrate each point?
c. Did I paste, colour, draw and print as neatly as I could?
d. Did I think about the question asked and write a good answer?

5. Knowledge
a. Do I know what employer, employee, customer and advertising mean?
b. Can I name the workers in the store and tell about their jobs and how their work affects others?
c. Can I explain the graph we made?

The following is a list of questions. Half of these can be used after Learning Experiences B1 and the other half at the conclusion of the unit.

Equality
1. Do you think that the person whose work it is to fill the shelves is as important as the person who is the cashier? (Everyone's job in the supermarket is important.)

Interdependence
2. If one of the persons who works in the produce department is away from work for two days, will this affect the other workers?
3. Will the person who is ill be missed by the customers?
4. Does it matter if the milk truck breaks down?
5. If the janitor has not cleaned the supermarket should the manager phone him to see what happened?
6. Does the carry-out boy who whistles while he works and hurries back into the store give bad service?

Responsibility
7. If you are a worker and you are going to be away from work should you tell the manager?
8. Should a customer who gets a can of spoiled peas get angry at the person who fills the shelves?
9. Is a cashier who never says anything doing a good job?
10. Would the manager feel tired at the end of the day?
11. A customer when getting a paper bag for apples, pulls out other bags that drop to the floor. Should he leave them on the floor for the produce worker to pick up?

Cooperation
12. Should the shelf worker help the customer find the products?
13. If employees do not cooperate with each other do you think the supermarket would run smoothly?
14. When the cashier becomes ill at work should another cashier take over for her?

Honesty

15. Baskets of tomatoes are selling for 75 cents. Should a customer exchange tomatoes in the baskets so that he will get all big ones in the basket he is going to buy?

16. When the sales clerk stays home to watch the N.H.L. finals should he phone in that he is sick?

17. Should the shelf boy take a chocolate bar when unpacking the candy?

18. Is Bob, the butcher, performing his duties if when he sees the price marker coming in late he hurries to tell the manager?

Loyalty

19. The workers in a supermarket have twenty minutes for coffee in the morning. One worker meets a friend at coffee. Should he take ten minutes more to visit with his friend?

20. It is one minute before closing time at the store. Should the cashier take time to wait on a customer?

21. Do you think you should shop in a supermarket in another neighbourhood if there is one in your neighbourhood?

Neighbourhood

22. If your father wanted the store to order him some garden fertilizer, would they?

23. Does a supermarket help people in a neighbourhood to be more neighbourly?

24. Do you think that a supermarket in your neighbourhood should stock Italian, Chinese, German, etc. food?

Goals

25. Should the manager hire Joe who wants to buy his family a Christmas turkey, instead of Jack who wants money to buy himself a pellet gun?

Division of Labour

26. Does everyone in the store have the same duties to perform?

27. Do you think a person in a little country store works harder than a person working in a supermarket?

Cleanliness

28. It does not matter how clean you are as long as you do your job well.

Advertising

29. We should buy only those products that are advertised by famous people.

30. You should always buy the cheapest product.

Notes:

BIBLIOGRAPHY

Note: Please see the catalogues of the Audio-Visual Services Branch, Department of Education, for lists of films, filmstrips, audio-tapes and video-tapes relating to the supermarket.

Kits

Language Development Program by David and Joseph Gladstone. Science Research Associates (Canada) Limited, 44 Prince Andrew Place, Don Mills, Ontario. (Approximate total cost of Kit—$97.50.)

Schools, Families, Neighborhoods. A multi-media readiness program. J. M. Dent and Sons (Canada) Limited, 100 Scarsdale Road, Don Mills 404, Ontario. (Approximate cost of Kit—$187.00.)

Pictures

Instructor *Community Helpers.* Posters. F. A. Owen Publishing Company, Dansville, New York, 1961, 1965.

My Community Teaching Pictures. David C. Cook Publishing Company, 850 N. Grove Avenue, Elgin, Illinois 60120, 1966.

Books

Braithwaite, Max, and R. S. Lambert. *There's No Place Like Home.* The Book Society of Canada, 4386 Sheppard Avenue East, Agincourt 742, Ontario, 1959.

Dennis, Lloyd A., and Mary Halliday. *Thank You Neighbour.* J. M. Dent and Sons (Canada) Limited, 100 Scarsdale Road, Don Mills 404, Ontario, 1958.

Durell, Thomas J. et al. *Living Together in the Neighborhood. Basic Social Studies Series.* Harper and Row Publishers, Inc., Scranton, Pennsylvania, 18512, 1964.

Goodspeed, J. M. *Let's Go to a Supermarket.* G. P. Putnam's Sons, 200 Madison Avenue, New York, New York 10016, 1958.

Hoffman, Elaine, and Jane Hefflefinger. *About Helpers Who Work at Night.* Children's Press, 1224 W. Van Buren Street, Chicago, Illinois 60612, 1963.

Marks, Mickey K. *What Can I Buy?* Dial Press, Inc., 750 Third Avenue, New York, New York 10017, 1962.

Pope, Billy N. *Let's Go to the Supermarket. Your World Series.* Taylor Publishing Company, Box 597, Dallas, Texas 75221, 1966.

Preston, Ralph C., Mildred M. Cameron, and Martha McIntosh. *Greenfield and Far Away.* D. C. Heath and Company, Suite 1408, 100 Adelaide Street West, Toronto 1, Ontario, 1969.

Preston, Ralph C., Eleanor Clymer, and Lillian Fortress. *Communities at Work.* D. C. Heath and Company, Suite 1408, 100 Adelaide Street West, Toronto 1, Ontario, 1969.

Senesh, Lawrence. *Families at Work. Our Working World Series.* Science Research Associates (Canada) Limited, 44 Prince Andrew Place, Don Mills, Ontario, 1964.

Senesh, Lawrence. *Neighbors at Work. Our Working World Series.* Science Research Associates (Canada) Limited, 44 Prince Andrew Place, Don Mills, Ontario, 1965.

Shaftel, Fannie and George. *People in Action.* Holt, Rinehart and Winston of Canada Limited, 833 Oxford Street, Toronto 530, Ontario, 1970.

Role-playing and discussion photographs

Thorn, Elizabeth A., and M. Irene Richmond. *Camera Patterns.* W. J. Gage Limited, 1500 Birchmount Road, Scarborough 733, Ontario, 1970.

Discussion of Sample Module

In evaluating this sample module, we find that it obviously does not contain all the components listed in the curriculum chapter as integral parts of a module. For instance, there are no time sequences and no alternative programs for the highly gifted or underachiever. The format is different from the examples shown earlier, but this presents no problem. Although the module is somewhat lacking, it has much to commend it. For example, it contains a rationale. Also, the classification of objectives into three different categories (value, skill, and knowledge objectives) is a useful way of stating the terminal skills required of the student. Although the objectives may not always be correctly stated, they relate directly to a specific concept given in parentheses at the end of each objective. The unit lists generalizations, suggests teacher questioning techniques, and provides possible activities. Most important, the module contains an evaluation measure that gets away from the usual conception that evaluation must take the form of written test items. In this instance, a rating scale has been used, especially useful for younger children. A list of questions is provided that the teacher can use in assessing the pupil's knowledge. However, it is not clear how the students should answer these questions or what form the questions should take. Should the questions be in the form of a true-false test offered for group response? Or can the questions be asked each child individually? In spite of this problem, the questions are put side by side with the concepts they represent.

Before designing his own module, the reader may want to consider a number of formats. The reader may want to design a module in which he develops all the objectives for the students. He may want to consider having the student develop his own program by writing his own objectives, stating his own activities, and entering into a contract with the teacher. The important point in writing any unit, especially one in which the teacher is designing the objectives, is to be sure that you are creative in the use of techniques and methodology. Inquiry teaching, educational simulation games, programmed learning, and multimedia are all tools that help operationalize the objectives. One module may incorporate a number of these tools.

In developing your own competency-based curriculum, you may

use the curriculum guides of your own school system. Remember these are probably content-oriented. Therefore, you must translate the content into concepts. Regardless of what help you get in developing your modules, be prepared to defend what you create.

SELF-EVALUATION ACTIVITIES

To complete the objectives of this chapter, the reader must build a competency-based curriculum model operationalizing the objectives of this book. The behavioral objective of this chapter was the following.

1. *The student will demonstrate his ability to synthesize competency-based theory in the development of a cluster of modules.*

   a. *The student will first state the subject area for which his curriculum is to be developed.*

   b. *In developing a synthesis of competency-based theory in curriculum development, the student will incorporate in his behavioral objectives activities and evaluate the conditions discussed in this chapter that promote pupil learning. The student will list and defend those elements in his planning that promote this learning.*

   c. *The student will field-test the modules in an educational setting and then make the necessary revisions in the modules based on his analysis of the students' performance, school resources, and the time alloted for instruction.*

The following checklist will be helpful.

Checklist for Building A Competency-Based Curriculum

_____ 1. Selection of a topic

_____ 2. Statement of rationale for teaching the topic and organizing it into a competency-based structure

_____ 3. Translation of the topic into generalizations, concepts, objectives, activities, and some type of criterion-referenced evaluation measure

_____ 4. Designation of a selected number of concepts and objectives into discrete learning modules that contain the following parts:

        _____ a. Sequencing of modules from simple to complex

        _____ b. Statement at the beginning of the module listing the necessary prerequisite skills

        _____ c. Development of pretests and posttests

        _____ d. Development of ways and means to handle remedial and accelerated students

———— e. Tentative estimation of time required for the average student to complete the module

———— 5. Selection of a variety of activities and methods or treatments that can be used to help students achieve the objectives

———— 6. Drawing of a flow diagram to help visualize the step-by-step process the student follows in his progress through the module

NOTES AND REFERENCES

1. Norman B. Murray and Robert D. Tennyson, *Conceptual Models of Complex Cognitive Behavior: Working Paper No. 14* (Provo, Utah: Brigham Young University, Department of Instructional Research and Development, 1971); Fredrick Roscoe Woolley, *Effects of the Presence of Concept Definition, Pretraining, Concept Exemplars, and Feedback on the Instruction of Indefinite Conjunctive Concepts* (Provo, Utah: Brigham Young University, Department of Instructional Research and Development, 1971). Although there are a large number of studies that presently illustrate the advantage of criteria-referenced evaluation of specific objectives over traditional norm-referenced testing of nonspecific .objectives, the research reports are the result of thorough experimental testing over the last several years.
2. William P. McLoughlin, "Individualization of Instruction vs. Nongrading," *Phi Delta Kappan* 53 no. 6 (February 1972), 378–382.

SUGGESTED READINGS

Ghiselin, Brewster. *The Creative Process.* Berkeley, Cal.: University of California Press, 1954.
   This gives a writer's view of creativity with articles by those who have created.

Pritzkau, Philo T. *On Education for the Authentic.* Scranton, Penn.: International Textbook Co., 1970.
   This contains an argument that, taken from a systems approach, requires such an approach to extend knowledge beyond lower learning levels.

Ryans, David G. "A Model of Instruction Based on Information Systems Concepts," in James MacDonald (ed.), *Theories of Instruction.* Washington, D.C.: Association for Supervision and Curriculum Development, 1965.

Torrance, E. Paul. *Creativity.* Washington, D.C.: Association of Classroom Teachers of the National Education Association, 1968.
   A brief pamphlet that discusses in a readily understandable form the components of creativity and ways of structuring learning to provide the necessary opportunities.

Torrance, E. Paul. *Encouraging Creativity in the Classroom*. Dubuque, Iowa: William C. Brown Co. Publishers, 1971.
This book gives specific means for building creativity into class instruction.

Whitehead, Alfred North. *The Aims of Education*. New York: Mentor Books, 1956.
Although the monumental work on Process and Reality is more comprehensive in respect to synthesis, the work above asks only that the reader define specifically Whitehead's terms and apply them to creating a curriculum based on a synthesis of the educational domains.

Glossary of Terms*

Activities: Tasks the student performs as he practices achieving the requirements of a behavioral objective. These activities should be developed directly from the behavioral objectives. The three types of activities are prerequisite, equivalent, and analogous.

Affective: Describing the behaviors that represent the "feeling" quality of experience. In measuring affective learning, we examine the behaviors that reflect changes in awareness, responding, attitudes, and value sets.

Analogous activity: This refers to an activity that gives the students practice in developing skills similar to those actually required in the behavioral objective.

Artificial learning: Learning that is short-term, usually involving only recall and memorization processes, and that cannot be applied outside the immediate learning context.

Authoritarian: This term applies to a classroom discipline system that is teacher-centered and punitively oriented, and that tends to treat only the symptomatic aspects of classroom problems.

Behavioral objective: A statement written in performance terms that describes the skills the student is to achieve and be tested on. A behavioral objective should be stated in terms of the (1) desired *student* behavior; (2) specific behavior to be performed; (3) conditions under which the student will perform; (4)

* These definitions are not necessarily meant to suggest universal application; they convey the meaning of the terms as used in this book.

239

criteria that will be used to evaluate whether the student has successfully completed the objective.

Behavior modification: The strategic use of any reinforcement technique designed to change an undesirable behavior to a desirable one.

Cognitive: Describing the behaviors that represent the various categories of knowing, going from the least complex to the most complex: knowledge, comprehension, application, analysis, synthesis, and evaluation.

Competency-based curriculum: A curriculum that involves the selection of objectives, pretesting, learning activities, posttesting and possibly remediation, with each phase involving a reassessment of its effectiveness.

Concept: An abstraction of a general idea representing a class or group of things that have common characteristics.

Contingency management: A behavioral modification technique that includes (1) observation to determine an individual's more likely and less likely behaviors; (2) application of reinforcement techniques (using the Premack principle) to promote the desired behavior; (3) assessment of results to determine the effectiveness of the reinforcement used in producing the desired behavior change.

Continuous progress: Refers to the progress or opportunity allowed a student to move through a course of instruction at his own pace. In competency-based programs, this progress is based upon the student's achievement of the behavioral objectives.

Creativity: The individual development of a new process or product by the application of skills in a unique way. The degree of difference may be a slight nuance of change from previous results or it may represent a complete break with previous experience.

Curriculum guide: A guide developed by a school or school district to communicate curriculum intentions. Such a guide should include generalizations, concepts, objectives, activities, resources, and modes of inquiry for a particular course or level of teaching.

Curriculum map: A diagrammatical representation of a curriculum that represents the plan of instruction in a sequential or vertical form.

Curriculum unit: In a competency-based curriculum, the term refers to a grouping or cluster of modules. The unit is distinguished by the fact that the modules are closely related in terms of the objectives and skills they contain. The unit has an average time designated in which the instructor assumes most students can complete the work. (A traditional curriculum unit consists of a number of lessons plans and covers a time span, but does not necessarily have recycling and pretesting capabilities.)

Discipline: Any behavior control system evolving from a lesser reliance on external controls to a greater reliance on internal controls.

Empirical: Relying or based solely on evidence gained by the systematic observation of behavior.

Equivalent activity: This refers to activity that requires the students to perform behaviors *identical* to that required in the behavioral objective.

Evaluation: Involves diagnosis of the student, the teacher, *and* the learning methodology. This assessment should take place prior to, during, and after the learning experience.

Extinction: The lessening of a response through nonreinforcement.

Flexible scheduling: The classroom day is divided into modules or units of time that may vary from day to day. The purpose is to allow the student and teacher varying amounts of time to work on assignments.

Generalization: A universally applicable statement at the highest level of abstraction, relevant to man's engaging in a basic human activity, past and/or present.

Goals: These are generalized statements written from concepts. Goals are then translated into behavioral objectives requiring specific actions on the part of the student.

Grading: One component of the evaluation process, which should include a specific statement of the student's various skill levels.

Individually guided instruction: Refers to programs in which students are given a set of objectives and are able to progress individually through activities that are perceived as the most facilitative in completing the requirements of the objective. The teacher in an individually guided program not only plans the instruction and the activities but also acts as a resource agent in helping the students work through the requirements.

Individualized instruction: In competency-based instruction, this term has two facets. The first refers to the individualized nature of a course once a student has taken a teacher-designed pretest and has had an individualized program developed for him based on the results of the pretest. His program may be different from any other student's or, because of the nature of the teacher-designed test, the student may find himself working at least part of the time with a small group of students who have somewhat similar tasks. The other facet of this term refers to either a teacher- or student-designed module that has been specifically created to meet the unique interests and skills of a particular student. This type of program is usually written to provide an application of higher taxonomic experience in which the student can integrate a variety of previously learned skills in a project that has special interest for him.

Inquiry method: A self-discovery learning methodology, based on a problem-solving approach. The teacher assumes a nondirective guidance role, and the student learns by asking and answering his own questions through research and discovery.

Learning: A desired or desirable change of behavior.

Linear (sequential) programming: The presentation of an equivalent activity followed by several analogous activities and concluded by a posttest. The students may or may not be excused from all or part of the instructional activities, depending on their pretest scores. The design is sequential in that it may imply that one must possess the skills in the first activity before moving to the next activity.

Mode of inquiry: The way in which practitioners of a given subject area develop activities and investigate data in order to develop generalizations and concepts within their fields of study.

Module: A module is a teacher-developed instructional (or learning) package. It includes a statement of the student prerequisite skills and behaviors needed before beginning the module, a statement of the behavioral objectives for the course of instruction, and accompanying student activities and evaluation.

Module cluster: A group of related modules on a given topic area. The cluster is often organized into a unit. Each cluster is designed to be completed in a specified period of time by the average student. The cluster allows for pretesting, posttesting, and recycling, and it may have individualized modules and group modules.

Motivation: This is reflected by an individual's increase in behaviors related to the attainment of a designated goal.

Multi-unit School: The multi-unit school uses teaching teams whose members represent different subject matter specialties. The members have designated planning time to develop individually guided instructional programs that may be competency-based. Integral parts of the multi-unit design include the assignment of a unit leader, student interns, instructional secretary, a planning team, and paraprofessional help.

Nongrading: The term is used to express two different processes. One use of nongrading refers to the removal of the structure of grade levels. In other words, for the idea of year-long grade levels (grades 1 through 12) is substituted some form of learning levels relying on the use of module clusters. The other use of the term refers to the elimination of the end-of-course grade. In place of the traditional letter grade, the student either receives a *pass/no credit* option or a written statement of his achievement. Both uses of the term are involved in competency-based instruction.

Permissive: Applies to a classroom discipline system that is pupil-centered and nonpunitive, and that tends to treat only the casual aspects of classroom problems.

Premack principle: A reinforcement strategy that makes a more likely behavior (*e.g.,* going out to play) contingent on the completion of a less likely behavior (*e.g.,* cleaning up one's room), thus increasing the likelihood of the less likely behavior occurring.

Prerequisite activity: The activity and skills from previous lessons that must have been achieved by the student before he can undertake more complex objectives and activities.

Pretest: An evaluation instrument designed to assess an individual's skills prior to entering a learning unit. A pretest should include both the necessary entering skills and the desired leaving skills.

Posttest: An evaluation instrument used at the conclusion of a course of study to measure the skills an individual has attained. The measurement technique used is developed from the behavioral objectives.

Probability factors: The "odds" in a given set of circumstances that a particular result will occur. In testing, we are concerned about the odds that a particular test score could be gained by chance factors alone.

Punishment: Any set of environmental circumstances (*e.g.,* teacher behavior) that reduces or eliminates the student behavior it follows.

Real learning: Learning that is long-term, involving higher cognitive processes, and that can be applied outside the immediate learning context.

Reassessment: The gathering of data, evaluation of its meaning, and the determination of the necessary changes of a competency-based curriculum. The need for this feedback at all stages of the program ensures continual evaluation.

Recycling: If a student fails to achieve the skill as measured on the end-of-course evaluation, he is provided with alternative work allowing him other opportunities to fulfill the requirements of the objective. This student receives more intensive help. This is also known as *remediation*.

Reinforcement: Any set of environmental circumstances (*e.g.*, a teacher "treatment") that results in an increase of the behavior which it follows.

Reliability: The consistency with which a test instrument measures.

Remediation: If a student fails to achieve the skill as measured on the end-of-course evaluation, alternative work is provided to allow him other opportunities to fulfill the requirements of the objective. This student receives more intensive help. This is also known as *recycling*.

Self-pacing: This refers to the process used in competency-based instruction in which a student is able to control his own learning rate by determining his own speed of accomplishing the skills outlined in the behavioral objectives.

Sequencing: This refers to placing objectives, activities, test items, and so on, in order from the least complex to the most complex.

Staffing: Refers to the assignment of teachers for instructional purposes. Staffing involves two categories: self-contained classrooms and differentiated staffing. In the self-contained classroom, a teacher is assigned to a room on a more or less permanent basis. This is what the layman refers to as the traditional classroom. The differentiated staffing arrangement involves one or more teachers being assigned to a classroom area and given a variety of designated roles and functions. Teachers perform in some variation of team teaching or a multi-unit arrangement. They may work in groups or individually with other professional and para-professional help. According to Dwight Allen and Lloyd Kline (in James Cooper (ed.), *Differentiated Staffing*, Philadelphia: Saunders Publishing Co., 1972, pp. 12-30), differentiated staffing is "really a frame of reference, a habit of mind, a non-traditional perspective, a rationale, a process with a great many patterns which can be devised, justified, and evaluated."

Structure of knowledge: This usually means the theories, concepts, generalizations, data, and modes of inquiry used by the practitioners of a particular discipline. The practitioner of a discipline knows the knowledge of the discipline, the principles, theories, and modes of inquiry or methods of collecting and evaluating data within his discipline.

Student contracting: The teacher and the student discuss the objectives and form a contract about the means necessary for the student to complete the task they have agreed upon. Achievement of the contract will result in the student's receiving a reward: money, released school time, or other extrinsic devices used to encourage rapid progress in the subject area.

Subconcept: The breaking down of a concept into more explicit elements.

Subject: A course of study such as history, English, business, mathematics.

Subject matter: The particular concepts and information contained within the subject area.

Synthesis: The putting together of previously learned skills so that they form a whole, a new pattern or structure—a creation unique to the individual performing the synthesis. The product or process demonstrated should also include elements of knowledge, comprehension, application, and analysis.

Teaching techniques and methods: Each subject area and discipline has its own specified methods and programs for teaching students how to inquire into the subject matter and learn the basic skills and content of the field. However, all teaching techniques can be grouped in a number of categories, which include:

a. *Programmed learning:* This includes teaching machines, programmed books, and sequenced learning programs that may include filmstrips, lab manuals, and other packaged materials.

b. *Inquiry materials:* This may consist of programmed kits that are largely self-contained learning programs. At the other extreme, inquiry methods may represent open-ended techniques in which teacher questioning provokes problem solving and student hypothesis formulation.

c. *Case studies:* This is a simulated view of reality. By isolating a problem in time, students can raise questions about the nature of the case and formulate possible ways of solving problems.

d. *Lecture-discussion:* The teaching method in which the teacher raises questions, considers various answers to the questions raised, and allows student reaction in either large or small groups.

e. *Audiovisual media:* This is not a method. The media include chalkboards, films, teaching machines, computers, and so on. The media are used by the teacher as aids for implementing a given technique.

The following two terms, while not teaching methods, relate directly to the techniques and how a teacher uses them in a classroom. The first is *microteaching,* which reduces the size of the classroom lesson to emphasize significant tasks in the lesson. Its function is to assess the adequacy of a teacher's instructional planning and methodology. It is used extensively in teacher training. The second term is *teacher self-appraisal.* This refers both to the teacher's view of himself and to his responses and reactions during the course of instruction.

Team teaching: This ordinarily refers to the organization of teachers in a subject area or grade level into a group for instructional purposes in which the classes are initially combined for instruction. Subsequently the students may receive large group instruction from one or more of the instructors. Teaming also allows these students to be placed in small groups or other combinations for instructional purposes.

Test: An instrument designed to measure whether a student can demonstrate the designated behavioral objectives.

Values: The beliefs and ideas an individuals holds; they are measured by evaluating the individual's choice of behaviors.

Validity: The extent to which a test measures what it intends to measure.

Vertical (simultaneous) programming: This involves the simultaneous presentation of activities that a student can engage in to achieve the behavioral objective. The assumption is that the student has the necessary prerequisite skills to engage in any or all of the activities that he chooses or is assigned. Learning stations using a variety of media are typical.

Index